SECOND TIME AROUND

The New Formula I:
The Turbo Era

By the same author:

FORMULA I The Art and Technicalities of Grand Prix Driving

FOR THE RECORD

Niki Lauda

Second Time Around

The New Formula I:
The Turbo Era

WILLIAM KIMBER · LONDON

This edition first published in 1984 by
WILLIAM KIMBER & CO. LIMITED
100 Jermyn Street, London, SW1Y 6EE

ISBN 0-7183-0199-4

Die neue Formel 1 by Niki Lauda © 1982 by Verlag Orac, Vienna
English translation copyright © 1984 by William Kimber & Co. Limited

This book is copyright. No part thereof may be reproduced in any form without written permission from the publisher except in the case of a reviewer who wishes to quote brief excerpts in connection with a review written for inclusion in a newspaper, magazine or radio or television broadcast.

Typeset by Grove Graphics, Tring and printed in Great Britain by
The Garden City Press Limited, Letchworth, Hertfordshire SG6 1JS

MANCHESTER
PUBLIC
LIBRARIES

84302422

The collaboration of
Diplom-Ingenieur Dr Fritz Indra
and Herbert Völker is gratefully acknowledged

English translation: E. J. Crockett

The Publishers would like to thank
David Phipps for his editorial advice

Acknowledgements to Illustrations

Alois Hans Rottensteiner (62), Thomas Streimelweger (38), Fritz Indra (10), DPPI (6), Bernard Cahier (3), Jutta Fausel (2), Joseph Reinhard (2), Walter Wachter (1), Chiel van der Heyden (1), Jeff Hutchinson (1), Keith Sutton (1). Renault (5), BMW (4), Martini (3), Talbot (2), Ford (1), Bilstein (1), Toyota (1), KKK (1), Marlboro (1).

Contents

Foreword

My first book eight years ago, *Formula I*, analysed the technical aspects of Grand Prix racing and explained how everything works in theory and in practice. *Formula I* was extremely successful and my collaborators and myself had the impression that everything that had been said would stand the test of time. We were wrong. Although the fundamental laws of physics are still valid, many of them have been subverted and outwitted. The technical landscape of Formula I today is wholly different from that of 1975 – not necessarily more beautiful, but certainly more exciting. Life is much more difficult and complex with the new generation of cars, and I can think of no era in Grand Prix history which has been so preoccupied with technical developments. In an effort to describe these and the rationale behind them, I realised it was essential to go a second time around.

Niki Lauda

Face to Face

Niki Lauda and Herbert Völker

VÖLKER: It's now been eight years since *Formula I*, your first book on the art of Grand Prix driving. As things have turned out, a remarkable amount of what was said back then no longer has any relevance. One thing is sure, the sport seems to have gone back to basics.
LAUDA: In the meantime we've seen the ground effect era come and go. We've been through a period where the laws of physics seemed to be subverted, judging by the way the cars handled.
VÖLKER: Wouldn't you agree that Formula I racing and all that goes with it – the sport itself, the show biz razzle-dazzle and the high finance – were turned upside down by a little something called ground effect?
LAUDA: That's a bit terse, but basically true. That is really what this book is about – the technical background and build-up.
VÖLKER: You yourself were very much in the limelight as being opposed to ground effect cars. You seem to have had your way. Lap times this year are slower across the board. Don't you think this is a step backwards? In other words, shouldn't Formula I exploit new technology to make sure that the cars lead the way in terms of both speed and advanced design?
LAUDA: The old suction-cup effect had little to do with technical progress as such. It was a very interesting dead-end. The engineers charged up a one-way street and we had to tag along with them. In next to no time aerodynamic R & D was developed and put into practice, but it was always a temporary aberration and a dangerous one at that. I go into all this in greater detail later on.
VÖLKER: Doesn't it bother you that you are slower now than last year?

LAUDA: No. Now we're driving cars that behave like cars. Take an example. We have 700-pound springs on the back, which means that the cars are still very stiffly sprung. But we used to have 4,500-pound springs on ground effect cars – you were driving on planks that had no give at all. As of this season, the cars have again started to handle predictably. You can sense *when* the car is starting to leave you – first you feel the longitudinal roll, then the side-slip. In a ground effect car you were jammed down on the track with no way of sensing any change in the car's handling characteristics. All you did know was that something really terrible, unnatural, unpredictable would happen if the airflow beneath the car was disrupted for one reason or another. I don't really see what that had to do with refinement of driving techniques, just because cornering speeds were way above what you might have expected in a normal racing car. I might just add that I am convinced we will soon be lapping even faster than in ground effect cars – albeit for different reasons. Above all, I'm sure some new way will be found to exploit aerodynamic design so that we can drive incredibly fast times which will nevertheless be practicable and safe.
VÖLKER: So the designers still have a trick or two up their sleeves?
LAUDA: Trick is the wrong word. There won't be a quick solution along the suction cup lines. True, we are now limited to exploiting downforce from conventional wings, but that still leaves the designers a lot of scope. The fact is, they haven't been paying all that much attention to other means of obtaining downforce, because they didn't need to in the days of ground effect developed by the underbody. Furthermore, engine and tyre developments will soon enable us to match the lap times recorded by ground effect cars. The real significance of the ground effect era was that it made us realise the importance of downforce.
VÖLKER: Don't you ever feel a twinge of nostalgia for the good old days before the turbos and all the cock-eyed aerodynamics?
LAUDA: Bull. I don't give a damn about the good old days. To me, it doesn't matter in the slightest whether they were good, bad or indifferent. What counts is today – and tomorrow.
VÖLKER: You feel that way about all your past successes?
LAUDA: Right. The next win is always the big one, not the ones you already have under your belt.
VÖLKER: Surely you can still say which win was your best – or your most important?
LAUDA: Always the most recent one.

VÖLKER: You always wipe the slate clean like this? Even about shunts like the one at Nürburgring in 1976?
LAUDA: That's right.
VÖLKER: Aren't you reminded about that one every time you look in a mirror?
LAUDA: No, this is just my new face. It doesn't remind me of anything. The only thing I notice in the mirror some mornings is that I haven't had a good night's sleep, and that does piss me off. Otherwise, there's nothing to see.
VÖLKER: I imagine some people might have thought about cosmetic surgery.
LAUDA: As a matter of fact, I did have a skin graft around the eyes soon after Nürburgring. And – at the same time – I got a cost estimate for all sorts of other repairs – new eyebrows, a hair transplant, a new ear, and so on. For one thing, it was all going to be very, very expensive and, for another, there was no sure-fire guarantee that it would work. Losing one ear almost completely never really bothered me all that much. Just the opposite – now it's easier to use the telephone. The receiver is a little bit closer to the eardrum, which comes in very handy when you are making a long-distance call.
VÖLKER: According to Enzo Ferrari, you would have been the all-time number one if you had stayed with him but, as things have turned out, you're only number four in the record books – behind Jackie Stewart, Jim Clark and Juan Manuel Fangio.
LAUDA: I don't lose sleep over that sort of league-table statistic because there is no real way of comparing one era with another. Back in Fangio's day there were seven or eight Grand Prix races a year. Now that inflation has taken hold, we're driving sixteen every season. Anyway, all Enzo Ferrari was trying to say is that his cars are the best ones around.
VÖLKER: He's right, isn't he?
LAUDA: Well, I was very angry at how the Ferraris which Villeneuve and Pironi shunted last season simply broke up completely. In a similar situation I certainly wouldn't have expected my McLaren to have been as unsafe from the driver's point of view. But, apart from that, yes, you're right: the Ferraris have always been tops over the years, or close to it, and they still are.
VÖLKER: When you left Ferrari in 1977 after taking the championship for the second time, some pretty harsh things were said on both sides. You certainly parted company with a bang. Enzo Ferrari complained loudly

and bitterly about you and you threw a few choice remarks his way. How are things between you now? Have you decided to forgive and forget?
LAUDA: Absolutely. The only tangible memories of those days are the good ones. Ferrari is a grand old man and you have to let him have his way. I see this now, but back then I didn't. And he seems to have taken a new liking to me. I saw him at Imola for the first time in years – that was in 1982 – and it was really fantastic how he came right over and put his arms around me. I was very happy and very touched at being welcomed like a prodigal son.
VÖLKER: Coming from you, that's downright sentimental. In that case, why did you turn down Ferrari's firm offer to come back into the fold?
LAUDA: Ferrari pays peanuts. I used to put up with it but those days are long gone. I just don't come that cheap any more. Apart from that, I was really keen to take on the challenge of starting from scratch with McLaren and getting the best out of the brand-new Porsche engine. I'm the right man for that job and I aim to prove it.
VÖLKER: In your two 'civilian' years between retirement and comeback did you experience anything or learn anything that was new or important to you?
LAUDA: Yes. Ever since I left school I was never anything other than a racing driver. In other words, I've always lived life up to the absolute hilt. When I retired in 1979 – because Formula I was getting on my nerves – I channelled all my energy towards a new goal, putting Lauda Air on the map. And that's when I learned what it's like being so dependent on other people. The wheels of commerce turn slowly and I had to put my own brakes on. In the highly competitive arena of Formula I there is an enormous amount that can be achieved by straightforward commitment and dedication. You are dealing exclusively with people who are geared to competition and who think and work and graft the same way as yourself. If an idea comes into your head one night you can go out and do something practical about it the very next morning. Out there in the world of everyday living, people don't realise that things can be changed at the drop of a hat. They plod along at their own steady pace. The average person doesn't have that chequered flag to go for every other week to force him to take stock of himself. Some people can go through life without that kind of challenge.
VÖLKER: There may be no chequered flag for you either as far as Lauda Air is concerned. Does it bother you that – for the first time in your life – you may fail to accomplish what you set out to do?

LAUDA: I don't see it that way. I went into the charter business at the worst conceivable time. It was the same all over the world, and I certainly had no idea how tough it would be for a private airline up against a repressive state monopoly – even if you steer clear of direct competition as I did. With things the way they are, you can't make it in the charter business in Austria. Lauda Air has been cut back and we are now focussing on expanding the executive jet side – which is already going well.
VÖLKER: And what about flying itself? Are you still as wildly enthusiastic about it as ever?
LAUDA: I don't have too much enthusiasm left. I still fly and I still get a real kick out of piloting a Mystère – which I do often. But the fascination of it all has evaporated. Flying is a very stolid pursuit and most people tend to overrate the skills it requires. There is no way that flying can live up to my expectations in the sense of fulfilling a lifetime's ambition.
VÖLKER: What happened? Was it a question of waking up one morning and saying to yourself: 'I'm going back into Grand Prix racing'?
LAUDA: No, it was all very gradual, more or less in step with growing awareness that flying wasn't the be-all and end-all. In 1980 – the first year after I retired – Formula I left me cold: I didn't even switch on TV to watch. By the next season, though, I was beginning to take some interest in TV coverage, but I still pitied those poor bastards out there. It was only when I did a TV commentary on the Austrian Grand Prix that I shook off that feeling for good and started thinking how appealing the idea was of getting back in there amongst them. That brought me up short, thinking that way, so I went off down to Monza to put the idea to the test. Monza worked out fine, so the next step was to give it a try again out on the track. And I did – in September 1981 at Donington.
VÖLKER: Was that an uplifting experience, getting back behind the wheel of a Formula I car?
LAUDA: Uplifting? Hell, no, it was humiliating. After one lap I could hardly hold the steering wheel. I don't think I ever came into the pits so often in one day, and every time I had a different excuse – this was wrong, that was wrong, this had to be changed, that had to be adjusted. I could hardly admit that I was all in. Later on in the day it got better and I discovered that speed wasn't going to be a problem. I wasn't at all worried about the physical fitness side, because that would sort itself out with the proper training routine. Willy Dungl worked out a fitness schedule for me right away and I was in peak condition before my first race.

VÖLKER: Was McLaren the only team interested in Niki Lauda's comeback plans?
LAUDA: Fortunately for me, Williams also showed an interest. If it hadn't been for that, my market value would have been lower.
VÖLKER: They must have had a lot of faith in you to expect top-class performances after that two-year lay-off.
LAUDA: Don't kid yourself on that score. I had to settle for a contract that ran only for four races at a time and a share of the prize money. That kind of deal is pretty tough, but I had no option. So much for faith.
VÖLKER: Did you talk over your comeback with your wife or did you just come right out with it one day and say, 'Oh, by the way, darling, I'm going back into racing'?
LAUDA: It came as a total surprise to her. At first I told her that all the comeback rumours were just that – rumours. She was quite happy to believe me because she knows how much rubbish gets into the press. Then, once the deal was finalised. I told her. All Marlene said was: You're off your head! It wasn't until a few days later that she blurted out how much she hated the sport and how stupid she thought I was to start all over again.
VÖLKER: She was all for it when you married back in 1976.
LAUDA: Well, she'd only seen the good side up to then. But along came Nürburgring a couple of weeks later – the burning wreck, the intensive care unit, and all the other horrors that this business can bring. It was a far, far greater shock for her than it was for me. I was ready for something like that, she wasn't. After that, she hardly ever came to the track with me, and now she doesn't come to any races at all. To Marlene, the only good race is one that has been called off.
VÖLKER: That puts extra pressure on you?
LAUDA: Naturally I'd be happier if my wife liked my job a bit more. A few days after her initial reaction to my comeback announcement we sat down together and talked it out. What I asked was whether a man – just because he is married – has to make concessions to the point where he gives up doing what he likes doing most. I was able to convince Marlene that everybody needs his or her freedom. If she wants to climb Everest, then good luck to her – as long as she doesn't do it while I'm racing. That wouldn't be fair on the children.
VÖLKER: I notice you automatically put yourself first.
LAUDA: For the moment, I put racing first. You can only race if everything else takes a back seat. I *am* terribly self-centred, but I know it and I do look

Marlboro
Marlboro
7

First colour illustration
John Watson (McLaren), Detroit
Left: Andrea de Cesaris
(Alfa Romeo)
Above: Elio de Angelis (Lotus)
Tom Byrne (Theodore)
Next page: Nelson Piquet
(Brabham-BMW)

parmalat
Santal

for give-and-take wherever possible – especially where my family is involved.
VÖLKER: How far would you go towards generalising that every good racing driver is self-centred by definition? That they never make it to the top unless they have a ruthless streak?
LAUDA: I'd agree. They're all the same. They all look out for number one. The ones who aren't ruthless don't make it.
VÖLKER: I must say that there doesn't seem to be a lot of friendship wasted among the drivers. Even those in the same team don't have all that much to say to each other.
LAUDA: True. That bunch won't even pull together enough to act in their own common interest.
VÖLKER: How did you find Formula I after your comeback?
LAUDA: The same old faces.
VÖLKER: You mean that jaded, been-through-it-all-before feeling?
LAUDA: No, no, not at all. The game is the same but I have changed. I have a positive attitude again, I'm freshly motivated.
VÖLKER: How do you explain that happening all of a sudden?
LAUDA: I can't, really. I just started enjoying it again. So much so, that I could get motivated about things that I don't feel all that good about.
VÖLKER: Such as?
LAUDA: Well, I go down to Imola for practice and the circuit is so bumpy that the car porpoises all over the place, and I ask myself, do I really need this, do I honestly have to put up with all this crap? But, because of my overall positive mental attitude, I talk myself into it and through it: it *is* important, it's part and parcel of the sport, so hang in there and do your stuff. Driving flat-out doesn't get any easier as you get older. But if you can't bring yourself to stay off those mental brakes, you may as well pack it in. Before my comeback I wasn't one hundred percent certain I could cope. It hasn't been easy, but so far I've been able to find the right positive attitude every time out.
VÖLKER: Let's talk about the driver's rôle in Formula I today. The suction effect was such in the ground effect era that the cars seemed to take the corners as if they were on rails. Did it really matter who was at the wheel?
LAUDA: It was really weird, believe me. The aerodynamic design meant that various factors were superimposed one on top of the other to the extent that they could hardly be distinguished. You had to be very skilful and work very hard if you were to be able to give your designer valid feedback on the

car's performance. By Spring '83, we'd gone back to 'normal' cars, but there were new kinds of superimposed factors to be taken into account. Technically speaking, we were back in uncharted territory. In the last few months, for example, we have been at the mercy of the tyres; winning or losing is a question of their make-up and, so far, we have only been able to guess how the complex factors involving loading, temperature and adhesion inter-react. We thought we had these problems licked years ago, but they have cropped up again as Formula I technology has evolved.

VÖLKER: You yourself made two mistakes in the 1982 season which led to shunts – trying to overtake Rosberg in Detroit and in practice at Hockenheim when you spun and ploughed into the safety fence. Are two errors of judgment per season worrying or just average?

LAUDA: I'm afraid that's about par for the course. I've spun out at least once a season since I started racing – more often than that, of course, in the early days. Twice a year is worrying but acceptable – as long as you can walk away from it.

VÖLKER: How do you find the peace of mind to accept this probability? And don't reply that you aren't scared because you are not intelligent or not imaginative enough. Do you have some special technique to keep your feelings under control – in this case, fear?

LAUDA: If you are really scared, and I mean scared rigid, then this is not the job for you. That kind of fear is probably well-founded, since it comes from awareness that you are not as completely in control of a situation as you obviously would like to be. That type of fear has no place in a Grand Prix driver's make-up. Still, having said that, there are definitely some grey areas. I sometimes wake up on the morning of a race with an unpleasant dry taste in my mouth. When that happens, I have my own routine which is based on a logical examination of the probable cause. I think the approach is valid for all kinds of 'funny' feelings, but let's stick to fear as a case in point. What I do is go off quietly by myself and think things through. What am I afraid of? That I'll make a mistake? I tell myself no, because I am on top of my job. That something will go wrong with the car? Answer: if I didn't have total confidence in our designer John Barnard and in the McLaren, I would have been with a different team ages ago. No, it won't be mechanical failure. Or am I worried that another driver will cause a shunt? Here I tell myself that I can trust so-and-so and so-and-so and that I'll simply have to keep my wits about me when I'm anywhere near the rest of them. This kind of rationalisation is normally enough to rid me of that queasy feeling.

VÖLKER: It surely can't be as simplistic as that. You mean to say, this is how you solve life's problems?
LAUDA: No, but it *is* my technique for getting rid of otherwise inexplicable feelings such as a case of the butterflies. If I came to the conclusion that I was a bad driver or that I was not physically up to the mark, then no amount of rationalising would help dispel that feeling.
VÖLKER: How about when you climbed back into the cockpit after the Nürburgring shunt – surely the most difficult moment in your entire career?
LAUDA: That was six weeks later. At Monza. I was scared stiff. The kind of fear when you think you're going to shit yourself any second.
VÖLKER: All the same, you brazened it out. You never owned up that you were scared at Monza.
LAUDA: Obviously not! What was I supposed to say in front of the TV cameras? Gentlemen, please excuse me for a couple of minutes. I'm so bloody scared I think I'm going to shit myself? Is that what I was supposed to say? At a time like that you just say the first thing that comes into your mind, something like 'there's a bit of oversteer, but I feel great'. And you stall for time, trying to pull yourself together.
VÖLKER: How did you?
LAUDA: By using the technique I've just described to you. I got myself away from all the hustle and bustle of Monza and thought things through in the peace and quiet of my hotel room. Why *was* I afraid? The answer was that, in practice that day, I simply wasn't up to handling a Formula I car: my reactions were all wrong and I was driving like a novice. Then I analysed the situation and decided that there was no way I could have forgotten all I knew about Grand Prix driving in the six short weeks since the shunt. All I needed was a bit of confidence. I had to take things slowly and calmly. And that's the way it was the next day in practice – as soon as I had that feeling of panic under control I was gradually able to open up. By evening I was the fastest of all three Ferrari drivers. Then I had enough confidence for the race itself – and for all the races that came after it.
VÖLKER: The 1982 South African Grand Prix was your comeback race after a two-year lay-off. It was also the venue for the biggest clash ever involving drivers, team bosses and race organisers. It so happened that you were behind that, and that you were also the most prominent figure in the drivers' strike that followed. Why is it that the most experienced driver of all turns out to be the one most vehemently opposed to the Grand Prix establishment?

LAUDA: I am an independent. No ties. If my team drops me it won't break my heart. So I'm in a better position than most to stand up to the establishment and fight for our rights as drivers. Kyalami was a classic situation. I was able to convince the others that the super-licence proposed for us actually gave the team bosses *carte blanche*: if we had said okay, then they would have had us in the palms of their hands. Despite the usual dose of paranoia, Kyalami was the first time that there was any real sense of solidarity, of a common cause. The outcome was a 'compromise' that really spelt victory for the drivers. Sad to say, the truth is that they very rarely agree to act in concert. There is always one or another that holds back. If only we could all stick together. And the same thing holds true for the team bosses, officialdom and all the Formula I politicos: none of them looks at the sport as a whole. They are all on the lookout for a personal advantage. Even the president of the ruling body – who should be aloof from this sort of thing – gets caught up in the perennial mud-slinging.
VÖLKER: The change in Formula I that you championed most passionately – a ban on skirts and aerodynamic underbodies – nevertheless seemed to come about as the result of exemplary co-operation.
LAUDA: I must admit it came as a surprise to me. I honestly didn't think that we – as a sport – had enough common sense. The fact is, everybody realised that ground effect cars would be the ruin of Grand Prix racing.
VÖIKER: Strictly speaking, you should also be opposed to the turbos. After all, they hardly help to make the situation any less crazy.
LAUDA: I would say that you can't penalise firms which opt for a technical solution which is within the rules, which invest millions and which – thanks to taking the right decision and putting it into practice – are getting better results. If someone comes on the scene with six foot legs and the ability to clear fifteen feet you can't simply rewrite the rulebook to prevent him competing in the high jump. What is more, turbo developments on the track are in tandem with automotive manufacturing innovation away from it. Lots of people drive turbos today, and it is only natural for them to be interested in what's happening. And don't forget that the technical development phase is far from over as far as the turbo engine is concerned, with the result that Formula I is finally back in a pioneering role. We have to learn to live with the turbos, they're not just a passing fad.
VÖLKER: That means in the longer term that the conventional engine will become extinct. But longer-term prophecies also see turbo engines generating 800 to 900 horsepower. Isn't that utter folly?

LAUDA: 800 or 900 horsepower would obviously be irresponsible on today's circuits. That would be a short-cut to the cemetery. The turbos will have to be held in check one way or another – not because they have to be kept race-compatible with conventional engines but because they have to be kept down to manageable proportions. Cutting back on engine capacity doesn't make much sense to me since that would mean squandering major investment to date. The phased reduction of fuel tank capacity in 1984 and 1985 does seem to be a viable solution. Once technology advances again to the point where we have gigantic horsepower at reduced fuel consumption, then we shall have to think again. For the immediate future, however, smaller tanks should be enough to keep things in check.
VÖLKER: You drove your first race as a 19-year-old in a Mini Cooper. Since then, you've had your full share of dreams and illusions about racing. How do you feel now as a 34-year-old?
LAUDA: Actually, I never had any illusions. Never. Because I never had enough imagination. And my dreams and ambitions always centred on the next stage. After that first race, where I came second in my class in the Mini Cooper, I made up my mind to win that class. Each goal, each challenge grew out of the one preceding it. But there was never any question of proclaiming to the world at twenty years of age that I would one day be world champion. No illusions, so no disappointments.
VÖLKER: We had a similar conversation in our first book together, eight years ago. I asked you at the end of it if you had any idea what you would do when you retired. You mentioned flying and said you couldn't imagine anything more beautiful. In the interim, you have already retired once and you've logged many hours in the air. Let me rephrase the question: have you any idea what you would like to do when you retire a second time?
LAUDA: I haven't a clue, except that it will be something completely different. It could be far removed from here and now, but I don't have any clear notion. Well, possibly – enough to say that it will be in a totally new sphere of activity.
VÖLKER: Are you happy?
LAUDA: That's something I never bother my head about. I always try to do what I like doing, something that I get a kick out of. Up to now, I've nearly always succeeded. If that's what happiness is all about, well, I suppose I'm happy.

Harmony

The Car That Gets It All Together

Harmony is a concept that has to be used with care in any discussion regarding Grand Prix racing. It is easy to appreciate why. To the innocent bystander, Formula I must seem like a madhouse whose inmates betray no sense of direction or purpose.

The total chaos spawned by labyrinthine rules and conflicting interpretations and all the resultant in-fighting and back-biting can be traced to a single root cause: a technical revolution that made a mockery of the physical laws that apply to conventional driving. The coincidental emergence of the turbos as a major force in Formula I only served to make matters even more complicated and confused. Grand Prix racing had jumped a gear. All of a sudden it was faster, more dangerous and more insane than ever.

The one plus in all this is that the technological side of things became more lucid and more innovative than at any period in the history of the sport. In some respects at least, Formula I emerged once again as a testbed for new materials and know-how. But, until recently, the end-product was something unnatural: a *machine infernale.*

The rule changes that came into effect at the start of the 1983 championship season helped significantly to defuse the situation. That these changes were recognised as being vital would seem to suggest that Formula I has not yet become totally irresponsible. There wasn't a single fatal shunt in the whole of the 1983 championship season despite the fact that lap times were gradually edging back up to those of the ground effect era. That seems to suggest that the cars have been 'humanized' again to the extent that they have become genuinely more drivable.

It is generally accepted that, to be successful, a car must be more or less 'balanced' or 'harmonious'. In other words, it doesn't matter how powerful your engine is if your brakes are liable to wear out during a race, or how perfect your suspension is if you've got the aerodynamics wrong, or how beautiful the overall design if your car is too heavy. Clearly, all the elements must be fitted together to achieve a proper balance and harmony.

The degree of harmony can be regarded as a function of the following eight factors and their interplay: engine and radiators; aerodynamic design; monocoque (chassis); suspension; tyres; brakes; overall dimensions (length, width, centre of gravity); and weight.

The technological transformation that has taken place over the last few years has necessitated a reappraisal of the relative importance of the above factors in the context of overall performance. Once upon a time, gravity, suspension and engine were dominant; then, in the ground effect era, everything played second fiddle to aerodynamic design. Today, aerodynamic styling is still extremely important, but it no longer outranks all other elements.

In the heyday of ground effect cars – from 1980 to 1982 – every designer knew only too well the immense potential of aerodynamic theory applied to a racing car (or, for that matter, to any road vehicle, primarily in terms of cutting fuel consumption); now that freedom of underbody design has been prohibited, however, the designers have to focus on other components (along with the precisely delineated 'flat' underbody) in an attempt to recapture at least part of the earlier downforce. There is no chance of attaining the full ground effect of a couple of years back because a key element is missing – the skirts. It was their job to ensure that the suction effect was never disrupted (see the chapter on ground effect); at the same time, the skirts played havoc with the car's normal, 'natural' harmony in the sense that it handled against all the laws of textbook physics.

To prevent damage to the skirts, ground effect cars had such stiff suspension that to all intents and purposes they were not sprung. A car that is incapable of assimilating the various external forces acting on it remains as rigid as a board and cannot react according to the normal laws of physics. Now that the cars are again sprung, a degree of harmony has been restored.

Building a car that is capable of exerting optimum downforce (now with the help of visible 'wings' as opposed to the invisible 'wing' of the underbody), yet with a sufficient semblance of streamlining to accommodate top speeds of around 195 mph *and* sufficient room for the driver and the engine – especially the ungainly turbo with its intercoolers and other accessories – quite frankly, that is a job for a genius.

It is probably symptomatic of changing priorities in Formula I today that the person responsible for 'getting it all together' is referred to not as a 'constructor' but as a 'designer'.

Ground Effect Cars

The Interlude That Ended in 1982

Ground effect cars started making their presence felt as of 1977. By championship seasons 1980, 1981 and 1982, virtually every car racing in Formula I used ground effect.

The best way to define a ground effect car was to say that it had an underbody shaped like an inverted wing in order to achieve negative lift or suction, as opposed to the positive lift used in flying. The downforce brought into play was so considerable that cars built along conventional lines were totally outclassed. An interesting analogy comes in the form of 'slot-car' racing, where electrically-powered scale models corner at incredible speeds on a grooved track. On each side of the grooves there are thin metal strips which carry the electric current. It was only a matter of time before someone had the bright idea of fixing a powerful magnet over the metal strips to pull the models down so firmly onto the track that practically every corner could be taken flat-out. If you didn't get in on the secret, your chances of winning were nil. The fact is, however, you can't keep this kind of subterfuge under wraps for very long: the magnetized models were soon banned from competition, and soon afterwards it was decreed that the metal strips be made of a non-magnetic material, namely copper.

Before going into technical detail, it may be as well to take a look at the jargon of the ground effect era, some of which is still current today.

Although Formula I is no longer the all-British affair it once was, English is still very much the *lingua franca* of the sport. The new breed of ground effect cars brought with it completely new concepts and terminology, among which the following expressions were perhaps the most frequently used.

The *underbody* determined the essential aerodynamic design to the extent that a distinction was made between the *flat bottom* of earlier generations and the *curved bottom* characteristic of the *ground effect car*. The aerodynamic principle exploited in the ground effect car created *negative lift*, referred to variously as *ground effect, downforce, suction* or *load*. The *centre of pressure* was the point on the underbody at which the greatest suction or downforce registered; *more load* was used to describe an increase in downforce, and was the opposite of *suction loss*.

Rubbing strips were attached to the bottom edge of the *skirts* to close the gap between skirts and track; properly adjusted skirts *sealed* the ground effect zone under the car, whereas a defective seal caused the zone to *leak*. Skirts which were in excessive contact with the track were prone to *skirt wear*.

Ride height or *clearance* was a key determinant of ground effect. *Bottoming* referred to contact between underbody and track, whereas *porpoising* could result from the formation of undesirable air pockets below the car, or any other such disruption or intermittent change in load which affected handling characteristics.

Less wing and *more wing* were used to describe variation in the angle of *rear wing* profile adjustment (whereby, strictly speaking, it was the rear wing *flap* only that was adjustable).

It is also worth mentioning that by 1982 the downforce developed by most cars was so great that they no longer needed conventional front wings, particularly on the faster circuits where these appendages interfered with the airflow to the underbody.

In the ground effect era, aerodynamic design assumed far greater importance as a criterion of Grand Prix success than even tyres or engine performance. The design revolution was so radical that lap times on some circuits were slashed by up to seven seconds from one season to the next.

It has to be made quite clear from the start that aerodynamic design problems in an open single-seater racing car are very much more complex than in the case of a conventional passenger vehicle or a racing saloon. The wide exposed wheels, the wishbone suspension, the open cockpit, the driver's helmet, the rollbar, and the multiple vents and apertures react and inter-react enigmatically. Sometimes where a design is altered – even fractionally – the overall impact on the car's performance is totally unpredictable, even with the benefit of long experience of both theory and practice.

Open, fissured design makes for a correspondingly poor drag (cw) coefficient, roughly twice that of a modern passenger saloon. What this means is that, given the same width of car at the front, the racing engine has to work twice as hard as its saloon counterpart to achieve the same speed.

The 'visible wings' – downforce-producing devices mounted front and rear (see chapter on aerodynamics) – lost much of their *raison d'être* in the ground effect era since their job was taken over almost entirely and much more effectively by the underbody (the 'invisible wings').

The real fetish in those days was, if you'll pardon the expression, the underbody: *fixed* parts of the car were specially designed on aerodynamic principles to generate improved downthrust or negative lift without unduly increasing drag.

The first car to use aerodynamic aids in the zone between the wheels was the 1970 March 701. This design acknowledged that there was no need to rely exclusively on conventional 'visible' wings to boost downforce. Accordingly, the fuel tanks were situated laterally between front and rear wheels and were given the form of truncated wings. Admittedly, the effect was still minimal because the car had a very wide, flat cockpit, with the result that the tanks were located in an unfavourable airflow path between front and rear wheels. Still, a first tentative step had been taken.

Colin Chapman took the idea up again in 1975 and, for the 1977 championship season, built the first real 'ground effect' car.

Expectations ran high. It was hoped that the new design would boost downforce without increasing drag, and might even permit the visible wings to be adjusted for even higher speeds. By this time it had been realised that, given the same downforce, the drag coefficient of a properly designed underbody was more acceptable than that resulting from an angled wing.

Before underbody ground effect could be fully exploited, however, a whole series of radical changes had to be introduced to overall racing car design.

Up to that point, the golden rule had been that the car's overall centre of gravity at rest had to be kept as low as possible. This ensured minimal lateral load displacement when cornering, *i.e.*, the load on all four tyres was distributed as evenly as possible and tyre temperatures kept as low as possible. All racing cars had been built accordingly.

What this meant in practice was that the fuel tanks were mounted low down along the sides of the car and were as 'flat' as could be; radiators were also sited low and flat alongside the driver, as was the oil tank; the engine and transmission were also installed as low down as possible, and the engine itself had to have the lowest possible centre of gravity. The 12-cylinder Ferrari V180° fitted the bill best, whereas high V60° engines were out and were withdrawn from racing (*e.g.*, the 12-cylinder Matra). What is more, the underside in those days was completely flat front to rear and lay parallel to the track. Finally, the driver sat relatively far to the rear with his back up against the engine.

Since all these low-lying components occupied precisely the area that was vital to the aerodynamic design of the wing car, it follows that they had to be redeployed. The broad monocoque with several lateral wing tanks rapidly became a relic of the past. Now there was only one fuel tank and all the designers soon realised that the best place for it was between the driver and the engine. There was a general unwillingness to lengthen the wheelbase, with the result that driver, pedals and so on had to be displaced forwards along the car's longitudinal axis to allow space for the tank to be installed. As a result, you had the driver in an exaggerated up-front position with the front wheels more or less adjacent to his kneecaps and his feet cantilevered out beyond the front suspension. The driver no longer had his back up against the engine but instead sat directly up against the centrally-positioned fuel tank which was built high and narrow – about as wide as the driver's back. The engine itself was located behind the approximately 75 cm-long fuel tank.

Most designers also chose to reposition the oil tank to preclude any disruption of the aerodynamic design of the underbody; the space between the engine and the gearbox proved to be ideal. Additionally, the lowest part of the engine, the oil sump pan, was moved forward to avoid an undesirable bulge as the underbody curved up towards the rear. Clearly, the main transmission shaft had to be fed through the oil tank, which was a rigid, lightweight casting forming a structural link between the engine and the gearbox. In terms of design, the oil tank was also ideal for its primary purpose – high and narrow, to ensure that the pump could effectively retrieve oil from the lowest point.

A similar observation can be made about the fuel tank: it used to be difficult to pick up the last drops from the broad, flat tanks, but the new high narrow tanks effectively eliminated this problem.

All the new Formula I cars other than the 12-cylinder models opted for the sequence driver-fuel tank-engine-oil tank-transmission. In the case of the long 12-cylinder Alfas and Matras, however, such a change would have entailed extending the car's overall length; accordingly, those engines were bolted directly to the transmission unit.

At the same time as this new sequence was adopted, the designers started to make the cockpits progressively narrower so as to exploit as much as possible of the 140 cms legally prescribed body width in order to instal aerodynamic aids. To ensure the driver a modicum of freedom of movement, the FIA found itself obliged to stipulate a minimum cockpit width of 45 cm.

The obsession with slimming down the mid-section of the car was such that Alfa switched from a flat-12 engine to a 60° V12 and the Matra V12 – which had been given up for dead – was resuscitated; Ferrari adopted a V6 layout for his new turbo-charged engine, and firms with in-line 4-cylinder units (BMW and Hart) made their first appearance on the Formula I scene. The stalwart Ford-Cosworth V8 made the transition virtually unchanged.

The advocates of aerodynamics were so strident that automotive designers such as Porsche (commissioned by TAG) and Honda gave top priority in new engine design to what we refer to as 'topography'. In plain English, this meant that they were obliged to build engines which were very narrow underneath, with the oil and water pumps switched from the sides to the front face. The V-angle of the two new 6-cylinder turbos also testifies to the exigencies of aerodynamic design: both firms settled on 80° as an optimum compromise solution.

Before the advent of ground effect cars, the lateral extensions for the fuel tanks had been utilised as part of the load-bearing structure and had played an important role in enhancing the cars' overall rigidity; front-to-rear-axle torsional stiffness had proved particularly important in terms of kinematics (wheel gear theory) and stability. Aerodynamic design considerations now posed the problem of building cars that were narrower than previously but even more rigid. In other words, a new materials technology had to be evolved in monocoque manufacture. As so often before, the quest for new rigid lightweight materials led to the aviation industry, where carbon fibre reinforced plastics and honeycomb sandwich-panel components had long been used.

Also born at this time was the concept of integrating the tanks into the monocoque as opposed to simply attaching them. It was realised that integrated tanks would also make for weight-saving and a more rigid overall superstructure.

The upshot was that the monocoque in the new breed of cars extended from the pedals, brake cylinders and front impact absorbing zone back over cockpit and seat to the rear of the fuel tank, behind which were the engine mountings; in other words, the whole formed a compact and rigid superstructure which gave excellent protection to the fuel tank.

I am one hundred percent convinced that my experience at Nürburgring in 1976 – when the car caught fire – would not have occurred had the fuel tank been positioned as described above. These days, it is very seldom that you see petrol escaping after a shunt, let alone a car catch fire. However, this safer location of the fuel tank came about less as a result of concern for driver safety than from the obvious advantages it provided for underbody aerodynamics.

The 1983 rule changes have not affected fuel tank location, no doubt because of time and cost considerations. It is only to be hoped that designers do not decide to move the tanks back to their previous vulnerable positions just because they want to lower the centre of gravity and shorten the car's overall length. In fact, the tank placement adopted in the ground effect era should be prescribed in the rulebook, despite the fact that there is no longer any aerodynamic justification for it. The only real consideration remaining is that of driver safety.

Once the new sequence of load-bearing components had been established (the pioneer, as so often before, was the late Colin Chapman) the designers turned their minds to the central issue of the ground effect era – building a successful underbody.

Seen from the side, the ground effect car as a whole took on the form of an inverted wing. Airflow to the car travelled a shorter distance across the (roughly) horizontal upper surface than it did across the underbody. Viewed head-on or from the rear, it was immediately apparent that ideal airflow conditions did not prevail: the car's mid-section was particularly disruptive, what with the cockpit, the driver himself, the rollbar, the tank, the engine and the transmission. Looking from head-on, it was also apparent that the centre of the underbody – in theory a smooth surface curving upwards towards the rear of the car – was necessarily disrupted by irregularities to accommodate the seat, the sump and the transmission. This was despite efforts to keep sump and transmission design as narrow as possible.

Afflux – airflow to and across the underbody – was not ideal, because the air was checked by suspension components, parts of the wheels and, where applicable, the front wing. To appreciate how important unimpeded afflux was in the ground effect era, you only had to look at front-axle design: in every case the springs, dampers and anti-roll bars were moved inboard as far as possible, and even the wishbones – the *sine qua non* of the entire suspension system – were aerodynamically profiled.

What is more, when you looked at a ground effect car you could immediately see that airflow over it was impeded even further by the various vents for water and oil radiators and intercoolers.

In short, conditions are far from ideal when it comes to designing for the primary prerequisite of a ground effect car – increased downforce. That there was any such effect at all can be explained in terms of the very large (approximately 1.4 x 2.0 m) effective surface of the underbody, roughly three to four times that of the visible wings. Because this surface was so large, a downwards pressure equivalent to as little a 0.02 bars was sufficient to double the car's weight, *i.e.*, the pressure it exerted on the track.

Invisible Aerodynamics in the Ground Effect Era

The second – and by far the most important – factor which contributes to downforce in a ground effect car is a function of the space and airflow conditions which prevail between the car underbody and track.

For purposes of flow theory, this space is referred to as a 'diffusor', *i.e.*, a more or less enclosed space that opens out in the direction of flow. The diffusor in a ground effect car is roughly rectangular, comprising the underbody, the 'walls' formed by the skirts, and the track itself, the whole opening out towards the rear. The amount of air entering the diffusor from the relatively low intake gap at the front is equal to the quantity which exits behind the car where the underbody ends. Thus, airflow speed is in inverse proportion to diffusor section : fast at the front, comparatively slow at the rear.

The object in ground effect design was to approximate airflow exit speed to driving speed or to just above it. If not, air would flow in under the tail and lift the car – to all intents and purposes, positive lift would be generated and this could only be offset by more (and clearly aerodynamically undesirable) wing. If it proved possible to boost airflow exit speed to above driving speed, the air leaving the diffusor conferred additional acceleration, at which point the entire process became particularly effective.

It goes without saying that the process doesn't function in a vacuum, but is dependent on the energy imparted to the car by the engine. In the case of ground effect cars, the big question was how much of this energy could be recouped to enhance the aerodynamic effect.

To get a better idea of what was involved, imagine to yourself an extremely free-running car equipped with an aerodynamically-styled underbody. When airflow is directed exclusively at the intake gap at the front, the car will begin to roll forward. This is because the forces directed at right angles to the underbody, particularly as it curves upwards towards the tail, act both vertically and horizontally; the lesser (horizontal) force pulls the car forward while the greater (vertical) force thrusts it down.

In order to achieve the desired downforce in a ground effect car, air had to be drawn into the diffusor at three times exit speed (corresponding to the 1 : 3 ratio between intake and exit profiles). This was achieved, first, by providing for as little afflux disruption as possible – I have already mentioned front axle design modifications to achieve this – and, second, by inclining the underbody slightly upwards at the front to 'attract' air to the intake gap.

High air intake speed generated the requisite downforce and ensured its effectiveness over the entire surface of the underbody – even in the mid-section where practical design considerations meant that the wing profile configuration could not be fully maintained. As the diffusor opened out towards the rear, air speed – and, with it, ground effect – dropped off progressively. Ambient airflow conditions were restored at the tail.

For all of this to work, the ground effect car had to have good afflux – the front intake had never to be too small – and consistent airflow to and across the underbody had to be maintained. This is why a typical ground effect underbody had relatively slight curvature; where it curved by more than 6 to 7°, the effectiveness of the diffuser principle was lost and turbulence set in.

All this makes it fairly obvious why we didn't fit spoilers, however handy and effective they might be in other types of car. A spoiler only makes sense if the underbody is irregular or fissured: in such cases, the spoiler directs airflow around the car where it encounters less resistance, thereby diminishing overall drag. In the case of a ground effect car, however, the smooth aerodynamically-styled underbody actually *feeds* on the air flowing across it: a spoiler would have been counter-productive.

Although ground effect applies more or less evenly across the entire underbody, it is possible to conceive of vertical downforce being concentrated on or at a single point – the 'centre of pressure'. In the Formula I ground effect era, pinpointing the centre of pressure and fully exploiting the downforce concentrated on it were the dominant criteria, to the virtual exclusion of all other considerations. Seen head-on or from the rear, the car's symmetrical design obviously suggests that the centre of pressure is located precisely at mid-point of the longitudinal axis; seen from the side, on the other hand, the centre of pressure falls not at the mid-point but somewhere in the front third of the wheelbase. Pinpointing it *exactly* was the key to improved performance, in the sense that it held the clue to otherwise inexplicable differences in lap speeds in one marque as opposed to another.

The centre of pressure could be displaced forwards or backwards by varying the curvature of the underbody. This, in conjunction with visible wing adjustments, often resulted in a two to three second difference either way. The remarkable thing was that the ground effect car's handling stayed incredibly neutral: it was the stopwatch rather than 'feel' which told you whether you were going faster or slower.

Getting To Grips With Downforce

The site of the centre of pressure is of vital importance; so, too, is the amount of downforce operating on it. Williams designer Patrick Head put together a few figures culled from leading Formula I cars in 1981. For example, that the ground effect generated by the cars' overall aerodynamics amounted to some 255 kilogrammes at 100 km/h. This figure quadrupled to 1,020 kg at 200 km/h, and reached almost 2,300 kg at 300 km/h, these 'weights' being additional to the all-up weight of the car itself. What we are talking about, in other words, is a quadrupling of the weight of the car at rest – complete with driver and, say, a half-full tank.

The increased wheel loading generated by aerodynamic design meant that corners could be taken significantly faster than in non-ground effect cars. To illustrate, let's assume a median friction coefficient (μ) of 1.2, *i.e.*, that a wheel subject to a vertical load of 100 kg will transfer horizontal force via the tyre equivalent to 120 kg (100 x 1.2) – an acceleration force amounting to 1.2*G* (acceleration due to gravity).

It is now quite simple to extrapolate values for different speeds and radii:

Speed km/h	Curve radius without ground effect	Lateral acceleration without ground effect	Curve radius with ground effect	Lateral acceleration with ground effect
100	66 metres	1.2 *G*	48.5 metres	1.6 *G*
200	268	1.2	107.5	2.9
300	589	1.2	140.5	5.0

The Design Revolution: The Quest for Enhanced Ground Effect

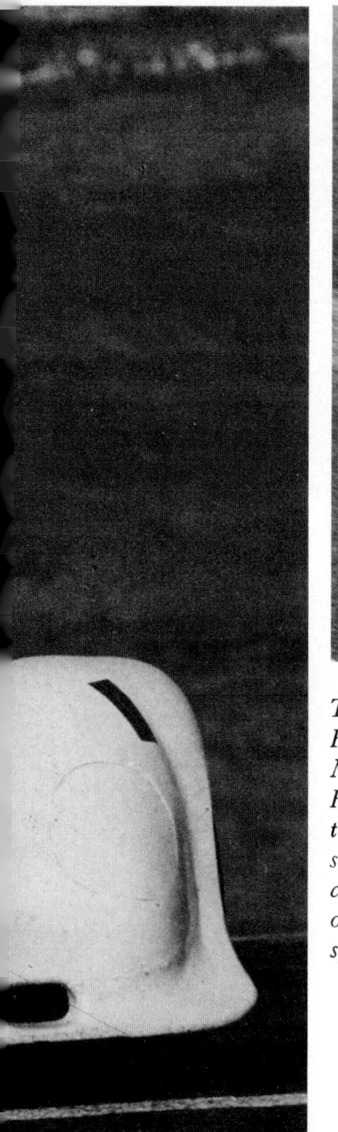

There was no hint of aerodynamic aids in mid-sixties Formula I cars (above: Jochen Rindt in a Cooper-Maserati). At that time, Texan designer and driver Jim Hall was hitting the headlines in his Chapparal: the towering Chapparal aerofoil (left) triggered a worldwide scramble for enhanced ground effect in the modern racing car. A few years later came the 'vacuum cleaner' version or 'fan' Chapparal (above: Jackie Stewart, 1970), symptomatic of every subsequent excess.

Right: Once Formula I had espoused the wing concept in 1968, the next championship season saw a series of grotesque designs such as the oversize aerofoils on this Lotus piloted by Graham Hill. The car would lose traction completely if one of these wings snapped, buckled or worked itself loose, and there were a number of serious shunts.

Above: Heyday and end of the road for double-decker fashion: the aerofoils on Graham Hill's Lotus, Jochen Rindt's Lotus and Jack Ickx's Brabham collapse during the 1969 Spanish Grand Prix. The two traumatic Lotus shunts in particular were enough to rattle the powers-that-be and high wings were banned eleven days later.

Far left: Wing fashion 1968: Jacky Ickx (Ferrari).

Left: Giant wings were banned as from the 1969 Monaco Grand Prix; Graham Hill's Lotus now looks very staid by comparison.

Top: The first Formula I car to apply the inverted wing principle to bodywork design was the 1970 March (driven here by Ronnie Peterson): the lateral ('wing') tanks are designed to provide a modest amount of downforce.

Above: The vacuum cleaner makes a short guest appearance: this Gordon Murray-designed Brabham was originally accepted as legal. I drove it to a very easy victory in the 1978 Swedish Grand Prix but it was banned soon after, along with other roadsweeper models.

Opposite: The first truly mature ground effect car was the Lotus driven to 1978 championship success by Mario Andretti.

John Player
Special
OLYMPUS
5
Valvoline

John Player Special
John
Player
Special
Andretti
NGK
Valvoline
Player Special
5

The difference in cornering speed for a 66 m radius curve is already considerable (126 as opposed to 100 km/h), but the gap increases enormously as the radius is enlarged. A conventional car will take a 140 m radius curve at 146 km/h, whereas a ground effect car will flash through it at 300 km/h – twice as fast.

The differences in lateral acceleration are also quite remarkable. Here, the values are a function of the tyres on the one hand and the loads forcing the car down on the track on the other. The actual weight of the car is immaterial. All other things being equal, you can corner at the same speed in a light car as in a heavy one. Lateral acceleration – gravitational pull – is determined by the friction coefficient of the tyres: where this is, say, 1.2, lateral acceleration will amount to 1.2 *G* – a typical friction coefficient for a non-aerodynamically-styled racing car on a dry track, although it falls off sharply in the rain or in snow to as little as one-tenth of the original value.

A car of non-aerodynamic design will exhibit a limit value which is constant (in our example 1.2), totally irrespective of the curve radius involved. In simpler terms, tight corners are taken more slowly than others. As the table shows, a 1.2 friction coefficient means that a 66 m radius curve can be taken at 100 km/h, whereas 200 km/h requires a radius of 268 metres, and 300 km/h a 'radius' of 589 metres – scarcely recognisable as a curve. In every instance, the driver will be subjected to 1.2 *G* at the apex of the curve – not a problem for the average healthy human.

It was a whole new ballgame, however, when you were driving a ground

The underbody, be-all and end-all of ground effect: a whole range of different airflow patterns can be achieved across the underbody by varying forms and contours. The indentations in the centre are designed to accommodate the driver's feet, the seat, the fuel tank, the sump and the transmission.

effect car. Downforce increased wheel loading immeasurably without increasing the car's mass. The tyres might still have a 1.2 friction coefficient, but the much greater downforce acting on them (four times 'normal' values at 300 km/h, for example) meant that they were able to handle greater lateral loads – up to four times as great at or around the 300 km/h mark. What it all boiled down to was gravitational pull equivalent to around 5 *G*: the 'weight' of the driver's body was increased five-fold. Clearly, this kind of stress can only be handled by someone in peak physical condition and, even then, only for very short periods.

It goes without saying that improved lap times on already fast circuits could be attributed to faster cornering. After all, not all that much had been done to the engines. But faster lap times also resulted from the improved braking and accelerating characteristics of ground effect cars. A ground effect car can be braked from high speed within a much shorter distance, the reasons being much the same as those which explain their faster cornering ability: in fact, a ground effect car travelling at 300 km/h can be braked four times as forcibly as a car without ground effect.

Skirts and Rubbing Strips

The lateral skirts and the rubbing strips attached to them played an important part in the development of ground effect cars. It was their job to seal off

An inadvertent glimpse of the underbody in a 1981 Arrows: the aerodynamic design exhibited a subtle curvature rather than a spectacular sweep. Less subtle, of course, were the dents and bumps caused by the crash.

as tightly as possible the vital ground effect zone between car underbody and track: the skirts enclosed the diffusor formed by underbody and (to a lesser extent) track, shielded the ground effect zone from disruptive ambient airflow, and thus ensured that downloading was distributed over an optimally effective underbody surface.

Clearly, you can get ground effect without skirts, but it is greatly reduced. Without them, the car handles in a radically different way: the immense longitudinal and transverse acceleration benefits evaporate and the car starts to drift through the corners again, responsive once more to the accelerator. This is obviously an attractive prospect for both driver and spectator.

Skirts were originally designed to be adjustable, *i.e.*, to ensure that they – or the rubbing strips – would close down against the track at all times and provide an optimum seal under any driving conditions. Obviously, the clearance between track and underbody (ride height) changed continually and, moreover, switched from one side of the car to the other to reflect variation in downloading, unevenness of circuit, or lift and droop caused by braking, accelerating and cornering. The adjustable skirts were developed to counteract these variations caused by load displacement; there was even some experimentation with brushes in this connection.

The completely adjustable skirt system didn't work out perfectly, however, and there were a number of shunts because the rubbing strips occasionally worked loose. The anti-skirt brigade managed to have them banned, and a new 6 cm clearance rule was brought in. This rule – applicable to the car at rest – might have been expected to take care of the problem except for the fact that crafty designers – never the ones to overlook a loophole – soon found a way round it.

The first move was to design skirts which were no longer almost rigid like their predecessors, but which were instead in two sections and elasticated. They were bolted rigidly to the sides of the car to conform to point 1 of the new regulation. Point 2 was also complied with by installing small hydraulic jacks, which acted on the suspension and brought the car up to the prescribed 6 cm clearance while the car was stationary in the pit-lane ready for inspection. Once qualifying laps and the race itself got under way, of course, the ride height was dropped to enhance the car's overall aerodynamic design. The powers-that-be turned to all manner of advance technology (even laser-beam equipment) to check ride height, but it all proved to be of little help in the long run. The whole farce was brought to an end in the 1982 championship season when the 6 cm ride height rule was abandoned.

One problem still remained, however, namely that of attaining a perfect seal in all conditions from rigidly-attached but more or less elastic skirts. This and underbody design were the hot issues in ground effect cars; all other considerations (such as suspension design, springs, differentiated shock absorber adjustment, anti-roll bars, and so on) had to take a back seat.

The springs were a case in point. In the ground effect era they had only one job – to maintain requisite clearance at optimum downforce, thereby ensuring constant airflow intake to take full advantage of aerodynamic design.

What this meant was that the springs had to be set to handle some 2,300 kg downforce plus some 700 kg of all-up car weight – about 3,000 kg in all. That explained their appearance: extremely short, with thick coils and a rigidity comparable to that of a small truck. The springs were brutally hard, and totally unadapted to any driving conditions other than flat-out. Strange as it may sound, however – cornering apart – the ground effect cars were relatively pleasant to drive at high speeds; it was only at slower speeds that you felt your brain rattling around inside your skull. Even watching on TV, you

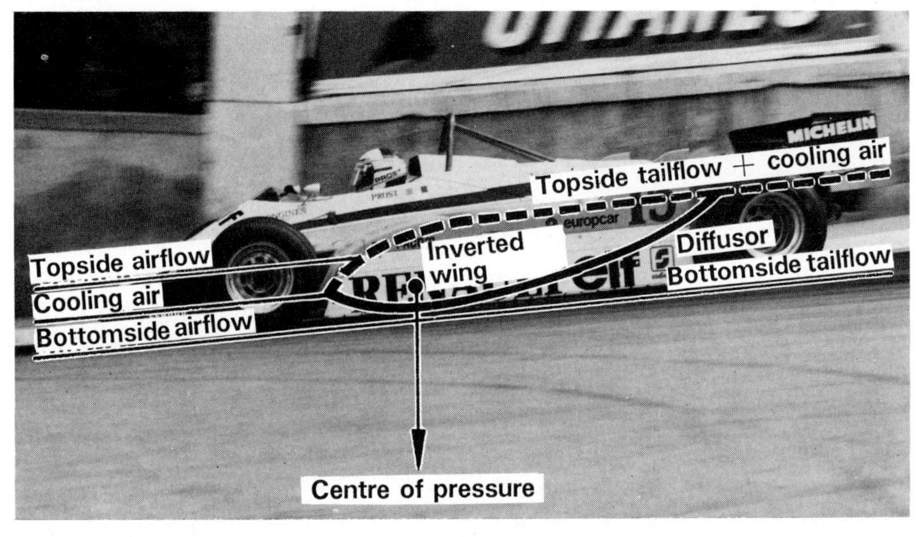

Bodywork and skirts concealed aerodynamic design details from view. Here they are superimposed. The quantity of air entering from bottom front (bottomside airflow) is the same – assuming a tight skirt seal – as the quantity of tailflow. The optimum airflow speed was recorded at the point where the space between the underbody and the track is at its narrowest. The approximate location of the centre of pressure is indicated by an arrow.

could see the cars bouncing about all over the place because the wheels no longer responded to the unevenness of the circuit.

Coming back to the skirts: if you took a close look at them, you would see how little play they could be expected to accommodate. On the one hand, they had to be elastic to some extent but, on the other, they couldn't afford to be *too* flexible since that would have meant that they were liable to be displaced by airflow along the sides of the car trying to force its way into the ground effect zone underneath it. When that happened, of course, your ground effect was dissipated.

The skirts were designed in two sections in an attempt to cope with the demands made on them. First, you had a rubbing strip about 2 cms thick which skimmed over the surface of the track, then you had 6 cm of skirt proper made of elastic or semi-elastic material. The two sections were bolted to the rubbing strip by countless tiny studs and the skirts in turn were secured by countless tiny studs to the sidepods. The skirts were mounted in such a way that they didn't hang down absolutely vertically – that way they would have had no play at all – but were angled slightly inwards. This meant that the angle could be increased as downforce built up. In effect, therefore, the skirts were somewhat longer than the actual ground clearance.

When a car was jacked up – to change a wheel for example – you would sometimes find that the skirts didn't angle inwards of their own accord but angled outwards instead: when that happened, you would see them being kicked or hammered back into place.

The choice of material for both the skirts and the rubbing strips was very critical. As far as the rubbing strips were concerned, the prime requirements were that they be somewhat elastic, tough enough to go the whole race distance and yet not so resilient that they slowed the car by dragging on the track surface. It was a mistake to underestimate the abrasion: it was so pronounced that it took four able-bodied mechanics to push the car when it was not under power. (This made a horrible noise, by the way, but had no ill effects on the car.) The important thing, however, was that the strips should wear evenly over their whole length – some two metres; if there was premature wear either at front or rear, the car's handling would change dramatically.

The start of the 1982 championship season saw a frenzied search for some kind of new 'super-plastic' for the rubbing strips. All kinds of wild ideas were floated until it dawned on us that the best results could probably be had by using wood. McLaren and the other leading makers switched to wooden strips – several thin slats bonded together to form a 2 x 2 cm block which was bolted to the plastic of the skirt. When the skirts were too long (*i.e.*, when the car was set too low), they folded in underneath the car at such a sharp angle that not only the wooden strips but also the skirts themselves made contact with the track; when that happened, of course, the skirts were soon worn beyond redemption.

Before the general switch to wood, all kinds of rubbing strip gimmicks had been tried. The regulations said that metal could not be used. One Spring day in 1982, however, Ferrari tested some new strips during qualifying: the car came thundering down the straight with smoke billowing out from behind it as if it were on fire. When we saw the blue smoke we all assumed that the engine had blown; not so – the smoke was coming from rubbing strips which had had tiny iron filings poured into them and which were showering sparks and smoke everywhere.

Changing the skirts was a routine chore for mechanics in 1981 and 1982. It was a reasonably difficult job, all the same, because it involved fiddling around with lots of tiny screws. This Talbot Ligier had an impressive V12 engine; note also the two rear brake calipers for each brake disc.

The skirts themselves were made as a rule of thin (approximately 10 mm) plastic material which corresponded exactly to the length of the rubbing strips. We always had a stock of skirts of different elasticity – designated hard, soft and medium. The aerodynamic effect was best with the hard skirt variety, but those made for most wear-and-tear on the strips. Choice of skirt material and the manner in which it was attached to the superstructure were co-determinant factors as regards even and overall wear.

During qualifying, everything depended on the rubbing strips. Anyone who ever followed the sport at all closely will have noticed that there was perpetual 'aerodynamic' adjustment all through a ground effect qualifying session. Previously, the focal points had been springs, anti-roll bars, dampers and suspension geometry, but the advent of the ground effect car meant that absolute and overriding priority was given to trying out skirt permutations: we all knew that there was a damned sight more to be gained that way than, say, by a few clicks adjustment to the dampers.

What none of us was in a position to afford, of course, was experimentation with various underbody units. Most teams were limited to two different 'standard' underbodies – one for fast circuits and one for slow – and had to make do with them.

Learning to Live with an 'Aerodynamic' Car

Earlier on I pointed out that ground effect cars handled comparatively reasonably only at high speeds, because it was only then that spring and damper settings were more or less right. When you eased out of the pit-lane at Kyalami, for example, passing over the two small bumps there was enough to put you off Grand Prix driving for good: there was no give in the springs and shock absorbers, with the result that you felt the jolt all the way up through the thin plastic seat.

On undulating circuits the cars leaped around so much that all the fun went out of driving. Worst of all was driving over the very high kerbs. I always tried very hard to avoid touching the kerbs, because if I did make contact, I never had a clue what the car would do next.

The wildest imaginable things could happen when you were behind the wheel of a ground effect car. For example, half way down a fast straight the nose would suddenly dip and hit the track. Your first reaction was to blame the virtually non-existent springing, which had not compensated for a small ridge on the track. But it kept on happening, at least on the straight – the nose dipped intermittently, and you got the feeling that the car's behaviour was totally beyond your control.

That was what we called 'porpoising', Formula I slang for irregular airflow conditions. The flow of air to and across the aerodynamically-styled underbody had been disrupted for some mysterious reason, and a cushion of air had started to build up beneath the car. This cushion got bigger and bigger until, at some unpredictable moment, the uneven ride broke the skirt seal and the air escaped. The nose was then sucked down briefly, and then the whole business repeated itself. The really traumatic part was that there was nothing you could do about this out on the circuit – there was nothing you could 'adjust', nothing you could 're-set'. All you could do was accept the fact that there was something wrong with the design of the underbody, and hope that one day your designer would come up with a better one.

We had this front axle lift problem at McLaren at the start of the 1982 championship season. John Barnard had already carried out some wind tunnel tests, and said that it was gradually coming good: everything would be all right in time for the South African Grand Prix. I had very serious doubts because it isn't good to bank on wind tunnel test data (mind you, being able to work in one is certainly a tremendous plus, and only a few teams can afford to do so). At any rate, I was sceptical when John proclaimed that he had 'found' 30 per cent more downforce. First of all, the behaviour of a racing car on the track can be very different from that of a quarter-scale model in a wind tunnel; in addition, the amount of downforce is not the only determinant when it comes to handling characteristics. You can come up with extra downforce and still have a car that handles badly – maybe because the centre of pressure is too far forward, with the result that the front of the car is held down beautifully but the back end gets very 'loose'. When that happens, you have to change the centre of pressure, which is one way of saying that you have to redesign the underbody. The closer the centre of pressure is moved towards the middle of the car, the better balanced the car: it is more 'neutral' and better equipped to exploit ground effect to the full.

It has recently become possible to run tests to check on centre of pressure location. Once Barnard had finished his wind tunnel tests and the new underbody was ready, we set off for the Michelin test circuit in Clermont-Ferrand. This fantastic circuit has a long straight with two measuring devices set into the track, for all the world like two manhole covers. It was my job to go over these with my left-side wheels at different predetermined speeds – 80, 180 and 280 km/h. We spent two whole days at this and it was unbelievably boring. I couldn't have anyone stand in for me, however, because the measuring devices have to be hit absolutely spot-on if you want accurate test measurements.

The precise location of the centre of pressure is extrapolated from these measurements. If the results more or less match those from the wind tunnel trials, the chances are that the car is set up right.

At any rate, we went off to Kyalami in 1982 with brand new cars in which McLaren's designer was the only one to have 100 per cent faith. He was right – they worked out from the word go, which was very impressive considering the problems other teams were having with porpoising.

On some of the circuits we drove that year (1982), McLaren certainly had the cars with the greatest downforce, *i.e.*, the fastest cars through the corners. However, we couldn't keep increasing downforce ad infinitum: problems start to multiply with increased ground effect. When you hug the track tightly you risk being thrown off line by the slightest surface irregularity. What is more, the rubbing strips start to wear much faster.

The material used for the strips was one problem area, skirt angle was another. It was a tremendously complicated business all round, since correct angling is vital if you want to avoid skirt leak. When the seal is broken in a ground effect car, the whole car immediately becomes unstable.

Another problem area related to the excessive demands made on the tyres due to extremely high cornering speeds. All of a sudden they were subjected to a weight of some 3,000 kg and they simply couldn't cope. The sidewalls gave under the strain, the tyre lost adhesion and you sideslipped until the tyre righted itself and gripped again.

It was always something of a mystery when you went into a qualifying lap with the car apparently set up right, an engine that was running well and the determination to give it everything you had, only to find that you were a second or so slower than some other Cosworth-engined car. All you could do was raise or lower the car by adjusting the spring collars – in other words, opt for less or more downforce. If you lowered the car, all the 'wing' elements were closer to the ground, the speed of the airflow under the car was increased, and the skirts gave a better seal.

The ride height you chose depended to a large extent on the condition of the track. If it was really bumpy you would tend to go for less pressure so as not to lose control when driving over the irregular surface. Another deci-

Keke Rosberg (Williams).

sive factor was the *type of circuit*, i.e., the relative predominance of slow corners and fast straights. If I increased downforce I could take the corners extremely fast but I lost out on the straight, because the car hugged the track so closely that its top speed suffered.

When you were setting up for a particularly fast circuit such as Paul Ricard, Oesterreich-Ring or Zandvoort, your thinking would probably be as follows. First, reduce rear wing to a logically acceptable minimum, then raise the front of the car to reduce front end downforce and balance the car. If you went for less rear wing and left the nose right down, there would be so much downforce on the front wheels that the car would oversteer wildly. That was why you had to reduce downforce by lifting the car via the spring collars – 3 to 5 mm was usually enough to strike a happy medium and allow a satisfactory top speed.

Cornering in a Ground Effect Car

To be honest, there was no such thing as 'cornering technique' in the ground effect era. 'Cornering' was a euphemism for out-and-out rape practised on the driver, the car and the laws of physics. Here's what happened.

You took a tight line up to the corner and, as you came in – that is, before the g-forces took over – you turned the steering wheel. That was it. The steering wheel was in position – for better or for worse – for the duration of the corner. As soon as the car was exposed to centrifugal forces, the steering wheel was locked in the chosen position and there was no way you could turn it. If – by some freak chance – you *did* manage to move it to take corrective action, the car – which was locked down as if it were in a vice – would start to bounce. Once that happened, the skirts began to leak, the aerodynamics were shot to hell, the car became completely unpredictable, and the chances were that you would end up in the shrubbery.

Let's run through it again: up to the corner, wheel over, end of story. If you didn't get it right, you would be far better off throttling back and braking than trying to correct via the steering wheel. The situation would still be hairy, but it would be easier to deal with than if you lost skirt seal or, even worse, hit the kerb.

There was a whole world of difference between driving a ground effect car and driving in the traditional style. The 'old-fashioned' approach meant that you could pull the steering over a bit, sense the tail starting to drift, steer into it fractionally, and drive on out of the corner. In a ground effect car, however, you had to be really precise in your selection of angle of approach. Once you got that right, the trick was to keep your foot hard down. I have already pointed out in the theoretical discussion that the aerodynamics improved the faster you went. As a driver, you got the impression that the car was wrongly set-up when you were coasting along but, once you stepped up the pace, you felt the car holding the road better and all systems were go. When you came into a corner you had to hit the accelerator as hard as you possibly could, build up speed as quickly as possible and, when things came unstuck, bite the bullet and give it even more. If you started to bounce you were in trouble, if you tried to steer out of trouble you only made matters worse. The only thing for it was to accelerate. But there was always that little question at the back of your mind: how far can I push it before I spin out?

None of us had the answer to that one. We could corner about 30 per cent faster in a ground effect car than we could in the old days, but previously we had always been able to work our way up very carefully towards the limit, bearing in mind that there were borderline situations where you could still steer or accelerate out of trouble. In a ground effect car, however, reaching the limit was synonymous with spinning out.

When you were really bang on form – completely alert, and with all the right instincts and the guts to go with them – you would drive the merest fraction below the absolute limit. But only for one lap in ten. In the long run you simply couldn't chance going flat out all the time because the slightest thing could trigger a shunt. All it took was for the man in front to take his foot off the accelerator and out you went. And when I say 'out', I don't mean an itsy-bitsy sideslip or a hint of a skid, I mean well and truly 'out' – at 280 km/h.

As you might expect, the designers had a pat answer to all this. Aha, they said, don't forget that the new aerodynamic design means that you can slow down faster than you can accelerate, because braking distances have become appreciably shorter. That was fair enough in normal situations, such as braking on the approach to a corner – the car did lose speed in a way you wouldn't have credited a few years previously, and which is no longer possible today. The braking of today's cars, and those of earlier generations, is dependent on the friction coefficient of the tyres, whereas ground effect cars had an additional advantage from their aerodynamic aids. The question was, however, how often did we spin out so favourably that the aerodynamics stayed intact? For that to happen, you needed a whole lot of asphalt and no major obstacles that might damage the skirts. In reality, the first spin would set in alongside the kerb; once you went over that your skirts were ripped away, you lost most of your ground effect, and off you went into the greenery. So much for coming to a standstill more quickly than before!

Another major problem area of ground effect cars made its presence felt on very fast circuits: excessive g-force loading on the driver. The car itself countered g-force thanks to its downloading and the driver's body was part of the car, 'bonded' to it thanks to the taut safety harness. It was only the driver's head that was exposed to colossal stress.

Take for instance the Rio de Janeiro circuit, with its long slightly banked corners. When you lapped in 1 min. 35 sec. you didn't run into any real problems. But when you stepped it up to 1:31 or 1:30, you found after about three laps that you couldn't hold your head straight: about halfway through a corner your head jack-knifed sideways and slammed up against the nearest fixed object – in this case, the bodywork. After a while, the whole thing became automatic – corner, half-in, thunk, round went the head. You watched the road out of the corner of your eye and waited until you came out of the corner before you could straighten up.

All of that was fairly acceptable, I suppose. But once you started to tire, there was more to it. The onrushing wind blasted into your face. It was more than just a case of your head being turned, now it was wrenched round and down. The net effect was that your field of vision was seriously curtailed: all you could make out were your thighs, the gear lever and the tiniest section of the track as it whipped by below. What you *didn't* see was the rest of the corner. There were only two things you could do – drive more slowly or call it a day.

If you still need convincing as to the unbelievable strain of driving at Rio, you only have to think back to Nelson Piquet's winning drive there in 1982. His head was slammed sideways in every fast corner, and he collapsed on the victor's rostrum after the race.

Rules of the Game

The Legislative Framework of Formula I

The technical specifications for Formula I were laid down by the *Fédération Internationale de l'Automobile* and are published *in extenso* in the Federation Yearbook. The key provisions as at May 1983 are as follows:
— *Engine*: Four-stroke, 12-cylinder maximum; capacity limited to 3 litres normally aspirated or 1.5 litres super-charged.
— *All-Up Weight*: Not less than 540 kg.
— *Length*: Wheelbase (distance between centre-lines of front and rear wheels) unrestricted, but coachwork (including front wings) must extend no more than 120 cm ahead of the centre line of the front wheels and must be no wider than 150 cm; coachwork (rear wing) may extend no more than 80 cm behind centre-line of rear wheels, and is subject to a width restriction of 110 cm.
— *Height*: Restricted to 80 cm (excluding roll hoop).
— *Width*: Maximum body width (outer rim to outer rim) restricted to 215 cm; maximum body width of substantial structure (*i.e.*, between wheels, see 'Length' above) restricted to 140 cm; cockpit width not to be less than 45 cm.

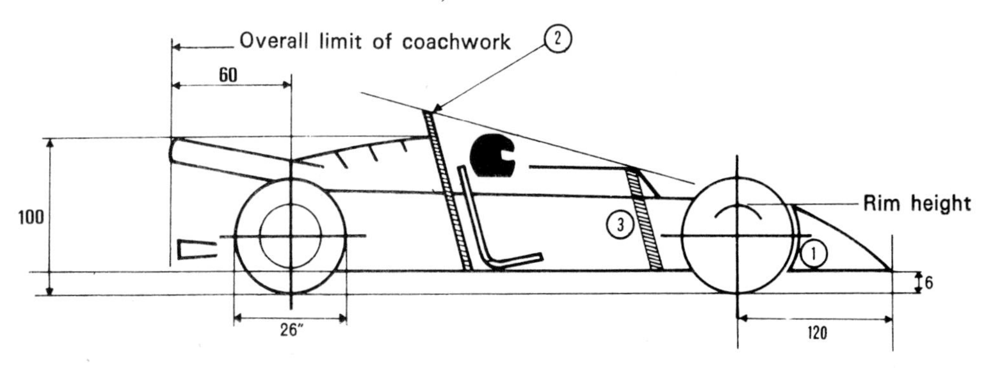

Dimensions in cms except those of wheels which must be given in inches

1 — For all parts wider than 110 cm.
2 — Safety roll bar
3 — Substantial structure

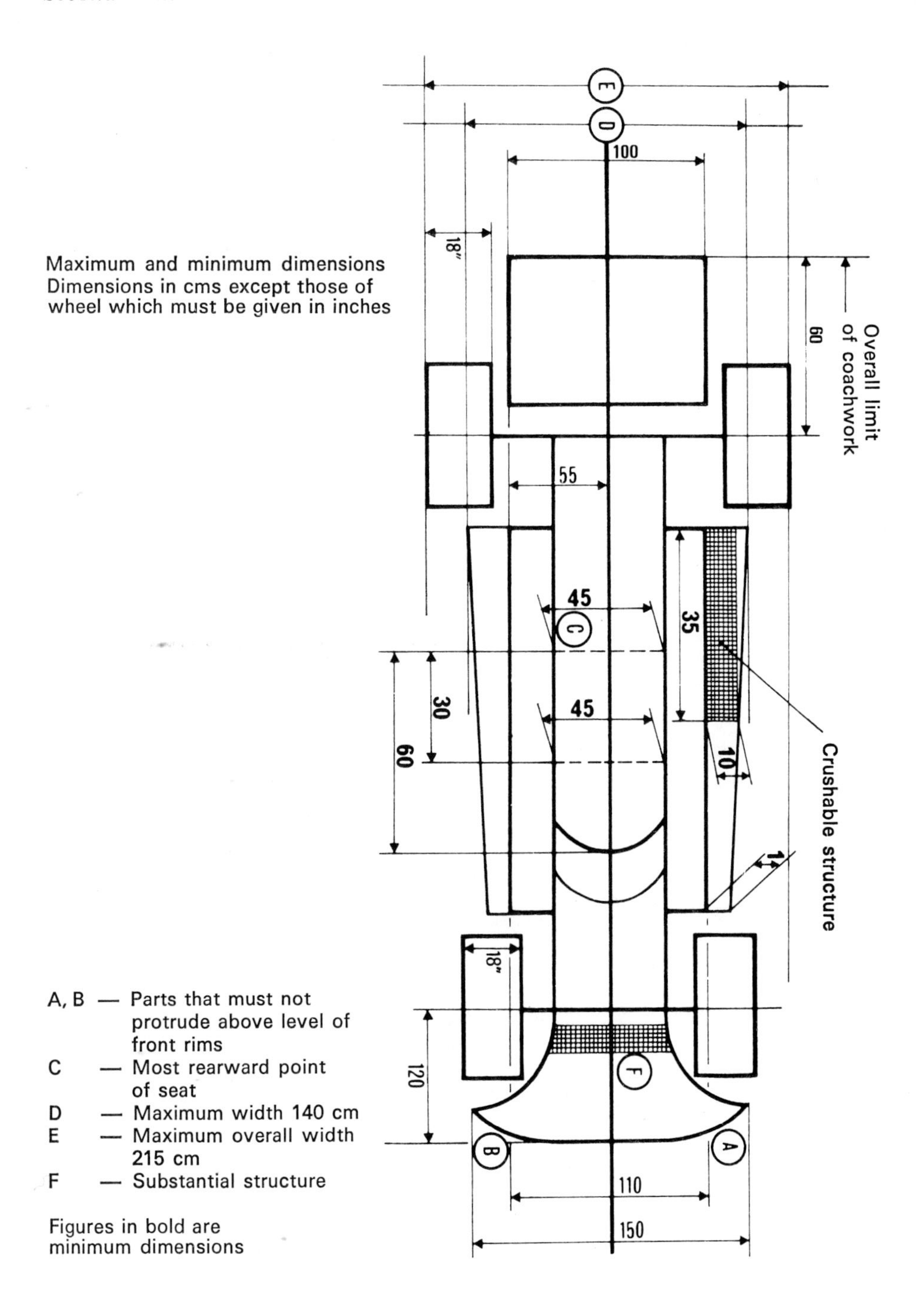
Maximum and minimum dimensions
Dimensions in cms except those of wheel which must be given in inches
E
D
100
18"
60
Overall limit of coachwork
55
45
C
35
30
45
60
10
1
Crushable structure
18"
120
F
B
A
110
150
A, B — Parts that must not protrude above level of front rims
C — Most rearward point of seat
D — Maximum width 140 cm
E — Maximum overall width 215 cm
F — Substantial structure
Figures in bold are minimum dimensions

Tyres: Maximum diameter 26″ (66 cm); maximum width 18″ (45.7 cm).
Tank Capacity: Maximum 250 litres.

Safety regulations, of which there are a growing number, are discussed in a separate chapter.

Since all the main dimensions are subject to tight specification, the designers have precious little scope to work in. Up until championship season 1983, however, there were no restrictions as regards underbody design and lateral skirts were generally permitted, subject to the rules discussed earlier.

Among the rule changes introduced for championship season 1983, the following stirred up most controversy: all-up weight was reduced from 580 kg to 540 kg; skirts were banned outright; and underbody design was subject to new proscriptions. An attempt was made to frame the rules in such a manner that it has become impossible or virtually impossible to design the underbody so as to create downforce.

To put it in a nutshell, what this means is that all today's Formula I cars have to have a flat, fixed underbody.

It seems to me that the question of fuel consumption has also been solved neatly. The rules for 1983 specify a maximum fuel tank capacity of 250 litres and permit re-fuelling; as of January 1, 1984, the overall tank capacity will be cut back to a maximum of 220 litres, and re-fuelling during the course of a race will not be permitted. The overall race distance has to lie between lower and upper limits of 300 and 320 kilometres respectively; if the prescribed distance is not covered within two hours, the leading car will be flagged down and the race considered over. Further, as of January 1, 1985, the tank capacity will be reduced even further, namely to 195 litres, and re-fuelling during a race will not be permitted.

Fuel is becoming an increasingly hot topic these days, not only in terms of quantity but also in terms of quality. The rules only admit fuel that is exclusively hydrocarbon-based, *i.e.*, no alcohol, nitrates or other additives may be used to boost performance.

It has been rumoured that some teams are using additives (alcohol and lead) to boost the octane count (the engine knock determinant) by some 5 to 6 percent. This ploy is favourable to the turbos in particular, since optimum boost pressure – and thus performance – is a function of fuel grade.

Normally-aspirated engines also benefit from the use of higher-grade fuel, but not to the same extent as turbo-charged engines.

Aerodynamics Today

Visible Wings

Earlier we dealt at length with the underbody and the 'invisible wings'. As far as aerodynamic design is concerned in the most recent generation of Formula I cars, however, we can limit the discussion to their 'visible' counterparts.

The wing profiles used in a modern racing car correspond to those used in aircraft design, the vital distinction being that – since they are intended to generate negative rather than positive lift – they are mounted upside down. In other words, the longer side of the wing section faces downwards. Because airflow speeds are identical ahead of and behind the wing, air flowing over the (longer) underside has to travel farther and thus faster. The net effect is to exert downwards pressure which forces the wing and the car down onto the track.

The inverted wing can be 'trimmed', *i.e.*, adjusted mechanically, to create varying degrees of downforce. Adjustment of the angle of inclination is by means of a composite spirit level/protractor device and is permitted only during a pit stop; wings that could be re-set directly from the cockpit or via the suspension while the car was in motion were banned in 1969 after a number of serious incidents.

Adjustment is effected via a row of slits or perforations on the wing mount; it can be done by the pit crew in next to no time. Adjustment of the wing angle is always carried out in very small steps, however, since downforce increases as the square of the speed at which the car is moving, which is to say that doubling the car's speed results in quadrupling of downforce.

As noted, the principle followed here is that used in aircraft design to exploit the fact that, within certain parameters, vertical forces (upthrust) increase in keeping with the angle of wing inclination. During take-off and final approach particularly, a jet aircraft will climb or descend steeply to preserve positive lift at low airspeed. The principle is at its most dramatic where the ratio of wing surface to overall weight is reduced – the classic example being the space shuttle, which makes its final approach with its nose pulled right up to compensate for negligible wing surface. While it is true that more wing would be useful on landing to shorten run-out, it would – quite literally – be a 'drag' during normal supersonic flight.

What actually happens can best be visualised by thinking of the wing as flat on one side and curved on the other. The curved surface is underneath in an aircraft wing and on top in a racing car. When the flat surface lies parallel to the ground, it is the curved side alone which generates negative lift in a racing car; when the wing is angled, however, the top surface also boosts downforce by checking topside airflow.

To get a feel for this, try holding the flat of your hand out of the window of a moving car and slowly angling it. You will feel quite distinctly how the rush of air past your hand is 'negated' in the sense that more pressure is exerted either upwards or downwards. You will also sense how much strength or counter-pressure has to be exerted to avoid your hand being jerked backwards: clearly, the amount of strength that has to be used against the onrushing air will increase with the speed at which the car is moving and the obliqueness of the angle at which you are holding your hand. This backwards pressure is 'drag' – the resistance generated by the hand (or wing) against relative wind.

Wings not only boost downwards pressure – which is both intentional and desirable – they also boost forwards pressure, which is undesirable in that it increases overall tractive resistance. Accordingly, you have to adjust the car for each individual circuit so as to strike a happy medium between downthrust and increased drag (= loss of speed). Never mind the theory: what counts is a faster lap time.

Wing width in the new Formula I is strictly regulated – no more than 150 centimetres at the front or 110 cm at the rear. Not surprisingly, every designer exploits these limits down to the last millimetre. To minimise wing tip drag, each wing is finished with thin vertical 'deflectors', end-plates which ensure even distribution of airflow over the entire wing surface.

Wings function best when airflow to and from them – 'afflux' and 'tailflow' respectively – is unimpeded. There is obviously no afflux problem as far as the front wing is concerned, but the rear wing is another matter entirely because of all the bits and pieces which lie ahead of it – wheels, roll-hoop, helmet, and so on – all of which contribute to a disruption of the airflow. One solution to rear wing afflux problems would clearly be to raise rear wing height: this is prohibited under current rules, however, to the extent that a maximum car height of 100 cm is stipulated.

Tailflow – airflow behind the wing – gives rise to a similar set of problems, albeit in reverse. As far as the rear wing is concerned, conditions are virtually ideal but, in the case of the front wing, the wheels, bodywork, suspension

The massive rear wing on the Brabham-BMW is reinforced by two thin cables to improve rigidity.

and so on exert a variety of disruptive influences on tailflow. Harping back to the airplane analogy, it is evident that the rear 'wings' – *i.e.*, the tailplane – are positioned much higher than the main wings to prevent tailflow from the latter disrupting airflow to the rear wings and so reducing lift and manoeuvrability.

The trailing edges of a racing car wing often have flaps which permit a build-up of air flowing over the upper surface, thereby increasing downforce. These flaps are particularly useful if airflow over the underside of the wing is less than ideal. Trailing edge flaps exact their own pound of flesh, however – more downthrust is generated but, equally, more drag. Occasionally 'split wings' are used – two thinner, independently adjustable wings mounted one above the other. The idea here is that air forced through the gap between them makes for better airflow conditions across the underside of the upper section.

As you come closer to the wing mount, the underside of the wing becomes less aerodynamically effective. For this reason, every effort is made to keep the mounts as slender as possible and to position them in an airflow 'zone' where conditions are in any case already unfavourable, namely in the centre section of the car. This is why wing mounts are almost invariably installed at the end of the transmission or somewhere in the centre of the rear suspension. Unfortunately, the wing mounts are designed so narrow that they inspire precious little confidence, particularly on an undulating circuit where they can be seen to wobble alarmingly.

If a front wing spoiler is used, the logical mount position is in the centre of the extended monocoque.

In the ground effect era before 1983, many designers tried to get by without using a front wing. This was easy enough to understand, because a properly designed underbody generated so much downforce that a front wing could be regarded as superfluous. This is no longer true – the new rules mean that there is no way you can do without a front wing. As of the 1983 championship season, the 'visible wings' have come back into the limelight because it is virtually to them alone that we look for downforce. Since the main dimensions are subject to stringent regulation, every effort is made to exploit their effective surface.

If you really want fast lap times today, you have to look again for the optimum wing configuration – 'less wing' or 'more wing': the former means less downforce but higher top speed, the latter increased downforce but a sacrifice in terms of speed. The 'best' wing configuration varies from circuit

Four-part 'Cascade' rear wing on the Lotus. The underbody is curved upwards as and where the rules allow.

An absolute must for the turbos: the rear wing has to be as large as the rules allow in order to generate maximum downforce.

to circuit. On fast circuits we use less wing, whereas more wing is used on circuits which feature a lot of corners.

The turbo-charged makes always use more wing – they can afford to with the extra power they deliver. The difference between the turbo brigade and the normally aspirated cars is most evident on fast circuits. In effect, the difference in lap times is due not only to higher top speeds because of greater engine power but also to the higher cornering speeds made possible by the use of more wing.

A simple calculation serves to illustrate this. On a long straight (2 km) a Formula I car travelling at 289 km/h will cover the distance in 24.9 seconds; at 308 km/h it will take 23.4 seconds, *i.e.*, 1.5 seconds less. These figures accurately correspond to Paul Ricard. In fact, however, lap time differences between turbo-charged and normally aspirated cars are significantly greater on that circuit than the 1.5 seconds postulated. Conclusion: there must be another element involved. Not only can the turbos corner faster, as noted above, they can also brake over a shorter distance because they have more wing and thus more downforce.

The above example also explains why the turbo-charged cars are already outdistancing the others even on some of the slower circuits.

Current Formula I regulations leave little prospect of any major aerodynamic developments as regards the visible wings. What this means is that engine performance is the decisive factor, just as it was in the ground effect era, despite the fact that it was widely assumed that the rule changes would benefit cars with normally aspirated engines. In effect, neither the new 540 kg weight nor the ban on ground effect has in any way altered the relative position of turbo-charged and normally aspirated cars.

The new fuel regulations earmarked for the 1984 and 1985 championship seasons *may* bring about a change.

Engines

The Relentless Challenge of the Turbos

The rules applying to Formula I engines date back to 1966 and will hold good until the end of 1985 – and probably even longer. There has been a lot of discussion as to possible changes, notably as regards limiting consumption, reducing fuel tank capacity or cutting back on engine capacity by fitting either fuel or air flow restrictors as in Formula 3.

For the meantime, the situation is as follows. Refuelling was permitted throughout the 1983 championship season, with the result that fuel tank capacity was of little direct relevance. In effect, cars with tanks that were too small (or with a fuel consumption rate that was too great) came into the pits about halfway through the race and sacrificed about 10 seconds at rest, plus another 10-15 seconds in slowing down and accelerating away, in order to refuel and change tyres.

This situation has given rise to an interesting tactical ploy – first used (of necessity) by Brabham. Starting with a half-empty tank confers a weight advantage (100 litres less fuel are equivalent to a weight-saving of 74 kg = more than 10 percent all-up weight) and thus permits a softer tyre compound to be used. However, even if a softer compound is not selected, there is still a tyre advantage to the extent that lower weight at the start means less wear-and-tear on the tyres through overheating and, clearly, faster lap times during the crucial in-fighting stage at the beginning of the race. After refuelling halfway through the race, the car is more or less the same weight as the others but has an edge in the form of fresh tyres.

If this tactic can add up to a net gain after taking the ±30-second pit-stop penalty into account, it is clearly to the team's advantage to make use of it. On an average circuit of, say, 80 laps at around 1 minute 30 seconds each,

In many cases it is no longer thought necessary to install even the most basic instruments (such as fuel pressure or even oil pressure gauges) where the driver can see them. Here they have been mounted next to the engine so that they can at least be checked during a pit stop. (Right) Connecting the compressed-air cylinder at the start. The driver's job is to switch on ignition and electrical fuel pump.

Central clutch disengagement is a standard feature in most current F1 cars, as is hydraulic operation. The disengagement mechanism is positioned in an intermediate casing between the engine (in front of it) and the transmission (behind). This casing also houses the engine oil tank, which has a capacity of approximately ten litres.

it follows that fractionally less than half a second per lap has to be made up to keep yourself level with the others. Championship season 1983, however, was very, very instructive in terms of pit-stop strategy and techniques, braking down into the pits and accelerating away again, and exploiting reduced all-up weight and softer tyre compounds.

One fact emerged from all the hot air : re-fuelling was quicker. Brabham – who pioneered re-fuelling – even threw in a new variant in the last (and deciding) race of the season in Kyalami. Championship contender Nelson Piquet started the race with a tank that was not one-half but one-third full – and with very soft compound tyres. This allowed him to take the race by the throat from the word go and put the pressure on the others to keep him in their sights. By the time he came in to re-fuel, it was all over bar the shouting.

As it happens, refuelling will be against the rules as of championship season 1984. At the same time, maximum tank capacity will be pruned from 250 to 220 litres, with a 195-litre limit scheduled for 1985. This is a timely move because it will oblige Formula I to give some thought to fuel economy : Grand Prix cars will have to get along somehow on a consumption rate of between 65 and 70 litres per 100 kms.

Another bread-and-butter job for the mechanics: changing gear ratios. The transmission is constructed so that the main shaft and reduction gears can be lifted out once the rear cover has been removed. Changing one or more gear ratios will take roughly half an hour.

In 1983 terms, this would seem to imply dire trouble for the turbos, but the technicians are already fairly well convinced that they will master this problem in due course. Nevertheless, the upshot will be that an end is in sight, at least as far as actual races are concerned (qualifying could be a very different matter!) as regards runaway horsepower. (I think it only fair to challenge the view that the turbos drink petrol, by the way: the major part of their additional fuel consumption can be ascribed to increased power output pure and simple).

Otherwise, the rules as they stand are short and to the point. Reciprocating piston engines up to twelve cylinders are permissible; volume is restricted to three litres in the case of normally aspirated engines and 1.5 litres for turbo-charged units. Rotary piston engines (chamber volume conversion ratio 1:2), two-stroke engines, and turbine and diesel engines were admitted up until 1982. For a long time, however – up until 1979 – the only real contenders in Formula I were the normally aspirated engines which had developed over the years not only high output per litre (some 166 bhp) but also a high degree of reliability. Overall, there was essentially very little difference in the characteristics exhibited by the various engines, the result being that lap times were close and there was some good racing.

A number of criteria are to be applied when evaluating the comparative performance of a Formula I engine, *viz.*:

* Power
* Weight
* Overall dimensions
* Height of gravity
* Fuel consumption
* Afflux conditions for intake of air-fuel mixture
* Tailflow conditions for exhaust gases
* Ignition spacing or firing sequence
* Crankcase vibration
* Crankcase oil separation

and * Balancing of masses

Clearly, only those engines which contrive to bring these elements into some kind of harmonious relationship will emerge as genuine contenders; the others, namely those that exhibit real shortcomings in any of the above respects, are expensive non-starters.

The front-runners in the 'induction era' were:

* The 8-cylinder DFV V 90° Ford Cosworth
* The 12-cylinder 312B V 180° Ferrari
* The 12-cylinder V 180° Alfa Romeo

and * The MS 120 V 60° Matra.

This cosy little world was turned upside down by two developments – the ever-increasing focus on aerodynamic design and the growing competitiveness of turbo-charged power units. In fact, aerodynamic design considerations became so dominant that they even dictated engine design. Anything that worked against the car's overall aerodynamics was viewed as unacceptable. Ferrari and Alfa Romeo are two excellent illustrations.

Ferrari had held out against the inevitable for the best part of a season before deciding that the fascinating, low, but very broad 12-cylinder – the legendary 'Sound' – simply had to go: the cylinder heads protruding way out into the lateral airflow path meant that it was impossible to achieve good ground effect – already recognised as being even more crucial in terms of performance than a very low centre of gravity. Ferrari may have taken his time to react, but when he did, he pulled no punches. If there had to be a new engine, then it would be turbo-charged from the word go, with a different number of cylinders and a new cylinder arrangement. Out he came with his 6-cylinder V 120° 1.5-litre engine for use either with a Comprex supercharger or with exhaust gas turbo-charging.

Alfa Romeo reacted less dramatically. The 12-cylinder induction engine was retained, but the two cylinder rows were angled up to prevent the cylinder heads disrupting the aerodynamics. Alfa's answer was a very high but – most important – very narrow V 60° reminiscent of the Matra MS 120 V 60°.

With the benefit of hindsight, Alfa is seen to have moved unwisely. They soon realised that there were no real long-term prospects for a normally aspirated engine: with their traditional penchant for many cylinders, they switched to development of a turbo-charged V-8.

Once ground effect cars were abolished there was no longer any need to build engines so high and narrow. Despite this, no one today is giving any thought to replacing the narrow turbos with the broad normally aspirated engines of the past.

Never before have there been so many firms active in Formula I engine design and construction or planning to become so. The leading manufacturers of the normally aspirated era – Cosworth, Ferrari, Alfa Romeo and Matra – have now been joined by Renault, BMW, Porsche, Hart and Honda. All the new boys have opted for turbo-charging, *i.e.*, the 1.5-litre variant.

Many people have great difficulty understanding how a turbo-charged engine with the cubic capacity of a VW Golf can deliver more power than 3-litre normally aspirated engines with more than a decade of R & D behind them. To be honest, 630 bhp developed by a VW Golf *is* hard to credit: I can only compare it with the jet engine which delivers enough thrust from a tiny aperture to power a huge aircraft.

At the same time, however, the turbo miracle has stimulated worldwide interest in Formula I. Every new country involved in Grand Prix racing – be it because of a driver, an engine or a car – boosts the overall appeal of the sport and makes it increasingly international.

The Dawn of the Turbo Era

Limiting the turbos to half the cubic capacity of their normally aspirated counterparts seemed to be too much of a handicap, particularly in the early days. There were very few engine manufacturers optimistic enough to believe that the performance gap could be closed.

There were all kinds of arguments against the turbos, notably in terms of stability, roadholding, fuel consumption and fuel compatibility – RON (research octane number) 102, i.e., a grade somewhere between super and aviation fuel, must not be exceeded – and overall horsepower. Still, Renault had been experimenting with a turbo-charged 6-cylinder engine for a number of years, basing it on the 2-litre version which had dominated the European Formula 2 Championship. Obviously, the engine had to be scaled down to 1.5 litres to comply with Formula I rules. It appeared, however, that in order to deliver 600 bhp – the amount believed essential to match the lap times of a 500 bhp normally aspirated engine – it would be necessary to raise boost pressure so much that RON 102 detonation resistance values would be exceeded.

On the other hand, it has to be recalled that the fuel grade demands made by a turbo-charged four-cycle engine are not only a function of compression and charging pressure values but are also – and to a very large extent – dependent on induction temperature. Inducted air is heated in the compressor

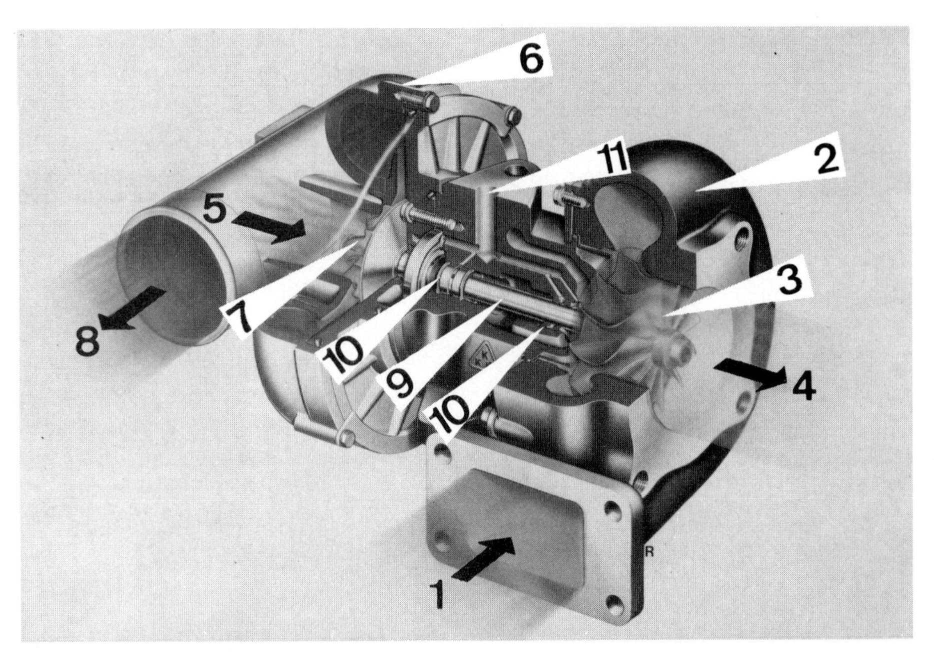

The magical turbo – strictly speaking, exhaust turbo-supercharger. This is the machine most widely used today to force air into internal combustion engines – ostensibly a simple enough affair, but in reality a highly-sensitive and complex device which must cope with very high thermal stresses and incredibly large quantities of air on both the inlet and exhaust sides. The German firm KKK (Kühnle, Kopp and Kausch) is the leading turbo manufacturer in Formula I; Brian Hart is the only one currently using the American Garrett supercharger. The vee-engine Renaults and Ferraris feature two smaller superchargers, whereas the BMW and Hart in-lines opt for a single larger supercharger. Searing (1000° C plus) exhaust gases enter at (1) into the turbine housing (T) where they actuate the turbine wheel (3) before leaving the 'hot' side through the aperture (4). The fresh air (5) which will be fed to the engine enters in the centre of the compressor housing (6), is brought up to pressure by the compressor wheel (7) powered by the turbine wheel (3), and exits from the spiral housing at (8). Compression has boosted the air temperature to some 180 to 200° Centigrade. This heated air is fed to the intercooler where its temperature is lowered to some 50 to 60° Centigrade before it is fed into the engine. The two-wheel turbo charge shaft (9) turns at up to 120,000 revolutions per minute and is held in place by two plain bearings(10) which are cooled by means of ports (11) connected to the engine oil circuit. Oil is pumped out of the bearing housing from the bottom.

and cooled back down in the intercooler: the more effectively this can be done, the greater the overall output, the more economical the engine, the less the total thermal load and the more modest the demands made on fuel grade.

Accordingly, every effort was made to improve the efficiency of intercoolers (in terms of temperature, flow resistance and overall size) while at the same time refining engine lay-out and tuning on the basis of race experience. Turbo lap times continued to improve: the first world championship points were scored in 1978, and the fastest qualifying time and first win came in 1979.

One of the biggest advantages enjoyed by the turbo driver is the feeling of 'smooth power' – not merely at maximum rpm but over a much wider range than the majority of normally aspirated engines. In addition to the more obvious factors, such as maximum speed, a car's acceleration is determined not only by peak output but also by its power curve – and this is where the turbos clearly have the edge.

Fitting a new exhaust turbo-supercharger. This is done not only when a unit is defective – which, incidentally, happens much more rarely than newspaper reports allege: in fact, most engine damage in the turbo cars can be traced back to the engine itself rather than the supercharger, because the engine has not been able to handle the high charging temperatures. Most common cause of damage can be ascribed to engine knock from worn pistons or cylinder heads, burnt-out valves or damaged cylinder head seals. Compressors or turbine housings can be changed to adapt the characteristics of the engine to specific circuits. Larger supercharger units will maximize power output whereas smaller units provide better low-speed response.

Another advantage is the way power builds up when the throttle is opened. In most normally aspirated engines you get an immediate, jerky reaction, whereas the turbo accelerates much more smoothly. The displacement of the car's centre of gravity towards the driven wheels, together with smooth, progressive torque build-up are particularly favourable both on the straight and when accelerating away from a corner. Wildly exaggerated wheelspin and jerky forwards and sideways movements very rarely affect the turbo driver.

For a long time, one of the biggest problems in the turbo was throttle lag – a delay of up to 2 seconds before the engine responded to movement of the accelerator. Now, however, thanks to improvements in intercooling and careful attention to the design of induction tracts, this problem has virtually been overcome. In the early days, the turbos also used to have terrible difficulty getting away from a standing start. Today, however, technology has advanced to the point where the turbos can get away just as effectively as normally aspirated cars. The hotshot in this respect is Alain Prost, who regularly guns his turbo out of the second or third row and wins the sprint to the first corner. He – and his engine – have it down to a fine art: come up to revs – clutch in – build boost pressure – extract maximum output – and go!

THE YEARS AHEAD

Prospects for Turbos and Others

It is fairly easy to put a figure on how much more power can be developed by the traditional 3-litre normally aspirated engine. Today's upper limit of 500+bhp at 10,500 rpm can probably be upped by a further 5 percent or so, assuming the same engine capacity. Having said this, let me repeat that 'optimum' performance and competitiveness in Formula I are not exclusively a question of engine power: there are a whole lot of other factors to be taken into consideration – and many of these act in favour of normally aspirated engines.

The conventional engine can be far more readily assimilated into Grand Prix racing than its turbo-charged counterpart. For the most part, the normally aspirated engine is 'independent', in the sense that data culled from bench tests will by and large be confirmed in practice: there are few unpleasant surprises. Further, it should not be overlooked that a normally aspirated engine needs relatively small water and oil radiators both of which can easily be housed in the car.

The normally aspirated engine also has a lot going for it in terms of longevity and ease of maintenance – and always will have. Taking care of a normally aspirated engine – and the car powered by it – is a very straightforward affair. Important races are not and will not be won, except in very unusual circumstances, because a normally aspirated engine gives up the ghost : this kind of engine is established, reliable and mature.

If the turbos one day become unbearably superior, however, then some new rules – *i.e.*, restrictions on the turbos – will have to be introduced. One of the suggestions most frequently heard is that turbo capacity should be cut back to 1.4 litres. In my opinion there have to be other ways of tackling the problem which do not involve wasting so much criminally expensive R & D. Surely it would be more reasonable to consider some other kind of restriction,

The turbo engine of the future? This eight-cylinder 1.5 litre V90° prototype was unveiled by Alfa Romeo back in 1980. It features a turbo-charger on each side. Individual cylinder volume is a mere 187 cm^3.

fuel formula or overall weight change which would be to the turbo's disadvantage. On top of all this, the problem cannot be viewed in isolation : once again we come back to the problems and implications of aerodynamic styling, often the decisive factor in determining overall performance.

A turbo engine is far more dependent on its immediate environment – its 'topographical surroundings' – than its normally aspirated counterpart. (This, by the way, is also one reason why it is more difficult to assess the true output of a turbo-charged power unit.) Every advance in terms of intercooling, supercharging, pipe design or fuel injection gives rise to an improvement in the overall performance of a turbo engine. Again, the turbo benefits more than its normally aspirated rival from new technologies in such sectors as ceramics, high-resistance thermal materials, fully electronic ignition and fuel injection systems, and so on. It is thus perfectly within reason to speculate that a 1.5-litre turbo will soon develop over 700 bhp – an incredible 466 bhp per litre.

One major contributory factor in this respect could well prove to be water injection. This technique has been around for many years (particularly in aviation) and is used selectively in Formula I, typically in short-burst qualification laps. Since water is by definition non-combustible, it is obvious that it is not directly responsible for added power : what happens, in fact, is that the intake air heated in the compressor is cooled most effectively. (The cooling down process can take place either as the air leaves the compressor – where it is particularly hot – or in the combustion chamber.) What you have is a double effect : on the one hand, air density is increased and the cylinder is thus filled better; on the other, the engine tends to knock less, with the result that boost pressure can be increased. This increase in performance naturally requires additional pro rata fuel injection.

Water is ideally suited to this process because it cools down the surrounding air significantly when it is vaporised. The water needed for the process has to be kept in a separate container. Calibrating the system is highly complex, since the quantity of water injected necessitates absolutely exact regulation of ignition, boost pressure and fuel quantity. To date, no single system has fully mastered the process, and the whole thing is still very much at the trial-and-error stage; the real breakthrough will only come with the introduction of completely electronic guidance systems.

Personally speaking, I am not in favour of water injection because it makes the already complex turbo engine even more involved and – coincidentally – represents a potential further advantage over normally aspirated units.

On top of all this, there is no direct relevance to the everyday car. Sooner or later there would also be inevitable problems as far as interpretation of the rules is concerned, because it is not clear whether or not the amount of water used should be calculated as part of the car's total fuel capacity.

As to how far performance might be boosted by a properly functioning water injection system, I would guess maybe by some 50 bhp. Water injection would be particularly effective on high-altitude circuits (for improving thin air density) and at high ambient temperatures (where its cooling properties would be enhanced). And even if it is not used to increase performance, water injection is capable of improving reliability by reducing the demands made on the whole power unit, including the turbo-chargers.

Brabham-BMW demonstrated in championship season 1983 that water is effective not only when directly applied to the combustion process: a significant cooling down of combustion air was also achieved by the simple expedient of spraying water directly over the outer skin of the intercooler. This tehnique is particularly useful when you recall that charge temperatures in the turbo can

The intercoolers on the Brabham-BMW are located right at the back. Left, the intercooler, right a combined water/oil radiator.

range up to some 200°C. The evaporation heat generated is such that relatively good cooling values can be obtained using very small quantities of water.

A key factor as regards the turbo engine is its immediate environment and how well it harmonises with it. In this respect it is much more dependent on ancillaries than normally aspirated engines, and these have the effect of increasing the weight and complexity of the car. If one firm makes the engine and another the rest of the car, it is almost inevitable that there will be conflicts. The engine designer has his own set of goals, namely to develop the best possible (and largest) radiators and intercoolers, and these clash with those of the car designer, who would prefer to have no intercoolers at all – to say nothing of the odds and ends that go with them.

The conflict situation really hots up if the engine has not been developed from the very beginning to meet the highly specific requirements of a single-seater racing car. The engine simply must harmonise with the overall car.

When you look at a Formula I design from the front or back, you cannot fail to notice its intrinsic symmetry. Ideally, the same degree of symmetry should prevail in the design of the engine and its ancillary equipment. (On that basis, V-engines certainly have the edge over the in-lines.)

It is also advantageous if the engine can be utilised as a structural member. For this to be possible, the cars have to be sufficiently rigid and compact, thereby saving weight and improving both access and design harmony. In this context, a vee layout for the engine is again appropriate.

If an engine cannot be used as a structural member, it is necessary for it to be surrounded by a sub-frame, which increases both weight and complexity. Strictly speaking, this extra weight should be regarded as 'engine' weight. What is more, the additional tubes and struts often prove incapable of being installed 'directly' – that is, in a straight line – because something or other is always in the way – exhaust or intake system, or water or oil pumps.

The most intelligent approach is undoubtedly for a turbo car to be developed by one firm – as is the case with Ferrari or Renault. A compromise solution would be to ensure that a new engine is tailored to the overall car design specifications – as exemplified in the co-operation between McLaren and Porsche. It isn't hard to foresee problems where an engine is developed in isolation, then fitted into a Formula I chassis: the Brabham-BMW is a case in point. There, however, the problems were largely ironed out once all concerned – and not least Bernie Ecclestone – acknowledged the new ground rules: the turbo engine is the dominant consideration now and in the years ahead and everything else about the car must be geared to it.

Common Denominators in Formula I Engine Design

The various engines used in Formula I have much more in common than first meets the eye.

The most readily apparent common feature is the arrangement of the cylinders in two rows. This design approach is essential in the case of multi-cylinder engines if the car's overall length is to be kept down, and has been followed in all the current Formula I cars others than those using the BMW and Hart 4-cylinder power units.

The angle between the two rows of cylinders varies from 120° in the Ferrari V6 to 60° in the normally aspirated Alfa Romeo V12. The 'vee' configuration is not immediately recognisable from the outside, and does not necessarily imply that the two cylinder rows are arranged in a 'V', but that two connecting rods from opposing cylinders each work on one common crankshaft throw. In other words, the crankshaft has half as many throws as the engine has cylinders. A major advantage of the 'vee' configuration is that the air below the pistons does not have to be compressed and expanded continuously, thereby consuming energy and forcing up the oil temperature; instead, the air is simply transferred from one side to the other, the net effect being that crankcase vibration is cut to a minimum.

Current engines also exhibit many common features in respect of the materials out of which they are made. Aluminium is usually the first choice for crankcases, cylinder heads and pistons – although Renault and BMW both have steel crankcases. 'Exotic' materials only find application for connecting rods and the occasional bolt or two – which are increasingly made of titanium. There is also a great deal of uniformity as far as valve-operation is concerned: with the exception of Hart, every engine manufacturer has opted for spur gears to drive the camshaft – a more expensive solution in terms of both weight and cost, but nonetheless one which offers more precision than chain or cogged belt drive. Renault has decided on a composite toothed gear/cogged belt drive system.

In the past, racing engines have featured a wide variety of valve systems – three valves per cylinder, desmodromic valves, radial valves, mushrooms and poppets – but during the seventies it became established practice for racing engines to have four valves per cylinder – two inlet and two exhausts. For safety reasons, each valve is provided with two springs, with the result that a 12-cylinder engine boasts the princely number of 96 valve springs.

The inlet and exhaust valves in the new TAG Porsche engine have been slightly angled, and the cams have been ground to a conical rather than cylindrical shape to accommodate this radial arrangement. The net effect, as in other racing engines, is to allow the valves to be driven directly from the camshaft, thereby ensuring really accurate timing.

The angle formed by the inlet and exhaust valves is a major bone of contention. It used to be very large – up to 90° – to accommodate large valve diameters; today, however, the trend is towards compact combustion chamber design, and accordingly the angle has grown increasingly narrow; in the Renault, for example, it has been reduced to 22°.

When you look at a racing combustion chamber from the piston side of the engine you will see a very flat top with a centrally-positioned spark plug; from this angle not even the *aficionado* can tell the difference between the various engines.

Cooling systems reveal yet another point in common. All Formula I engines are water-cooled. This makes for a sacrifice in weight terms, but is indispensable if four-valve cylinder heads are to be used – air-cooling would be totally inadequate for the four tightly-grouped valves. This explains why Porsche – who, after all, pioneered air-cooled engines – never even considered four-valve air-cooling.

In the final analysis, today's engines have so many features in common that they can really only be distinguished in terms of cylinder number and deployment, and whether or not they are turbo-charged. The perennial argument as to the ideal number of cylinders for any given engine size will never be resolved satisfactorily, because it is just about impossible to vary the number of cylinders in one and the same engine design.

There is no doubt, however, that engine design configurations have a considerable influence on performance, so it would seem that a definitive answer will only be found when someone takes a particular design type – preferably an in-line – and runs consistent trials with varying numbers of cylinders. You might well ask, of course, who would be crazy enough to build a 12-cylinder Formula I in-line just for the hell of it. . .

Ford Cosworth DFV

We have established that it is much easier to build a normally aspirated engine than it is to build a super-charged one. Eloquent proof comes in the guise of the V 90° Ford Cosworth DFV, the design of which must surely rank among the greatest achievements in the annals of modern Grand Prix racing. Even today, this engine can still be a passport to championship success.

The Cosworth is the oldest power unit currently raced in Formula I, but the remarkable thing about it is the extent to which its original specification has remained unaltered. The Cosworth was first raced in the Dutch Grand Prix on June 4, 1967, and there is something symbolic about the fact that it triumphed on that very first outing, when Jim Clark drove the Lotus 49 to victory. Since then, the Cosworth has been used by the winners of twelve World Championships, missing out only three times in fifteen years – in 1975, 1977 and 1979, when Ferrari took the title.

As a power unit the Cosworth is extremely compact overall. There is virtually unlimited space for judicious design of the inlet and exhaust systems. It is worth mentioning that the four crankshaft throws are on one level, so that the crankshaft looks exactly like one from a 4-cylinder in-line engine. As a result, secondary inertia forces are not counterbalanced; on the other hand, each cylinder row has the same angular ignition spacing – a *sine qua non* for a properly-functioning single-exhaust system. The four exhaust pipes from each row of cylinders can thus be of equal lengths and can feed into one tailpipe at each side.

If the 8-cylinder V 90° Cosworth had been intended for use in a saloon car, the uniform firing sequence would have been sacrificed to permit full balancing of the masses and there would have been two crankshaft throws, one at right angles to the other. Free moments of inertia are not so significant in a racing car, however, always assuming that they are not of sufficient magnitude to prompt oscillation failure in the engine or chassis.

The counterweights on the crankshaft faces have been scaled down to such a degree that the resultant weight increase in the main bearing is just barely adequate. A major reduction in rotational weight is also vital in terms of torsional oscillation: the longer the crankshaft and the greater the rotational weight it assumes, the more vulnerable it will necessarily be to torsional stress and fracture.

The Cosworth is not only the least complicated, it is also the least expensive

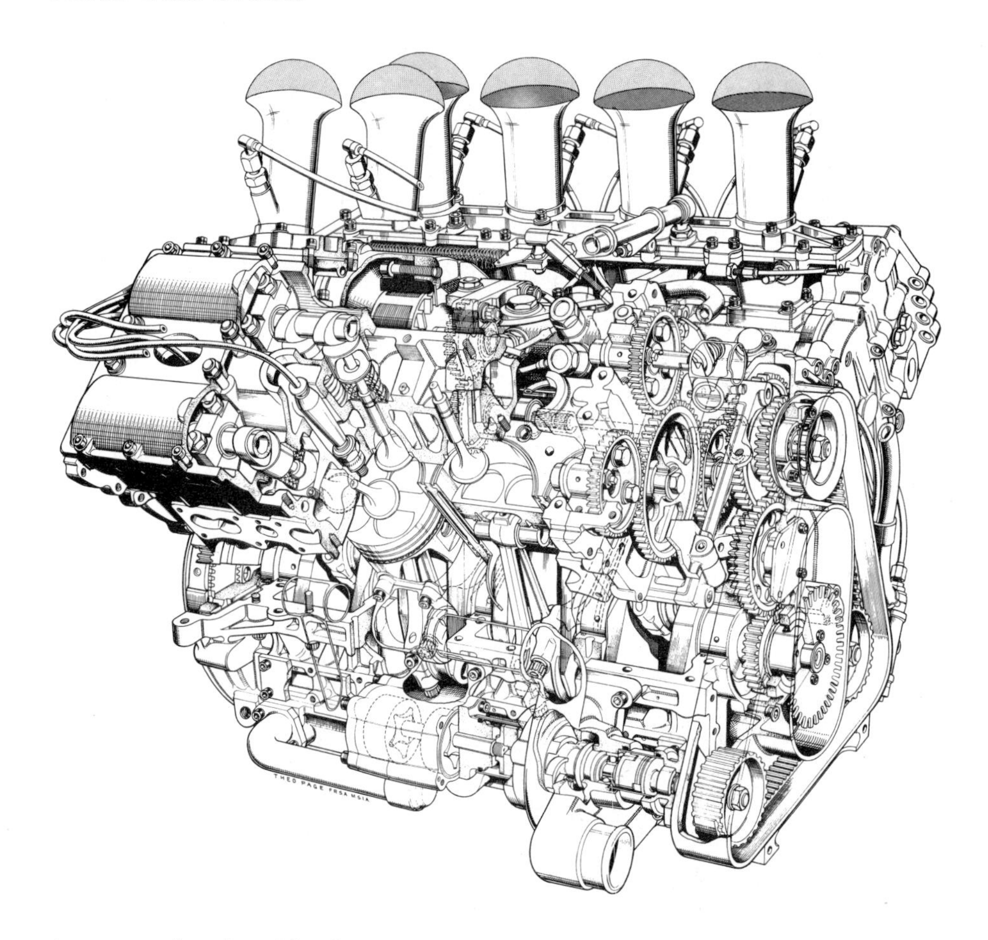

A contract signed on March 1, 1966 by Ford, Cosworth Engineering and Keith Duckworth paved the way for a project that was to prevent Grand Prix racing from stagnating due to lack of suitable engines. It culminated in the Cosworth DFV (Double Four Valves), an eight-cylinder V90° engine that has since proved to be by far the most successful in the history of motor racing. By comparison with other non-turbo engines, the Cosworth DFV exhibits the best overall characteristics in terms of output, weight, size, reliability and fuel consumption. The four valves are driven by a total of thirteen spur gears. The crankshaft is set extremely low, as are the various laterally-mounted oil and water pump units. As of mid-1982, 375 such engines had been built. The Cosworth DFV, which celebrated its 150th Grand Prix victory in the 1982 Austrian Grand Prix, is the only Formula I engine which can be bought on the open market – at a current cost of £27,296.

One of the fastest normally aspirated cars in the 1983 championship season was the new Tyrrell Cosworth DFY. The narrow cylinder heads are particularly striking. This is also one the first Formula I designs for a long time in which the rear brake discs were mounted inboard next to the transmission.

The most successful Formula I engine of all time – Cosworth. But has its latest variant come too late? The DFY is a natural progression from the Cosworth DFV and features a shorter stroke and, above all, completely redesigned cylinder heads: the very small (22.5^0) valve angle allows the heads to be narrower, lighter and more rigid. Only time will tell whether this variant – which develops approximately five per cent more power than its predecessors – can give the turbos a run for their money once the new fuel restrictions come into effect.

Up to 1981 the prescribed minimum all-up weight of 580 kilogrammes was largely academic, since there was no way to get below this limit and still build a car that was viable and safe. By the beginning of 1982, however, lightweight construction techniques had been developed to the point where some designers of Cosworth-powered marques (the turbos are heavier) had managed to get below the 580 kg limit. The teams involved (notably Williams and, to a lesser extent, McLaren) soon realised that this gave them an opportunity to make up some of the ground they had lost to the turbos. The big problem, of course, was to find a loophole in the 580 kg limit regulation.

The answer lay in what came to be known as the water tank ploy. In the illustration above, a 25-litre water container was installed behind the oil cooler and next to the fuel tank, ostensibly to promote better brake cooling. When the tank was filled, the weight of the water brought a light car back up over the 580 kg limit. Immediately after the start, however, the water was jettisoned from the tank by means of an electric pump and the car raced 'light'. When the race was over, the tank was filled up again so that the car weighed at least 580 kg in the event of officials carrying out a spot check.

The powers-that-be stamped out this practice by outlawing any topping-up with liquids (including oil) after the car had crosed the finishing line. At the same time, cars that were found to be underweight had to carry ballast to bring themselves up to the limit: the ballast took the form of lead plates securely fixed to the car. (As a matter of fact, the claim that the water was necessary to 'cool the brakes' had some legitimacy to the extent that this technique 'is' used in touring car racing, where cooling problems are significantly greater: depressing the brake pedal triggers an electrical pump which injects a fine water spray into the brake disc cooling ducts.) Subsequently the ploy has been rendered unnecessary because the minimum weight limit has been lowered to 540 kg.

and most economical of Formula I engines. Additionally, it is the one Formula I engine that can be bought off the shelf. Because the Cosworth can be bought over-the-counter like this, it tends to dominate the Grand Prix scene: more than half the cars in Grand Prix races in 1983 were Cosworth-powered.

In terms of performance, however, the Cosworth is actually one of the least powerful Formula I engines. It delivers some 500 bhp as a rule, or allegedly 520 bhp in its most recent short-stroke variant. Where the Cosworth really scores is in its compact design, which allows easy integration into the chassis and optimal exploitation of aerodynamic design. It is also important to note that the Cosworth uses less fuel than any of the other Formula I engines, with the result that Cosworth-powered cars have a weight advantage on the starting grid. Above all, however, the Cosworth is a glutton for punishment: it is going to be around for a long time yet.

In Spring 1983 Cosworth came out with a radically reworked version known as the DFY, an expensive variant thought justified to the extent that the new fuel limits set for 1984 and, particularly, 1985 would work against the turbos and prevent them from capitalising on their power advantage over full race distances. (Any hopes of closing the power gap itself had clearly had to be dismissed as wishful thinking.)

The DFY has a shorter induction stroke than its predecessor, the result being that piston speed is cut back and rpm raised. The totally redesigned cylinder heads exemplify the trend towards increasingly narrow valve angles. The DFV used an inclined angle of 32°, but on the DFY it is reduced to only 22.5°. This extremely narrow angle permits the use of smaller, lighter cylinder heads, the total weight saving being 6.4 kilos.

The short-stroke variant had a sensational debut when Michele Alboreto's Tyrrell won the 1983 Detroit Grand Prix. After that, however, the performance gap between the normally aspirated engines and the turbos opened up more than ever. Now, Cosworth hopes are pinned on limiting fuel consumption, and it is conceivable that this might just bring about a shift in the comparative performances of the two engine systems.

The Cosworth teams were the first to exploit the design variant which enabled the engine to be moved forward in the car, thereby making for very simple and very compact construction of the car as a whole. The 10-litre oil tank used to be mounted in front of or alongside the engine; now it has been squeezed in between the engine and the transmission. What this means is that the engine is no longer mounted directly on to the transmission, but is separated from it by a 30 cm long casting, with a shaft through the lower part of the casting to link the clutch to the gearbox.

This feature is a throw-back to the ground effect era, when it constituted an attempt to improve aerodynamic styling of the underbody. It was so elegant in its simplicity, however, that other designers adopted it and have carried it through into the new, non-ground effect era.

Alfa Romeo 12-Cylinder

This engine is a typical offshoot of the ground effect era. The narrow V 60° design was a natural in a ground effect car, hence the modest renaissance. In 1983 the Alfa Romeo team switched to a V8 turbo, but the 12-cylinder engine is still used by Osella.

Cars powered by the V12 Alfa Romeo are very impressive performers thanks to their twelve cylinders – the maximum number permitted – and their high revs. The upright structure of the engine also makes for good oil return to the sump.

The 60° Alfa V12 came into being by the relatively simple expedient of folding upwards the two cylinder rows of the 'flat' or V 180° engine; all in all, key engine components such as the crankshaft, connecting rods, pistons and cylinder heads needed little adaptation. The firing sequence is such that each set of three adjacent cylinders has the same angular ignition spacing : the exhaust pipes from these three cylinders are separate at first but are brought together in the tailpipe section. In other words, the Alfa 12-cylinder has four tailpipes which have a very distinctive exhaust note – much more aggressive than that of the Cosworths – although they, in turn, eclipse the turbos, whose roar is muted by the ultra-fast rotation of turbine and compressor wheels, as well as by the fact that they have fewer cylinders.

It is only when you strip off the outer skin, however, that you realise how impressive the Alfa engine really is. The twelve cylinders lie relatively close together and give the impression of awesome power and authority, much more so than the Cosworths and the turbos – the latter actually look a bit on the puny side. There is also a beautiful harmony about the Alfa to the extent that it seems to fit perfectly into the overall design of the car. For me, the Alfa V12 is the type of car that approximates most closely to the classic concept of a single-seater racing machine.

Because of its length, the Alfa engine has to be bolted directly up against the transmission – there is no intermediate oil tank as in most other current cars – and this serves to enhance the overall impression of power.

The Alfa works team car was very clean, very tidy and very flowing. The record books for 1982 also testify that it was fast.

Matra 12-Cylinder

This engine has been mothballed for the time being, but it might be premature to write it off completely since it came back from obscurity once before. At any rate, its design features are sufficiently interesting to merit some discussion.

The 12-cylinder Matra MS 120 is a V 60° engine developed from the sports car variant and from various prototypes dating back to 1967. It first came into Formula I in the 1976 championship season but was never particularly successful, hence its retirement in 1978. It got second wind during

The 1983 Osella continued to rely on the normally aspirated 12-cylinder Alfa.

the ground effect era, however, when it was used in the Talbot-Ligier-Matra which Laffite drove to victory twice in the course of the 1981 championship season.

The comparatively wide (32°) valve angle betrays the fact that the Matra is a bit long in the tooth: the trend nowadays is towards narrower angles – 26° in the 12-cylinder Alfa, for example, and 22° in the Renault. This apart, the Matra comes very close to the Alfa in basic overall design.

The camshafts have been bored out to cut down weight, and are driven

The twelve-cylinder Matra brought the twin exhaust valve outlets together in a welded exhaust system (1) rather than at the cylinder head. The rest of the exhaust were not bolted on rigidly but is simply slotted together and secured by metal flap screws (2). The tail pipes were secured by spring clips to the rear suspension unit (3). The huge distributor driven by the intake cam on the left row of cylinders is clearly visible. The intake trumpets were covered by a fine-mesh gauze to keep out stones.

by no less than twelve toothed gears from the front end of the crankshaft. Toothed gears are also used to drive the low-set oil pump. The engine block is cast in aluminium. Cylinder liners are countersunk, and are in direct contact with cooling water. The design of the exhaust tracts is of interest. Normally the ducts from each exhaust valve are brought together in the cylinder head so that each head has only one outlet per cylinder; in the Matra, however, the two ducts emerge separately, requiring two exhaust pipes per cylinder, and these are not brought together until the first section of the tailpipe.

There is never any question of installing an engine before its performance has been checked on the test bench. It is essential that test bench conditions approximate as closely as possible to those which will apply to the engine once it has been installed, i.e., *that induction and exhaust, airflow and temperature conditions correspond to actual operating criteria. The free end of the crankshaft (flywheel) is connected to the dynamometer by means of a short universally-jointed drive shaft which, for safety reasons, has been enclosed here in a thick steel jacket. The power delivered to the dynamometer by the engine is absorbed by an electrical retarder or a hydrokinetic turbo closed-flow power absorber. The requisite torque is delivered via a torquemeter. Engine output is calculated on the basis of recorded torque and revs. No one is admitted to the test area while the engine is being bench-tested: technicians shelter behind a special reinforced glass window or observe the test on video screens. The engine shown here is a twelve-cylinder Matra.*

Classic racing engine design: the twelve-cylinder 3-litre Matra V 60° – four tail pipes make for an infernal roar.

The engine is very clean: the smooth cam covers and the beautifully-gathered fuel injection and ignition cables are a real delight for the connoisseur.

Renault Turbo
(*And Some Basic Thoughts On Formula I Turbos*)

Turbo-charged engines were first used in automobile racing in the United States, and turbo-charging of series production cars came about via the race track: there is thus a clear link between the sport and everyday driving. There are more turbos around today than ever before, both on the track and off it; virtually every passenger car manufacturer has at least one turbo model in his range, and some have several.

Of all European manufacturers Renault has been the most active in promoting the turbo – to the extent that turbo-charged models are available throughout the company's range. At the same time, most of today's rally events are being won by turbo-charged cars like the Audi Quattro, the Lancia or the R5 Turbo. Every newcomer to Formula I has opted for the turbo variant. There is no need to belabour the point further: the turbo can no longer be dismissed as a passing fad.

It was Renault who took the first positive step towards using a turbo in Formula I, long before any other manufacturer. I witnessed Renault's debut as my 'first' career was drawing to a close. In the early days, Renault posted good qualifying times, but seemed to get off to a bad start in the race proper and be plagued by technical problems which forced them to retire. Renault managed to overcome these teething troubles in brilliant style, even although their race results in the 1982 championship season were strangely undistinguished. Nevertheless, the Formula I Renault Turbo is now good enough to win any Grand Prix anywhere in the world.

What exactly makes the 6-cylinder Renault V 90° turbo tick?

First of all, let's take any engine and turbo-charge it, in other words, do what any of today's manufacturers would do if he wanted improved performance on the road or on the track. It is not absolutely essential to develop a new engine – you can readily turn to one that has already been developed and, all things being equal, modify it in such a way that it can cope with the thermal and mechanical demands brought about by turbo-charging. Incidentally, a real breakthrough in turbo technology has now come in the form of the TAG Porsche Formula I engine, the first such engine (apart from the Heidegger, which has not yet raced) to be designed from the outset as a turbo-charged unit.

In Renault's case, the engine they fell back on was the 2-litre 6-cylinder V 90° which we all knew from Formula 2 racing, in which it had been used since 1973. Its first major successes came in 1976 and 1977, when Renault-engined cars won the European Formula 2 championship, and then, in 1978, a turbo-charged version of the engine won the 24 hours at Le Mans. By that time, Renault was already gearing up for a full-blooded assault on Formula I using this engine and the company's own single-seater racing car design.

An experimental version had been raced in 1975: with its 49.4 mm stroke and 80 mm bore (ratio 0.62), it had delivered 503 bhp at 10,800 rpm. Every effort was then made to capitalise on this prototype's performance by increasing maximum torque and, at the same time, contriving to reach it at lower

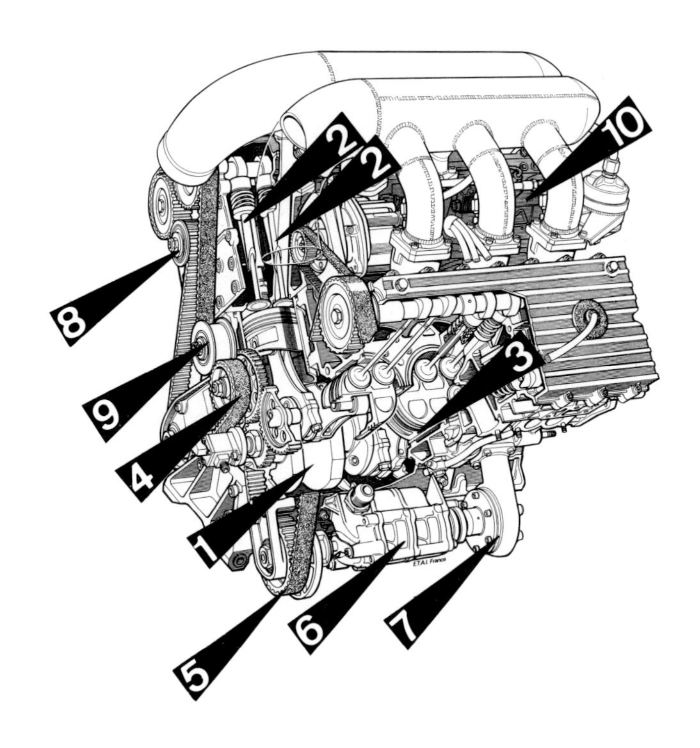

The Renault-Gordini Formula I engine which ushered in the turbo era. This engine, developed at considerable cost, exhibited all the ups and downs of turbo development and thus influenced, directly or indirectly, all subsequent turbo R and D. It was the Renault-Gordini that proved that a 1.5-litre turbo could make the grade against a 3-litre induction engine. The engine itself is a Formula 2 unit, with an approximate 2:1 bore (86 mm) to stroke (42.8 mm) ratio. The six cylinders are arranged in two groups of three at an angle of 90°. Two cylinders act on one common crankshaft throw (readily identified at the front connecting rods (1)), so that the crankshaft has only three throws and four main bearings. The valve stems (2) are extremely long. Intake and exhaust valves (two per cylinder) form a very narrow (21° 30′) angle. The cylinder block is in cast steel, whereas the case-hardened wet-polished cylinder bearing bushings (3) are in aluminium to afford better heat dissipation. The four camshafts are actuated by a combination of toothed gears and belts. The cogged belts run on each side of the toothed-gear drive wheel (4) extending diagonally down to a cog drive (5) powering the oil (6) and water (7) pump units, then back up over a reverse-transfer roller (8) to the two camshafts and over a further reverse-transfer roller (9) back to the drive wheel. In the open vee formed by the two engine halves you will note the ignition system and the electronically-actuated fuel injection pump (10). The drive gear also features cogged belts. The entire engine is extremely compact (480 mm long, 680 mm wide and 650 mm high) and, together with all accessories, weighs 180 kilogrammes. Renault claimed in mid-1982 that this engine delivered 585 PS at 11,200 rpms.

revs. (In the prototype, peak power revs and maximum torque revs had been virtually identical.)

A crucial step forward came with the decision to increase bore to 86 mm and reduce stroke to 43 mm, giving a stroke-to-bore ratio of 0.5; this ratio has been maintained to the present day.

The reasoning behind this unusual step emerges clearly when you stop to consider the individual cylinder volume of a 1.5-litre 6-cylinder engine – a remarkable 250 cm^3. Naturally, the four combustion chamber valves have to be made correspondingly small. With its 86 mm bore, the Renault has virtually the same dimensions as the Cosworth (85.7 mm) and as a result it was possible to increase valve size accordingly.

Another point in Renault's favour is the extremely narrow angle (22°) between the inlet and exhaust valves. This has permitted the design of a very compact combustion chamber, which reduces the engine's susceptibility to detonation, a key consideration in a turbo-charged engine.

It is perhaps as well to recall briefly what 'detonation' actually means. The compression ratio of both normally aspirated and turbo-charged engines is restricted by the onset of irregular combustion, *i.e.*, knocking. This occurs when combustion is not triggered by the ignition spark alone but when – usually because of excessive heat – the mixture ignites spontaneously at various points in the combustion chamber. There is a characteristic 'pinging' sound which signifies that at least two different points in the chamber are igniting at one and the same time. When this happens it gives rise to extremely high pressure peaks at the onset of combustion, which then fall off rapidly. These peaks damage the engine – in particular the cylinder head gasket, pistons and piston rings. Once knocking sets in, it is only a matter of minutes before the engine is done for.

The more compact the combustion chamber and the shorter the flame travel (the optimum plug position is in the centre of the four valves) the more resistant the chamber will be to knocking – thereby allowing a lighter compression ratio in a normally aspirated engine and increased boost-pressure in a turbo. It goes without saying that a number of other factors also influence combustion efficiency, notably combustion chamber cooling, types of valve (solid or sodium-filled), types of piston and piston cooling (perhaps via injection nozzles) and so on.

In the second, revamped version of the Renault, the engine delivered 510 bhp at 10,500 rpm. Of considerably more significance, however, was the colossal 400 Nm at 8,200 rpm – an unattainable figure in a normally aspirated engine, where the limit lies around 340 Nm. This version had a single exhaust driven supercharger, with all six exhaust pipes brought together behind the engine.

This engine was first raced at Silverstone on July 14, 1977. Then came a long and very difficult development phase. On occasion, the Renault Turbo would put up the best qualifying times and even lead the field in the initial stages of a race. Its potential was never in doubt, but it was not until July 1979 that it won its first Formula I race, albeit a singular triumph for France since it happened to be the French Grand Prix at Dijon – won by an all-French car with a French driver (Jean Pierre Jabouille) at the wheel. July 1, 1979 is the date to remember as the real beginning of the turbo era.

In the meantime, Renault had put in a staggering amount of R & D, which other teams will have to match if they are to cut back Renault's lead. Renault's competitors do have one advantage, however, to the extent that the fundamental question has been answered: yes, turbo engines *do* have a future in Formula I.

The boost pressure indicator (in this case, in the Renault) is the most important instrument on a turbo car apart from the rev counter.

The Renault F-1 Turbo. The engine is completely symmetrical in design. The turbo-supercharger compressor (1) sucks in fresh air from below through the duct (2). The compressed air is then fed to the intercooler (3) where it is first water-cooled and then air-cooled from below. The cooled air is forced into the engine via the plenum chamber (4). The water radiator (5) lies ahead of the intercooler. The waste gate (6) expels exhaust gases via the pipe at (7), and the exhaust turbo-supercharger discharges via the outlet pipe (8).

Apart from changing bore and stroke, Renault took another decisive step in switching from one to two exhaust-driven superchargers. This made for a completely symmetrical, compact and aerodynamically effective arrangement of exhaust pipes, turbo-chargers, intercoolers and induction systems. The twin KKK turbo-chargers are positioned alongside the two rows of cylinders, and are symmetrically actuated at every 240° of crankshaft revolution by the exhaust from each alternate set of three cylinders. The individual exhaust pipes are kept as far apart as possible and come together only immediately before the turbine housing. In this way, the imparted exhaust flow energy can be exploited individually and to the full.

Intermittent flow is effected by opening and closing the waste-gates, so that the turbo-charger is powered not only by the mean pressure built up before the turbine wheel but also by regular pressure peaks which impart additional acceleration to the wheel. This action is particularly effective where you have three cylinders with identical angular ignition spacing, because the exhaust valves open and close without overlapping: as one closes, the next is just beginning to open. The net effect is that exhaust gas energy can be exploited to the full. This so-called 'high-rate' or 'intermittent' charging system is derived from diesel truck engine design, a sector where fuel efficiency is particularly important.

Renault is currently concentrating its efforts on the improvement of acceleration and reduction of fuel consumption. Both these factors can be positively influenced by means of a basic compression ratio set as high as possible; in effect, the 7 : 1 ratio in the Renault engine makes it the highest compression turbo around. Clearly, this is far removed from the 11.5 : 1 ratio of normally aspirated engines, but the important thing is not the compression ratio on paper but the effective mean (as opposed to peak) pressure which the combustion process exerts on the piston over the latter's entire working range. This is where the turbo engine is way ahead of its normally aspirated counterparts – otherwise it would not be possible for it to deliver more power from half the cubic capacity.

Calculations have shown that the Cosworth has a mean or median pressure of 14.8 bars at full output, whereas the Renault Turbo has 33.1. By comparison, a standard passenger saloon engine will have a typical pressure-reading of 9.5.

A high basic compression ratio in a turbo-charged petrol engine is not necessarily indicative of extremely high performance. With a compression ratio of 7 : 1 the Renault Turbo develops a maximum of 580 bhp, whereas the Ferrari produces over 600 bhp with a lower (6.5 : 1) compression ratio.

The emphasis on acceleration is immediately apparent in the 1982 and 1983 Renaults, whose turbo-chargers have been moved closer to both the cylinder heads and the intercoolers. This may result in slightly lower peak output, but it improves engine pick-up because the 'dead volume' in the inlet and exhaust tracts has been reduced. It has already been stressed in our comparison of eight and twelve cylinders that peak output is not necessarily the sole criterion in engine performance. On the contrary, the key is to find a proper harmony by striking a compromise between often conflicting requirements. It goes without saying that there are circuits – predominantly the very fast ones such as Kyalami or Oesterreich-Ring – where peak output ('top speed') is particularly important. But when you switch to tortuous circuits such as Long Beach and Monte Carlo, good pickup and low weight on the starting grid are prime factors. A good racing engine should be able to cope with any set of conditions.

Intercooling

The intercoolers on the F1 Renault are intriguing. Intercoolers are essential to reduce the temperature of very hot combustion gases. Depending on the make of engine and the type of turbo-charging, we are talking in terms of temperatures of some 180 to 200° Centigrade in the turbo-charger – and the engine would not tolerate this hot air being fed directly to it. Accordingly, a turbo-charged racing engine will only be as good as its intercooling. This implies not so much that the radiators have to be large but that the afflux to them must be extremely efficient; this is one of the most important areas in which the functions of turbo-charged engine and chassis inter-react.

To avoid having to design excessively large intercoolers (one on each side of the engine), the solution is to install composite water-air-air-coolers, which is to say coolers which are actuated one-third by water and two-thirds by the passage of air. In this way the hot gases – at give or take 200° Centigrade – can be cooled to some 115° quickly and compactly thanks to the excellent convective properties of water, and then brought down to about 30° above ambient temperature by the cooling action of air-flow. To keep things as simple as possible, the engine cooling system is used for the initial process – the size of the water radiators having been increased accordingly.

It is obvious that a separate water cooling unit could be installed for this purpose, and equally obvious that a separate unit might be more effective since it would not be subject to the high operating temperature (some 95° Centigrade) of the engine cooling system. But doing this would necessitate the installation of additional water radiators and pumps and, for the time being at least, does not seem worthwhile to Renault. Instead, the effective cooling surface of the air-air intercoolers was increased in 1982 by installing them at an angle (a fairly common ploy used for water and oil radiators).

The weight of a Renault engine is not as low as one might expect from its very compact dimensions. The first reason for this is the fact that Renault uses cast steel for the cylinder block in the interest of rigidity, whereas most other makers opt for aluminium. Although the block walls are thin (3.5 to 4 mm), there is a distinct weight disadvantage by comparison with the aluminium block of a Cosworth V-8. The wet cylinder liners (which are directly water-cooled) are made of aluminium, in order to disperse as quickly and effectively as possible the heat generated during the combustion process.

The second reason for the unexpectedly high weight lies in the 'environment' necessary to a turbo-charged power unit. Everything which contributes to the operation of the engine must be regarded, in the final analysis, as 'engine weight'. Strictly speaking, therefore, you have to consider not only the actual engine but also the two turbo-chargers and their piping, the two intercoolers and their ducts, and two water radiators with an appreciable weight of water in each – which all adds up to a total 'engine weight' of some 180 kilogrammes, about twenty more than an eight-cylinder Cosworth Ford and roughly the same as a normally aspirated twelve-cylinder engine.

All of this boosts the overall weight of the car. Over the last few seasons, Cosworth-engined cars clearly were the lightest, and some bright designers (notably Patrick Head of Williams) were able to get appreciably below the prescribed minimum weight of 580 kilogrammes or, as of season 1983, 540 kg.

A turbo-charged racing engine consumes enormous quantities of air – about 0.6 cubic metres per second, or roughly the equivalent of a medium-sized room every minute. For this reason, a single exhaust turbo-supercharger has to be very large and is correspondingly heavy (14.6 kilogrammes in the early Renault version). If the work is divided between two units, these can be made smaller and lighter and are correspondingly easier to mount and anchor (weight = 2 x 6.7 kg). In addition, engine behaviour – notably in respect of acceleration – is considerably better with two turbo-chargers, and heat is more easily dissipated.

The throttle butterfly on the Renault's turbo-chargers is located just before the air intake into the compressor housing, and is operated by two simple lightweight slides rather than the complicated roller bearing systems used in normally aspirated engines. By positioning the butterfly just ahead of the compressor, acceleration values have also been improved. Run-on is longer when the butterfly is closed, because the compression wheel is vacuum-limited: this means that you have higher initial revs when the throttle is opened again.

It is only some six years since the first turbo-charged engines made their debut in Formula I – not really enough to establish many areas of comparison. Despite this, it is clear that Renault has made a good move with its in-house 6-cylinder V 90°. Turbo-charged V-6 engines seem to be as good all-round as the normally aspirated 3-litre 8-cylinder Cosworth. The V-design means that they can be integrated harmoniously into the car, and their whole environment can be built up symmetrically on each side. They also have very short inlet and exhaust tracts and correspondingly small turbo-chargers.

A further plus in V-6 design is the reduction in engine length. All today's Formula I cars have their fuel tank positioned in the centre of the car between the engine and the driver's seat. Clearly, the shorter the engine, the shorter the car overall – which is to say that greater fuel tank capacity can be achieved within the same overall length of car or wheelbase, provided that engine length can be reduced. This is vital for the turbos, which currently use more fuel than their normally aspirated counterparts. As to the peculiarities of 4-cylinder in-line turbos, these we shall look at in more detail when we come to discuss the BMW engine.

Renault currently employs 170 people in its racing division, all dedicated to the goal of French victory in the Formula I World Championship. The budget for all this runs into millions, but it would appear to be money well-spent because Renault has carried its turbo technology over into series production, and can thus fully exploit the 'Grand Prix' image.

It can be argued, however, that Renault's over-zealous commitment to new engine technology may have crossed the demarcation line between day-to-day feasibility and downright wishful thinking. Renault engineers have piled one idea on top of another: taken in isolation, each new idea may seem sensible enough; taken together, they tend to add up to an over-technical, excessively complex final product. The interplay of ideas and solutions is such that it has become increasingly difficult to sort out certain basic problem areas. Even allowing for the occasional driver error, the results in the 1982 Championship season seemed oddly at variance with the company's investment, technical expertise, overall potential and longer-term goals.

Admittedly, things brightened up a bit in 1983 but – let's face it – Renault still didn't take the title.

Ferrari Turbo

As far as number of cylinders (six) and engine configuration ('vee') are concerned, Ferrari's engineers have clearly been thinking along the same basic lines as their rivals at Renault. Apart from the angle formed by the two rows of cylinders – 120° in the Ferrari and 90° in the Renault – there is one very distinct difference between the two. In the Renault, compressed air is fed to the engine in the middle, *i.e.*, in the space between the two rows of cylinders, and exhaust gases are discharged low down at the sides. In the Ferrari, exactly the reverse is true. The two exhaust turbo-chargers are not positioned alongside the engine but are mounted symmetrically above it in the free space between the two banks of cylinders. It was to achieve more design freedom in this area that the 'vee' angle was opened out to 120°.

It is very unusual in automotive engine design for the air/fuel mixture to be fed *up* to the combustion chamber rather than – as one would logically expect – down to it. The racing car engine is a special case, however, and there are some very interesting ramifications.

Ferrari works with two turbo-charging systems – exhaust turbo-charging and Comprex super-charging.

The Comprex System

As I write, the Comprex system is still at the trial stage. Although it has yet to be tried out in an actual race, it is interesting enough to discuss in some detail.

Like a lot of other supercharging techniques, the Comprex system has its origins in the diesel truck sector. It might appear something of a paradox that what is good for diesel trucks is also good for thoroughbred racing cars. However, the heavy diesels and the racing car engine have at least one thing in common – both types of engine have to operate within a very limited rev range. Neither mode of transport is designed with the driver's comfort in mind: both are built for a specific purpose, and the driver often has to change gear repeatedly to keep the engine working effectively. In a diesel, operating efficiency is gauged by fuel consumption; in the new Formula I, the acid test is that of improved performance.

Comprex supercharging is relatively ill-adapted to the needs of a standard petrol-engine passenger saloon, but it is easy to see that it can offer very good results in a diesel engine or a racing engine. Essentially, this type of supercharging is designed to accomplish the same as turbo-charging, namely to exploit the latent energy of exhaust gases to feed compressed air to the engine.

The Comprex is a pressure wave engine. Its one advantage over the exhaust turbo-charger is that the energy derived from the exhaust gases is utilised directly rather than via relatively heavy components such as a turbine wheel, shaft and compression wheel, all of which have to overcome inertia – a process that results in less satisfactory engine pickup.

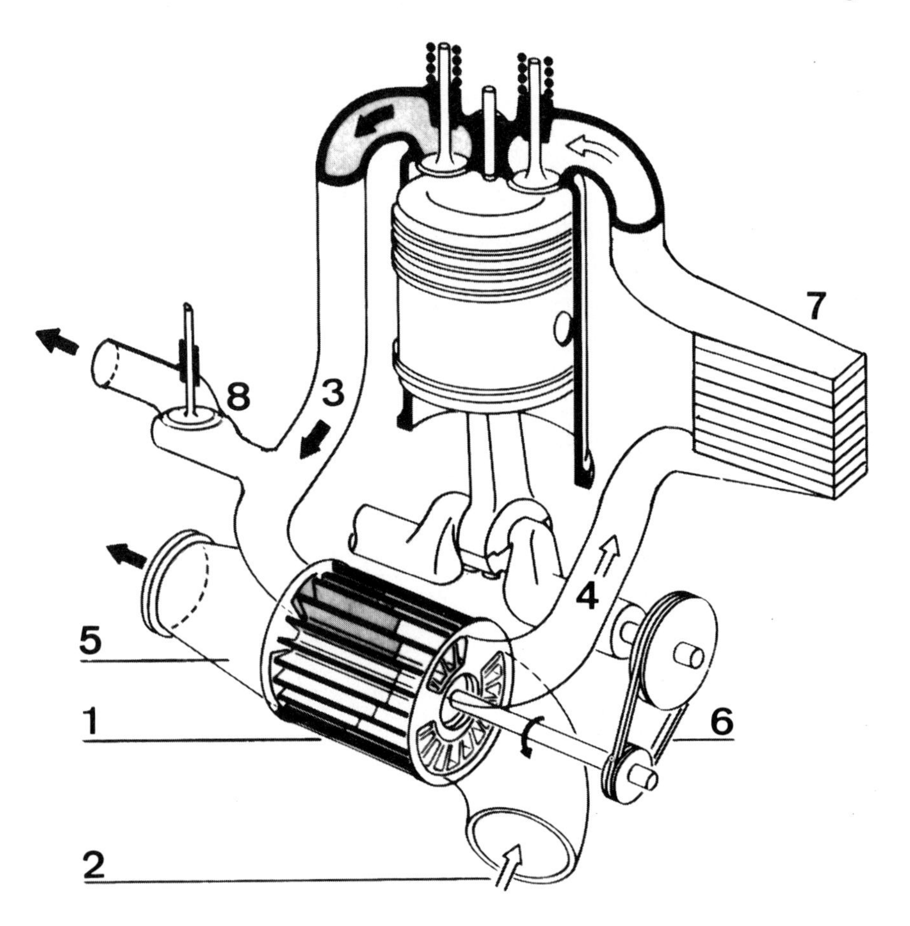

The Comprex System. In a conventional exhaust turbo-supercharger there is a clear separation of the (hot) exhaust gas side and the (cold) fresh-air intake side. Not so in this Comprex pressure-charging system developed by Brown Boveri of Switzerland: here there is direct contact between exhaust gases and inducted air – although there is absolutely no question of the two being mixed. The contact comes about in the (1) where the fresh air inducted at (2) and conveyed by the wheel (1) is compressed by exhaust gases introduced via (3). The compressed air is fed to engine via manifold (4) and the exhaust gases which have transferred their energy to the inducted fresh air are expelled at (5). The wheel is drivn by a low-powered drive mechanism (6) which might, for example, be powered by an electric motor. The compressed air becomes just as hot as in the case of a standard turbo-supercharger, with the result that an intercooler is necessary at (7) to operate on the induction tract (4). Note also the indispensable waste gate (8) already encountered in exhaust turbo-superchargers.

The actual Comprex unit consists of a mechanically-powered turbine wheel rotating in an enclosed chamber. The rotational speed of turbine is not a decisive factor in the supercharging system. What is more, the power needed to drive the wheel (about one percent of total engine output) is extraordinarily small.

The exhaust gases enter on one cylinder face and exit at a somewhat different angle on the same side; the same process applies on the opposite face, this time with inducted air. The intermittent pressure of the exhaust gases thus comes into direct contact with the inducted air in the turbine and compresses it. The rotating bucket wheel carries the compressed air to the next aperture where it is forcibly expelled. The same thing happens to the exhaust gases, except that these were initially compressed and are relieved (*i.e.*, decompressed) in the bucket wheel. The key to the whole concept is that exhaust gases and inducted air each flow in and out of one and the same side of the turbine: the exhaust gases enter and exit on one cylinder face, the inducted air enters and exits on the other.

Under no circumstances must there be direct contact between exhaust gases and inducted air. If the two did mix the inducted air would be contaminated by the exhaust – which would not only increase charge temperatures but would also reduce combustion efficiency by depriving the cylinder of oxygen.

In the Ferrari, the Comprex unit is mounted in the same place as a turbo-charger, namely on top of the engine.

Up to now, the improved engine pickup made possible by the Comprex system has taken its toll in terms of weight. The unit as a whole weighs some twenty kilogrammes more than a complete exhaust turbo-charger system. In addition, it uses more fuel. On top of all this, there is obviously no getting round the need for intercoolers – compressed (and therefore hot) air has to be cooled drastically.

There are other problem areas, notably the mechanical drive unit for the turbine. V-belts or cogged belts are used, and these are particularly susceptible to dislocation or fracture when there is a sudden change in engine rpm – for instance, during a gear change. As I mentioned, the actual power required to drive the wheel is very small, just enough to start it turning and keep it rotating, and it might be feasible to dispense with the mechanical drive and actuate the Comprex unit by external means such as an electric motor.

The 'Normal' Turbo

To return to the turbo. Comprex supercharged engines have performed well in testing, but Ferrari is not primarily committed to this system. Exhaust turbo-charging has proved to be even more effective, at least in the short term, so it is appropriate to focus our attention now on the 'normal' Ferrari Turbo.

The mounting of the Ferrari's turbo-chargers above the engine does not do too much for the engine's centre of gravity, although this is somewhat offset by the low down location of the induction system. In addition, the positioning of the turbo-chargers is beneficial for heat dispersion, and the layout of the exhaust system is extremely compact. For reasons of space and simpler pipe arrangement, the turbo-charger powered by the exhaust gases from the left cylinder bank feeds air to the right bank and vice versa.

The fact that the two Ferrari turbo-chargers lie close together is also an advantage when it comes to adjusting boost pressure. Almost all turbo engines – whether petrol or diesel, road or racing – use the same kind of boost-pressure limitation, the essential component of which is the so-called 'waste gate'.

This regulating valve comprises a duct running through a high thermal resistance housing. The valve – just like a standard inlet or exhaust valve, only larger – is positioned so as to close off the duct or open it as required. The end of the valve shaft is enclosed by an aluminium casing which houses a spring (to close the valve) and a membrane. When the membrane chamber is under pressure, the valve opens; when the pressure falls below the requisite amount (as determined by the spring and membrane surface area), the valve closes again.

The waste gate is built into a conduit that surrounds the turbine housing. As long as the valve is shut, all the exhaust gas passes through the turbine. Depending on the extent to which the valve is opened, more or less exhaust gas will circumvent the turbine and pass directly to the tailpipe.

A turbo-charger could be designed large enough to dispense with a waste gate, *i.e.*, the flow of exhaust gas over the turbine would be consistent and undiminished. However, a turbo-charger large enough to accomplish this would deliver very little boost pressure at low revs. For this reason, it is preferable to use smaller units which deliver a high boost at low rpm. As the revs increase, of course, there would be a danger of over-charging – subjecting the engine to so much pressure that something would have to give.

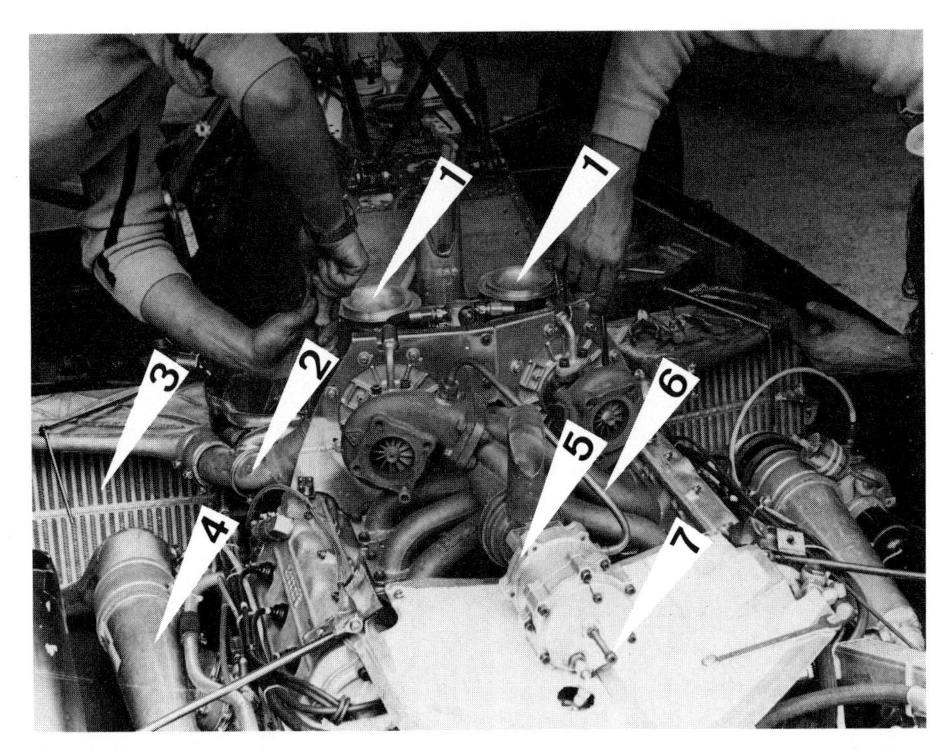

Here we can appreciate the simple, clear and symmetrical lines of the six-cylinder V 120° Ferrari. Air is inducted into the trumpets (1). After compression, the air moves through duct (2) to the vertical intercooler (3) and is fed to the engine via the low lateral plenum chamber. The exhaust gases are expelled through the centre of the vee and are fed to the turbo-charger units via very short individual pipes. The turbo-charger for the left-hand bank of cylinders is positioned on the right and vice versa. Since the exhaust tail pipes have been removed in this shot, we have a fine view of the turbine wheels which can turn at anything up to 120,000 rpm. At the other end of the turbo-charger shafts are similar turbines which rotate at the same speed induct fresh air, compress it and feeds it to the engine via the intercoolers. There is only one waste gate (5) for the two exhaust gas flows. Any superfluous exhaust gas is expelled directly through the diagonal aperture. A control cable (6) regulates the system. If the boost pressure (and, with it, the counter-pressure from the turbine) is too high, the waste gate will open, with the result that less of the exhaust flow is fed to the turbine wheel. Boost pressure can be adjusted by means of a long screw (7).

To prevent this, a waste gate is clearly indispensable. The size, pressure, spring and membrane of the waste gate are so designed that the gate opens when the engine reaches high boost: from that moment on, excess exhaust gases do not pass through the turbine but are channelled directly to the tailpipe.

To all intents and purposes, boost pressure is now kept constant. It is also possible to allow the driver to vary boost pressure from the cockpit, but this is a shabby practice, particularly when it is abused in order to set a fast qualifying time. In my opinion it should only be possible for boost pressure to be regulated by the mechanics from outside the car. And it should be illegal to change it between qualifying and the race proper.

On most cars there is one waste gate per turbo-charger. On the Ferrari, however, the close proximity of the turbo-chargers means that only a single waste-gate is required; even though it is necessarily larger than the waste gates on the Renault, it is, overall, simpler, lighter and more easily reached.

Like the Renault, the Ferrari has two intercoolers. Unlike Renault, however, they are pure air-air coolers. The air exits from them relatively low down and is fed to the engine via two inlet manifolds, one for each intercooler.

The Formula I Ferrari differs from other makes in that air passing through the radiators and intercooler is expelled from the side rather than the top. This means that the top surface of the side pods can be kept completely smooth.

When it comes to performance, Ferrari has always gone for peak power, and the V6 Turbo delivers over 600 bhp at 11,000 rpm on a compression ratio of 6.5 : 1. This makes the Ferrari one of the highest-revving turbo power units: in fact, only the normally aspirated 12-cylinder engines and the V8 Alfa Turbo reach higher rpm.

Running at 11,000 rpm is no problem for the 6-cylinder 1.5-litre Ferrari Turbo because the mean piston velocity (taken as a measure of frictional loss) is extraordinarily low. The small cylinders and, above all, the tiny piston stroke in the Renault (43 mm) and the Ferrari (48.4 mm) mean that respective piston velocity (15 m/sec. for the Renault and 17.7 m/sec. for the Ferrari) is down in the range of a standard passenger saloon. By contrast, piston velocity in other engines is significantly higher – 22.6 m/sec. in a Cosworth, for example, or 21.2 m/sec. in the BMW 4-cylinder turbo.

BMW 4-Cylinder Turbo

Like Renault, BMW simply took a compatible engine and turbo-charged it. In both instances, BMW and Renault, the engine was one that had originally been developed to compete in the European Formula 2 Championship, the difference being that the BMW had enjoyed more success there than Renault, as confirmed by BMW's five championship titles. The engine in question was one that no longer features in BMW's range – a 4-cylinder 2-litre in-line with 89 mm bore and 80 mm stroke.

The familiar four-valve cylinder head with the unusually wide 40° valve angle was taken over virtually unchanged from the Formula 2 engine. For all that, the shape of the combustion chamber is quite favourable, given the larger cylinder size (375 cm^3) by comparison with the 6-cylinder turbo and the lower (6.7 : 1) compression ratio. In this case, reduced valve angle is not so crucial as it is in highly-stressed 12-cylinder normally aspirated engines.

The 89.2 mm bore was also taken over practically unchanged from the 2-litre engine but, to get cubic capacity down to the prescribed 1.5-litre limit, the stroke was reduced from 80 to 60 mm. The shorter stroke requires the use of uncommonly long (153.6 mm) titanium connecting rods.

A certain amount of experience had already been had with turbo-charging to the extent that a 1.4-litre version of the engine had raced in the German Championships in a modified BMW 320.

In theory, there was very little to commend the use of a turbo-charged four-cylinder in-line engine in Formula I – and a whole lot to be said against it. There could be no doubt that BMW had set itself a difficult task in preparing engines for Grand Prix racing. Nor can there be any doubt now that the Munich firm has convincingly demonstrated its fantastic prowess, bearing in mind that Nelson Piquet used a BMW engine in the world championship in 1983.

A number of things are immediately apparent when you compare the BMW 4-cylinder in-line with 6-cylinder V-engines such as the Renault, Ferrari, Honda or Porsche.

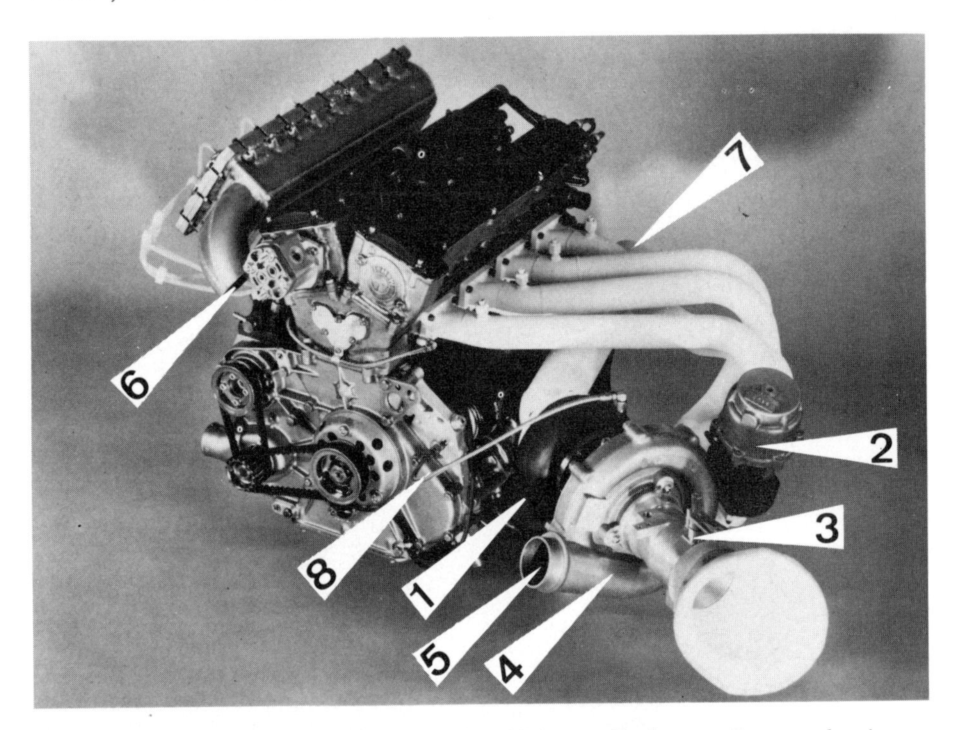

This BMW engine block derives from the old four-cylinder two-litre production unit, and the cylinder head has been adapted from Formula 2. The extremely long, carefully calibrated exhaust pipes are brought together just before the turbine casing (1) next to the waste gate (2); later the exhaust pipes were shortened. The throttle butterfly (3) is positioned ahead of the compressor (4). The intercooler is located between the compressor exit (5) – where temperature is around 190° Centigrade and air pressure 2.8 bars – and the inlet manifold (6). The exhaust gases leave the turbo-charger unit via a thick tail pipe (7). The turbo-charger shaft rotates some 110,000 times per minute; its bearings are lubricated via the oil pipe (8).

The number of cylinders in the BMW – four – is less than favourable because the individual cylinder units are relatively large. This has the effect of limiting peak revs because the combustion process is longer and mechanical demands are greater. In effect, the BMW has nominal top revs of 9,500/min, making it the lowest-revving engine in Formula I.

To get the best out of turbo-charging, the BMW opts for two sets of cylinders (1 and 4, 2 and 3) with identical angular ignition spacing. These link up just outside the turbine housing and the combined ducts are fed separately deep into the turbine housing. In other words, BMW has come out in favour of what we know as a 'two-flow' turbine housing, otherwise used only in diesel engines on account of the heat problems which arise in the wall between the two ducts. In the diesel engine, of course, exhaust gas temperatures are distinctly lower, so that there is far less danger of failure.

Another problem for BMW was the installation and anchoring of the large, heavy (14.6 kg) turbo-charger. In the Brabham-BMW, the unit is mounted on the left and served by four long exhaust pipes. Precise calibration of exhaust pipe length makes for a particularly impressive performance in a turbo, albeit at the expense of optimum engine response.

To improve engine response and integrate the engine more completely

Absolute precision is vital in engine assembly. This illustration features a BMW cylinder head.

ATS switched to the BMW engine in the 1983 championship season but with no spectacular results. Overall, the car is not a patch on the Brabham-BMW.

into the car's overall design, the exhaust pipes were shortened by some 100 mm for the 1983 season, and overall performance improved to the extent that the engine now delivers an effective 600 bhp.

Just ahead of the turbo-charger – still on the left – is the one large intercooler; just behind the turbo-charger is the waste-gate and the short exhaust tailpipe. Air exiting from the intercooler is fed round the front to the four intake ducts on the far side of the engine.

Although the intercooler is mounted upright and only slightly inclined, it is very effectively cooled by air-flow, because the rear wheels check the rush of oncoming air: the left rear wheel then forces the air inboard through the intercooler.

The plenum chamber and inlet manifold are made of carbon fibre reinforced plastic – a material notable for its combination of high strength and low weight. The injection nozzles are bolted directly to the manifold and thus project freely into the centre of the intake trumpets.

The whole engine is firmly suspended in a secondary frame which forms a connection between the back wall of the monocoque and the transmission. Accordingly, the engine does not assume a full load-bearing function – it was not designed to do so and, in any case, in-line engines are so narrow on top that they are ill-suited as load-bearing components.

The big plus in the BMW is the amount of power it can deliver – 600 bhp at 9,500 rpm with a basic compression ratio of 6.75 : 1 and 1.8 bar boost pressure. Its biggest weaknesses are difficulty of intallation, acceleration (engine pick-up) and fuel consumption.

To improve pickup, the BMW now makes use of two throttle systems. The original large butterfly in front of the compressor intake was retained, and four other small ones were installed in the inlet ports. By careful balancing of the two systems it proved possible to regulate pressures and improve engine response.

A not inconsiderable portion of the fuel used by a turbo engine goes purely and simply towards cooling the inducted air. What this means is that, in the critical heat range, the engine will be fed an over-rich air-fuel mixture. Where conditions are poor (*e.g.*, high charge temperature, inadequate inter-cooling or poor combustion chamber design), the engine will burn excessive amounts of fuel.

Starting with the 1982 British Grand Prix at Brands Hatch, the Brabham-BMW team used a special ploy which involved starting the race with a half-empty tank and soft tyres and then coming in half-way through the race to refuel and change tyres. This was not so much shrewd tactics as an admission that the 240-litre fuel tank might not be large enough for a long race – particularly where a lot of fast gear-changing was involved.

One thing is sure, however : the BMW is the most impressive 'afterburner' of all the F1 turbos. The afterburner effect is seen mainly in the braking zone coming up to a corner. Even though the throttle is virtually closed, the sharp fall of pressure in the remaining gap (vital to idling) allows some air to force its way into the combustion chambers. At the same time, a little fuel is still being fed over the ignition unit, albeit not enough to be ignited by the spark. What then happens is that ignition and combustion tend to occur around the red-hot parts of the turbo exhaust and at the tailpipe. Turbo exhaust gases are distinctly hotter than those from a normally aspirated engine – some 1100° C as opposed to 900°. The alarmingly dangerous-looking flames are a result of this delayed combustion, but they are actually unimportant other than in their contribution to heightened spectator enjoyment.

Hart Turbo

The first person to experiment with a turbo-charged 4-cylinder engine was England's Brian Hart. The car it was used in – the Toleman-Hart – was unsuccessful at first because of a substandard chassis, but it hit the headlines during the British Grand Prix 1982 at Brands Hatch, when Derek Warwick held on in second place behind me for lap after lap. The Hart delivers a lot of power and is interesting in many respects. It derives from the 2-litre 4-valve power unit used by Toleman and others in the European Formula 2 Championship, where it was a serious challenger over the years to the BMWs and Renaults.

Once Hart started to develop this engine as a turbo-charged Formula I unit, he ran into all manner of difficulties with cylinder head sealing. Finally, he decided to cast the cylinder head and block as one unit. The whole is in cast aluminium (*i.e.*, conveniently light) with no seal between head and block. This 'monobloc' design is not new in racing engine construction: Mercedes-

The Hart four-cylinder turbo used in the Toleman is an interesting new development. The engine has a different look about it because it is built in one piece: block and head are cast together, so there is no cylinder head gasket. The valves are operated by two cogged-belt driven camshafts.

1983 saw some good performances by the Hart Turbo once the roadholding of the Toleman chassis had been improved. The Toleman team's results were very impressive in view of the restricted budget at its disposal.

The Hart Turbo compressed air starter unit (1): compressed air is fed to the 'air engine' via a bolt connection (2). The pressure advances the pinion (3) and rotates it, thereby actuating the flywheel ring gear and drive coupling. This system is used by all Formula I teams other than Ferrari, which employs an electrical starter unit.

Benz used a similar layout in 1954, and there were other, earlier, examples.

Up to the close of the 1982 Championship season Hart featured an intriguing technical solution to the problems of intercooling. An exclusively water-cooled system was used, but Hart achieved particularly good results by using an independent system rather than – as in the Renault – one which utilised the water from the engine cooling system. This meant using a separate water pump which was belt-driven from the engine. The water was fed through aluminium tubes below the normal radiator and into large heat exchangers. Since water-air heat transfer values are good, Hart was able to keep the intercooler unit down to remarkably small proportions. It was installed to the right of the engine.

By 1983, however, Hart had shelved this system, probably because the circulating water represented excessive weight. Now he has decided to let air do the job for him: the air flow impacts directly on the two large intercoolers positioned on either side of the engine and slightly ahead of it – in other words, just as in the 'vee' engine variants. The result is something of a jumble of pipes and tubes, because the compressed air has to be fed from the turbo-charger down to the intercoolers and then the two airflows have to be reunited and fed to the inlet manifold. The water and oil coolers are located at the front of the car, ahead of the front axle.

This engine – complemented by a completely new chassis – achieved some very good lap times during testing and qualifying at the start of the 1983 season, and twice finished fourth in the latter part of the season.

Alfa Romeo V-8 Cylinder Turbo

Italian racing engine designers have always had a soft spot for high-revving power units and multiple cylinders. BMW and Hart opted for the 4-cylinder approach, the lower limit for turbo-charged 1.5-litre engines; by contrast, Alfa went to the other extreme, and risked developing a 1.5-litre 8-cylinder. Cylinder volume in a 4-cylinder engine is hardly what you would call large (375 cm^3), but the 8-cylinder Alfa has an individual cylinder volume of only 187.5 cm^3.

Alfa opted for a 74 mm bore and a very small 43.5 mm stroke. If you stop to consider that you then have four valves per cylinder, plus valve springs, caps and sundry regulating gear, you begin to realise that we are talking about real miniaturisation. In terms of a 3-litre normally aspirated engine, the Alfa V-8 corresponds to a 16-cylinder unit, currently prohibited under the maximum 12-cylinder rule. (Incidentally, BRM did experiment with a 16-cylinder engine some years back, albeit with precious little success.)

The new Alfa engine (which, as of championship season 1983, has now replaced the 12-cylinder normally aspirated engine in the works team) has a V 90° cylinder arrangement, undoubtedly the best solution in an 8-cylinder power unit (*vide* Ford Cosworth).

Induction is from above. The two turbo-chargers are installed at either side, and each is driven by the exhaust from one bank of cylinders. KKK turbo-chargers were used initially, but there has now been a switch to Alfa Avio units designed in-house. The Alfa is the highest-revving of all the turbo engines, and instead of the characteristic slightly-muted turbo sound it has a rather more aggressive exhaust note, almost like that of a conventional engine.

The 'vee' design means that the engine blends nicely with the car's overall lines. The intercoolers are mounted on either side of the engine and are inclined slightly forwards. Now that the Alfa Turbos are beginning to make their presence felt, very little attention is being paid to development of the 3-litre Alfa V12.

Heidegger Turbo

The Heidegger Turbo is a 6-cylinder in-line engine designed by Austria's Rolf-Peter Marlow, who has worked extensively on high-performance engines at Porsche, BMW and Oettinger and who has now settled in Liechtenstein with the Max Heidegger development group.

In fact, the Heidegger is the first engine to be developed specifically for the 1.5-litre turbo category in Formula I. This is a very courageous project which, like the Hart, is characterised by boundless enthusiasm and a lot of good new ideas but suffers from lack of funds. The Heidegger engine has attracted several interested parties, but none has to date taken the plunge and built a Heidegger into a Formula I chassis.

The problem for small firms such as Heidegger is rather different than is widely assumed. Developing their own engine and the various (for the layman) sophisticated parts that go into making it, is *not* the real problem: the real problem, in fact, is in coping with what we have called the engine's 'environment'. Turbo-charged engines are becoming increasingly dependent on electronically-controlled ignition and injection units, not to mention specially-developed turbo-chargers. All of this is very expensive, not least because the various units have to all intents and purposes to be developed individually for each engine; as a result, suppliers prefer to work with firms who already are series production customers.

The Heidegger design focuses on extreme lightness, ease of construction and proper choice of cylinder number. The Heidegger uses six cylinders – like Renault and Ferrari – but these are in line rather than in a 'vee'. As far as bore and stroke are concerned, however, the Heidegger takes no chances: the respective dimensions (86 and 43 mm) are identical to those selected by Renault.

It is an entirely different matter when it comes to the design of the crank-case. The cast steel case favoured by Renault is rejected by Heidegger and substituted by magnesium (which is four times lighter than steel). By saving weight also on other components in the engine, the manufacturer can claim

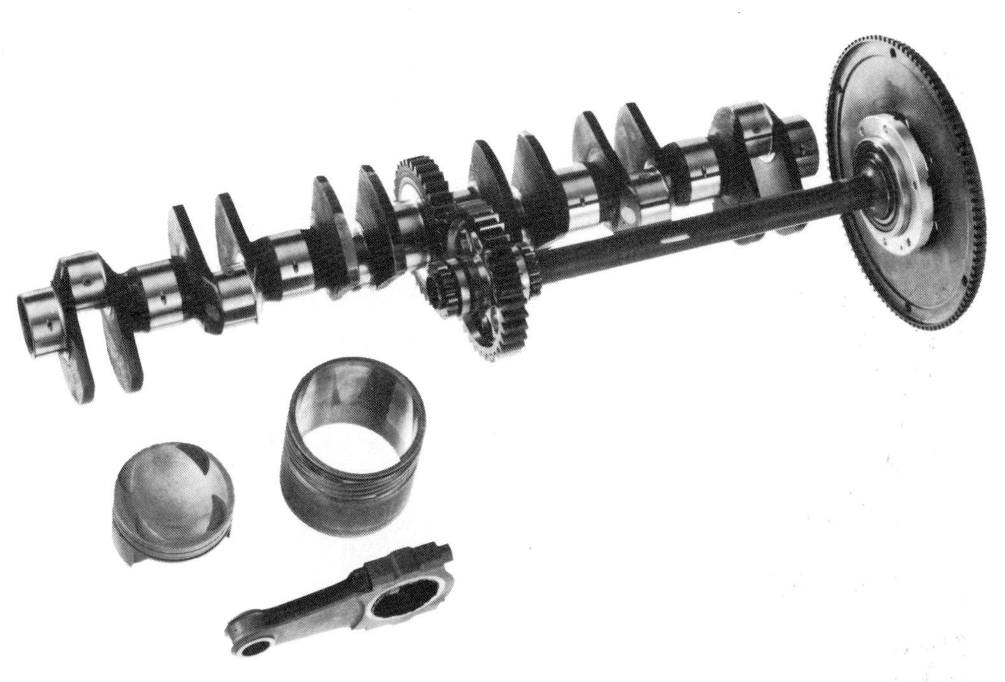

The Heidegger is a very expensive piece of engine. The crankshaft with its 43 mm stroke is extremely light and features a central power take-off. The pistons run in oil-cooled liners and the connecting rods are made of solid titanium.

overall engine weight to be 130 kilogrammes – nothing short of sensational. This is some 30 kilogrammes lighter than the lightest Formula I engine currently in use; it has to be said, however, that part of the weight-saving is cancelled out by the fact that the long, narrow design of the Heidegger means that it cannot be used as a structural part of the car.

Long six-cylinder crankshafts react violently to high revs – particularly in excess of 9,000 rpm – so Heidegger has opted for a central power take-off. This means that the engine is, practically speaking, two three-cylinder units. A powerful cog-wheel is located exactly in the centre of the crankshaft to deliver power outwards to a link-shaft which runs parallel to the crankshaft back to the transmission.

This arrangement goes a long way towards solving the 'long crankshaft' problem and also has a further, significant advantage. Normally, the centre of the transmission is in line with the mid-point of the crankshaft. In the Heidegger, by contrast, there is complete flexibility in positioning engine and transmission: depending on the effect desired, the engine can be installed

The comparative sizes of the Heidegger six-cylinder and the BMW four-cylinder graphically illustrate the latitude enjoyed by a designer – such as Heidegger – in devising a power-unit specially for a Formula I turbo. It goes without saying that the difference in size is also reflected in weight.

lower or moved sideways relative to the transmission. The cylinder head is made up of two units of three cylinders each, the overall effect being one of compactness and rigidity. The overhead camshafts are actuated by toothed gears, which are also driven from the centre of the engine.

As far as performance is concerned, a 6-cylinder in-line offers the same potential as a 6-cylinder 'vee' although – as repeatedly stressed – the latter is more symmetrical and compact and thus better integrated into the car's overall design. Nevertheless, it can only be hoped that the Heidegger will soon find an appropriate partner or, failing that, a wealthy sponsor.

Porsche V6 Turbo

A number of years back Porsche attempted – with no great success – to develop its own Formula I engine. Today, however, Porsche is one of the most experienced firms in the field of turbo-charging; its potential was recognised by Porsche at a very early stage and has since been exploited both on the racing circuits and in series production.

Today, Porsche not only builds cars but has also carved a niche for itself as an engineering 'subcontractor'. There is an understandable reluctance on the part of those who contract out to Porsche to publicise the fact: it is a matter of record, however, that some 40 per cent of Porsche's development capacity is today earmarked for outside contracts.

The development contract initially entered into by McLaren is now administered by TAG (Techniques d'Avant-Garde), a group that specialises in new technologies. TAG first became involved in motor racing as a sponsor of the Williams team. Clearly, Techniques d'Avant-Garde doesn't get involved in this sort of thing just for the fun of it: the money invested is scheduled for recuperation at a later date through commercial exploitation. At any rate, the official designation of the Porsche engine is now TAG Turbo Engine TTE PO1.

I have already stressed repeatedly how crucial the interrelationship is – particularly when a turbo is involved – between engine and car: only when the two are in harmony do you have any chance of Grand Prix success.

Co-operation between McLaren and Porsche was particularly close during the development stage in 1982. On the British side, Ron Dennis dealt with project management and John Barnard with technical matters; Hans Metzger is senior project development executive at Porsche. The prospect of the new engine becoming available was certainly one factor which clinched my decision to drive for McLaren in 1983. Like its counterparts at Ferrari and Renault, the new engine is a V-6 – a 'real' vee-engine, to the extent that each crankshaft throw is actuated by two connecting rods. Thus, the crankshaft has only three throws, each offset by 120°.

The angle between the cylinder banks was hotly debated by both sets of designers (car and engine). John Barnard was absolutely insistent on designing a wing car *par excellence*, whereas the engine boffins pressed their claim for sufficient latitude to house turbo-chargers, intercoolers, intake manifold and so on. The engine entered its development phase during the ground effect era, but did not suffer in any way because of aerodynamic design

Electronic ignition and injection systems making their presence felt in Formula I. My McLaren Turbo has two drive units (for safety reasons) positioned on either side of the driver. (Opposite) A mechanic uses a monitoring unit to check ignition and injection units on the McLaren TAG Turbo.

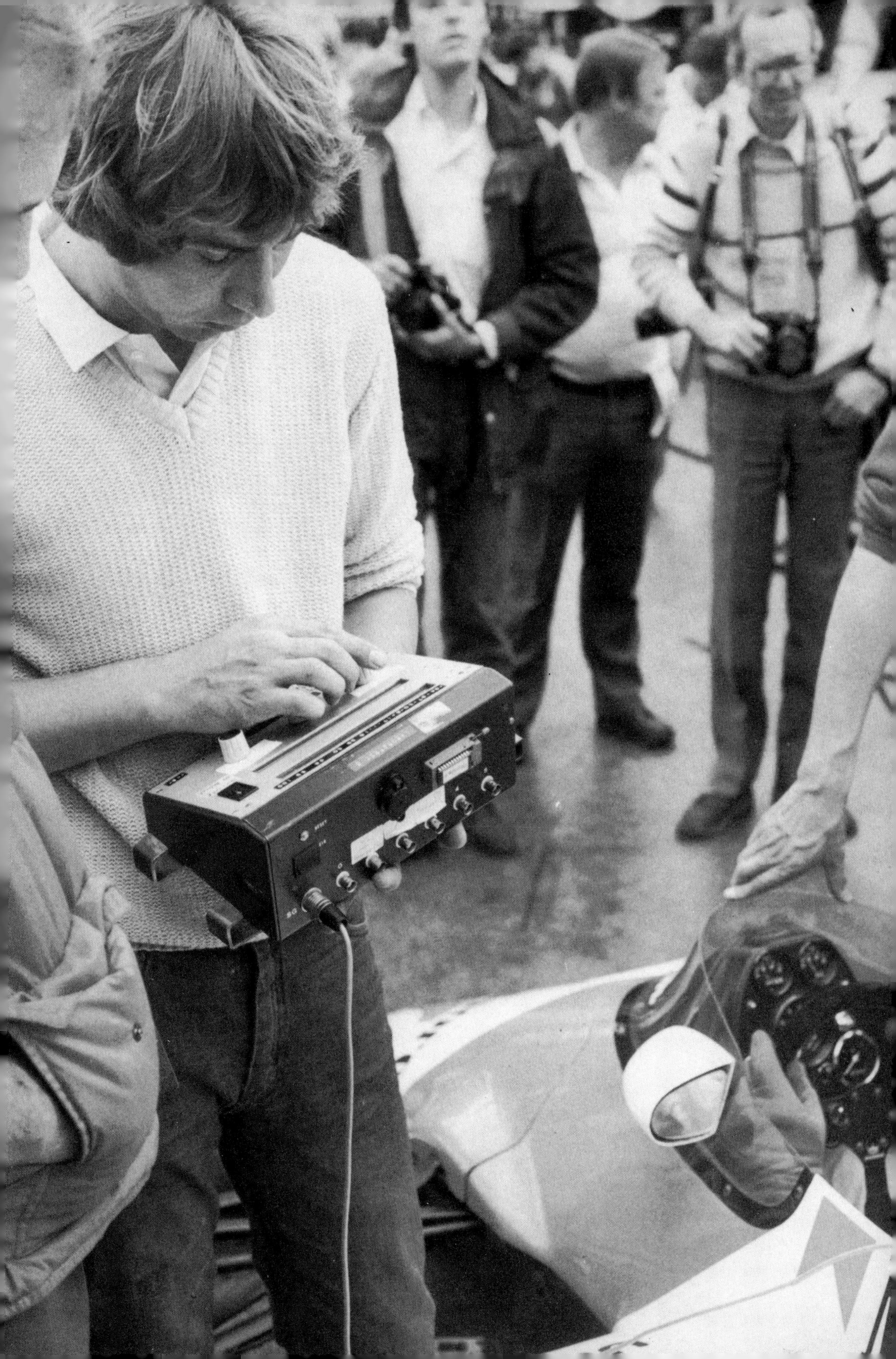

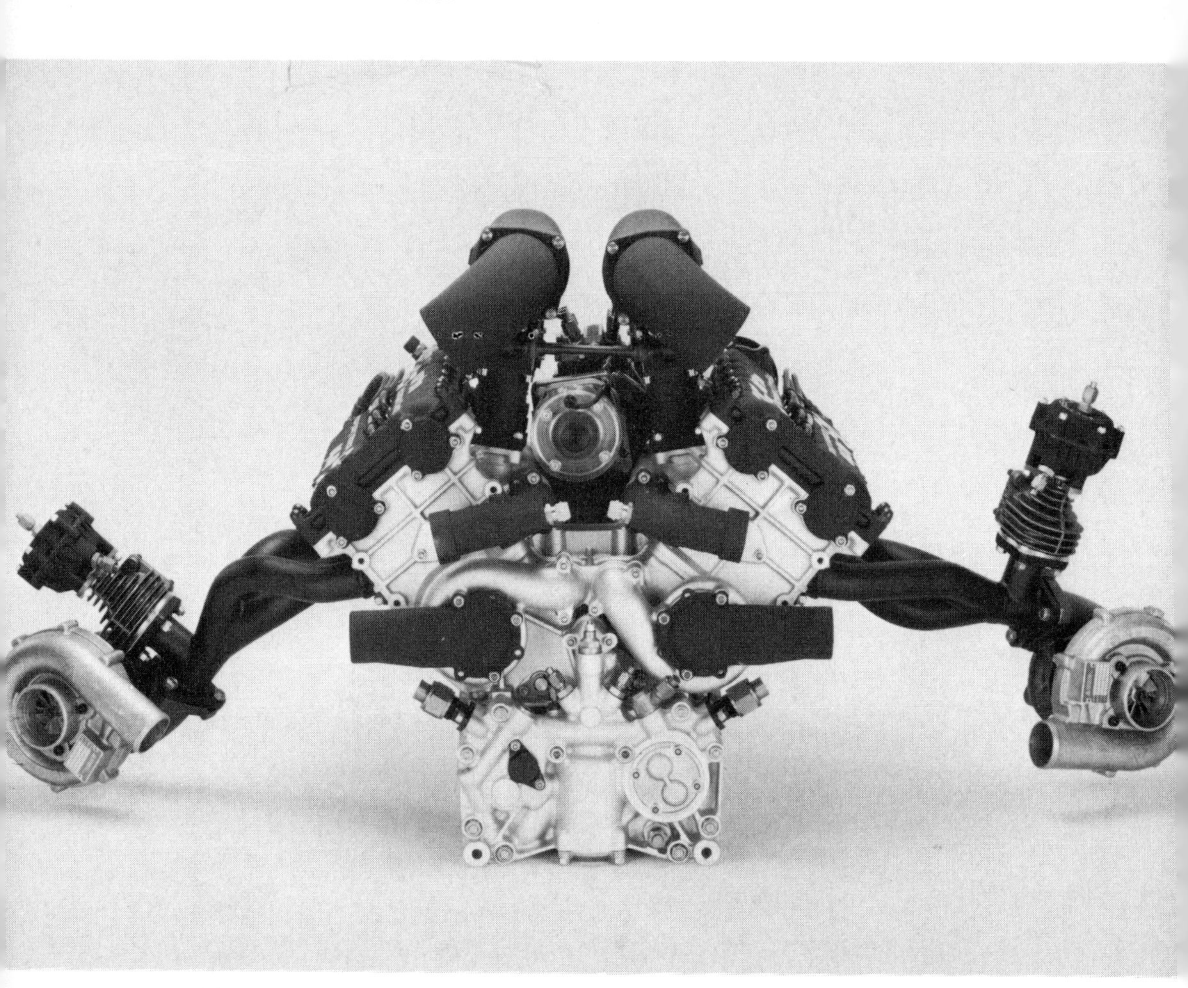

The TAG-Turbo is a masterpiece of engine design. Everything is integrated into the engine. The engine itself is extremely light and compact. The 6-cylinder V 80° is completely symmetrical and sufficiently rigid to act as a fully stressed component of the car.

constraints. In the end, it was agreed to make the angle 80°, something that had never been tried up to then in a vee-engine.

While this does mean that the engine has both primary and secondary free moments of inertia, it also means that it is ideal in terms of installation. The free moments of inertia – which are common to all 6-cylinder vee-engines – are in fact relatively unimportant, as is the irregular firing sequence in a high-revving engine. The important thing – and this is provided for in the Porsche – is that the angular ignition spacing be identical for each cylinder row, thereby making for equal actuation of the two turbo-chargers (one for each bank). An additional factor – which has now become largely irrelevant – is that the small 'V' permitted the turbo-chargers to be installed sufficiently high up so that they do not interfere with the aerodynamic design of the side-pods.

McLaren also had specific notions as to the underside of the engine, *i.e.*, left and right of the crankshaft. What was wanted was an engine built as narrow as possible to enhance airflow conditions across the underbody. In other words, a new position had to be found for the oil and water pumps – another item which has become irrelevant with the change to flat bottoms.

To economise on weight, the engine block is in aluminium. It is divided into two sections at crankshaft level. The underside is also in cast aluminium: it houses the main bearing caps and, at the same time, serves as the oil sump. The extreme rigidity suggests that the main load stresses can be readily accommodated, with something in reserve. The pistons run in wet cylinder liners, which are also made of aluminium for reasons of heat dispersion. The running surfaces – as has long been common – are nikasil-coated.

High rigidity was a must not only for the block but also for the cylinder heads. John Barnard was adamant that the engine assume a full load-bearing role, just like a Cosworth. In the event, an enormous degree of rigidity has been achieved by casting the cylinder heads in one piece – a complete departure from convention as regards 4-valve cylinder heads in a racing car engine. Thanks to a bit of technical wizardry, it has proved possible to get away from the traditional (and finicky) approach which entails dividing the cylinder head. The Porsche has a 30° valve angle and a bore/stroke ratio of 0.576 – which puts it somewhere between the Renault and the Ferrari.

The four overhead camshafts are driven by toothed gears only (thirteen in all). Two of these also serve to drive the water pump, thus saving a little on space and weight. Gear drive has also been selected for the two oil pumps set low down at the front. Overall, the emphasis is on optimum reliability, extremely rigid construction and scrupulous attention to detail – so much so, that there is not one single component, not so much as a connecting rod, which has been taken over from another engine design.

The air-fuel mixture is fed to the engine from above, *i.e.*, from within the 'vee'. This would have been the place to install a Bosch fuel injection pump *à la* BMW but Porsche opted to go electronic to the extent that both fuel injection and ignition system are computerised. The requisite quantities of fuel to be injected and the ignition timing sequences are thus called up immediately and 'fed' to the engine.

I have to admit that, unfortunately, things don't always happen as quick as one might like – even at Porsche. We simply haven't had time as yet to try out some of the ideas buzzing around in my head and in the heads of the Porsche designers. The engine still has some components that are prototypes and we can expect to see further distinct improvements once they are perfected. On the other hand, the name of the game – obviously – was to get the car on the track as soon as humanly possible. At any rate, the engine already shows such enormous potential that I expect to be a front-runner in the 1984 championship season, just as I used to be back in the Ferrari days.

The engine itself is still the same as the one we unveiled in Geneva at the start of 1983, very compact and very tidy. Virtually everything has been integrated into the engine and there are no outboard ducts, pipes or drive units. There are also some new subtleties as far as exhaust design is concerned, but these are still a trade secret.

Even if it does not have any spectacularly new features, I am convinced that I now have the engine with the greatest overall potential. And that makes working on it and testing it a very special pleasure.

Let's quickly run through the engine's history. The original development contract was signed in September 1981 and, exactly one year later, we were bench-testing the first prototypes. Before you can really start gauging performance, a whole battery of tests has to be completed as regards ancillary equipment (water and oil pumps, dynamo, injection unit, oil and water circuitry, and so on). One thing that is absolutely vital is to determine the engine's drag coefficient, since that is a decisive factor in overall performance. The drag coefficient is measured in terms of the power needed to turn the engine at a specified number of revs. In essence, it is determined by friction in the bearings, piston rings and auxiliary drive units and by internal 'pulsations', *i.e.*, compression and expansion of air beneath the pistons. The lower the coefficient the better, because that not only means better performance but also lower oil and water temperatures.

The TAG Porsche engine came through all these tests with flying colours. The complete engine ran independently as of February 1982, and immediately delivered the desired 600 bhp.

Honda V6 Turbo

The new TAG Porsche Formula I engine was unveiled at the 1983 Geneva Motor Show. The new Honda engine made its formal debut about one hour previously. As we said at the Porsche press conference, we hope this is the first and last time that Honda will be ahead of Porsche.

Honda's decision to return to Formula I was not a spur-of-the-moment affair. After all, Honda had raced before and had notched up Grand Prix wins in 1965 and 1967. After that, Honda took a long break from Formula I, but maintained a strong presence in Formula 2 and took the European championship in 1981. The Japanese V6 engines are now back in the hunt and are the toughest challengers to the BMW 4-cylinder engines which – speaking purely in performance terms – they edge out.

The 1967 Honda Formula I engine was a 12-cylinder 'V', immediately recognisable on account of the jumble of tailpipes which jutted up from it. Now, Honda has opted for a turbo-charged 6-cylinder unit, obviously in the belief that the future belongs to the 1.5-litre turbo engine rather than the 3-litre normally aspirated type. Honda also believes, however, that the development of this kind of power unit can offer new technical insights, the prospect of which is especially appealing to the younger generation of engineers.

The Honda and the TAG Porsche are very much alike at first glance. Even the 'vee' formed by the two banks of cylinders is the same – 80°. Induction takes place in the middle of the vee, exhaust below on either the side. The exhaust pipes are distinctly longer in the Honda.

For purposes of turbo-charging, Honda falls back on the redoubtable KKK (Type K26) unit manufactured in West Germany, but ignition and injection equipment is manufactured in Japan; the injection system, in fact, has been developed by Honda itself. The emphasis is on electronics. The Honda PGMF 1 (Programmed Fuel Injection System) is used not only in the Honda F-1 and F-2 engines but also in the series production City Turbo.

The other technical specifications of the Honda are very much up-to-date: 4 valves per cylinder, overhead camshafts, dry sump lubrication, multiplate clutch, two turbo-chargers, etc. The Honda is reported to deliver in excess of 600 bhp.

The Honda engine was first raced experimentally by the Spirit Team using a modified Formula 2 chassis. The switch to Williams was virtually trouble-free and Rosberg placed fifth in his very first race with the Honda, the final Grand Prix of the 1983 championship season at Kyalami.

Honda has sunk an incredible amount of money into this project, and there is every reason to expect the Honda-Williams-Rosberg combination to be a formidable one.

Living with the Engine

First of all, let me describe what life was like with a normally aspirated Cosworth. It all came down to one thing, really: the damn thing had to function and it had to function consistently. As it happened, the Cosworth had matured over the years to the point where this simple – yet basic – requirement could genuinely be met. The Cosworth very rarely let you down.

When I found that I was slow in practice or in qualifying, it hardly ever occurred to me to blame the engine. We very rarely fiddled around with it, *e.g.*, varying ignition sequences, fuel injection rates, intake or exhaust systems or camshaft. The McLaren team didn't lavish the same care and attention on the engine as you might find, for example, over at Ferrari, where the engine is viewed very much as an integral part of the car. With McLaren, there was no long drawn-out inquest into why a Cosworth engine wasn't up to scratch: we simply changed it. The main reason we didn't waste too much time on the engine was that we knew how quickly and easily a new one could be installed (we normally allowed about 100 minutes). The only real bit of fine-tuning that might prove necessary after a new engine had been installed was adjustment of the metering unit if the new engine should start to splutter and back-fire – in which case the mixture was too lean and was igniting at the exhaust rather than in the combustion chamber.

My experience of Cosworths dates back to 1972, with March. By comparison with that engine, today's Cosworth delivers an additional 40 bhp or so – up to a maximum of some 510 bhp – and has a useful range which is some 2,000 rpm greater. One Cosworth did, in fact, deliver 520 bhp.

The mature design of the Cosworth was such that very little power was lost in the course of a race – not more than 10 bhp, which is appreciably less than is usual in, say, a Ferrari. Maintenance, repairs and bench-testing are carried out both by Cosworth themselves and by several independent companies.

In qualifying laps and during the race itself I kept the revs between 7,000 and 11,500. An electronically-operated rev limiter engaged at 11,500; I could no longer switch this off from the cockpit as I used to be able to do. When the limiter cut in it eliminated individual ignition impulses and prevented damage from over-revving.

One thing I couldn't complain about was too much power. Other than at the start of a race – assuming the track was dry – the only wheelspin you experienced would be in an exceptionally tight corner. On the long straights, of course, all you could do was respectfully watch the turbos flash past you and then say a prayer for better days.

Starting the engine had long since ceased to be a problem. It fired as reliably as a Volkswagen Golf, although the actual procedure involved was just a shade more complicated. I had to switch the ignition on and remember to engage the electric fuel pump (which was switched off again at around 3,000 rpm to save electricity – above 3,000 rpm all you need is the mechanical pump powered directly by the engine). The actual starting process was carried out by the mechanics who stood behind the car with a huge compressed air cylinder which operated the pneumatic starter motor.

Things got a little bit trickier if the engine died on you somewhere out on the circuit – which could quite easily happen, for example, if you spun out. The compressed air cylinder which each car is required to carry was so tiny that the starter motor generally gave up after a few turns and failed to bring the engine back to life. The on-board cylinder is operated by means of a lever/ cable-pull mechanism.

Starting a hot racing engine somehow seems to be more difficult today than it ever was. It is something that we as drivers simply have to learn to live with, since no really effective answer has yet been found. You simply have to be inordinately careful to keep the engine alive in tricky situations by disengaging the clutch and accelerating out of trouble.

Coming to terms With the Turbo

The prospect of racing a new engine had a major bearing on my contract extension at McLaren. Working with something new has always had a great appeal for me: Ferrari back in 1974 is a case in point.

It was not until the fourth time out that I was able to show just how much potential the new engine has. That was in Kyalami, in the last race of the 1983 championship season. Clearly, however, we are still a long way away from what we feel the new engine can do.

The fact that I had to call it a day just four laps from the end and with the leader – Patrese – in my sights had nothing whatever to do with the turbo engine. It was simply a matter of electrical failure. The regulator had packed up, with the result that voltage dropped off steadily. When we checked after the race we found that we were running on 7 volts as opposed to the requisite 12. The fuel injection and ignition systems no longer function at that low voltage, the net result being that the engine simply stops running.

As a matter of fact, one of the particularly good features about the new engine is its reliability. Other teams travelled to Kyalami with sixteen engines (there were test sessions scheduled before the race weekend) but we only took along the same five engines that we had already used in testing and in three previous races.

Another thing that came good right from the word go was top speed. On the straight we were always up there with the leaders. By the same token, one thing that was clearly unsatisfactory was poor engine response at low revs. The engine seems to have something of a split personality. In the rpm range between start and 7,000 (*i.e.*, at virtually no boost pressure) the car was next to impossible to drive. I say 'was' because I am sure that spring 1984 will be a different matter entirely.

At the end of the 1983 championship season, however, the situation was as follows. Once the 7,000 rpm mark had been reached, the car suddenly started to perform. Coming from a normally aspirated engine, I had got used to a direct relationship between accelerator position and power. The turbo was something else again. Just imagine, you're at 7,000 revs with your foot to the floor, the engine is performing miserably, your foot stays down and then, as you come up to around 8,000, the engine goes wild. Believe me, this delayed action effect takes some getting used to. It entails a completely new driving style. It is not just the engine that you have to cope with, of course, but the car's whole set-up, the aim being to come out of a corner with the revs up as high as possible.

This is the point where somebody usually mentions the legendary 'left foot braking' used by many rally drivers to keep their speed down without killing off the revs. No way in Formula I. Brake, clutch and shift operations are so rapid that there is simply no question of complicating matters further by being on brake and accelerator at one and the same time. Anyway, the brakes wouldn't take that kind of treatment for very long.

In the brief time I have driven with the new engine we have already managed to cope much better with this problem. A breakthrough came at Kyalami where, with the aid of a larger rear wing, I really got up some speed and even set the fastest warm-up time on the race morning.

I also have a brand new toy in the cockpit with me – a boost pressure gauge which keeps me in the picture as regard pressure in the engine intake. Boost pressure is a function of several factors (ambient temperature, engine temperature, air pressure, altitude, and so on), so the first thing I have to do is find the correct setting during test and qualifying laps. The 1.9 bar pressure we use in the race itself can be set directly from the cockpit. I take my time over this to make sure I get the setting right. The best opportunity for trimming boost pressure usually presents itself on a long straight. A quarter turn of the regulator wheel makes for a pressure change of some 0.2 bar.

As yet we are not ready to play games as far as fastest qualifying laps are concerned: the engine is set up in such a way that it won't 'digest' higher pressures – unlike the Renaults, Ferraris and BMWs that can deliver 700 bhp and more over short periods thanks to incredible (2.5 bar) boost pressure and additional intercoolers. Of course, there is another reason why we can't get in on the act for the time being – there is always the risk of blowing an engine and we have too few of those for the time being to chance it.

Speaking of increased boost, it is also worth mentioning that higher boost pressure seems to make for slower engine response. 'Seems', because this is totally subjective; technically speaking, it is impossible. It is nonetheless a bit disconcerting for the driver because braking, shifting and gear ratios don't seem to 'fit'. Boosting pressure would only seem to be meaningful in a car with a mature engine, one where power is better spread over a greater rpm range than in mine – at least, as of end-season 1983.

In any case, one thing that is really fascinating is that my turbo vibrates less and runs more smoothly than any normally aspirated engine unit I've ever had dealings with, despite the fact that its 6-cylinder V80° configuration doesn't balance the masses as well as, say, the Ferrari V180° 12-cylinder. This bears out what passenger saloon designers have long maintained, namely that a turbo engine will deliver power more sweetly and more evenly than its normally aspirated counterpart.

Once the pressure has built up I can tell by a very faint whine that the two charge units have come up to peak revs. What happens next is really out of this world: there is an incredible kick that leaves even the best conventional engines standing. This is evidenced in terms of top speed, which can be anything up to 30 km/h faster with a turbo. It is important to add, however, that the distinctly faster lap times in a turbo are only attributable in part to its power down the straight. In fact, just as much is a result of faster cornering because we can put on more wing. The wing translates extra speed into increased downforce and allows us to corner faster.

Normally aspirated Marques: Teams and Specs

As at Monaco 1983

	FORD COSWORTH	MATRA	ALFA ROMEO
Teams	Arrows, Ensign, Fittipaldi, March, McLaren, Osella, Theodore, Tyrrell, Williams	None at present	None at present
No. of cylinders and configuration	8 V 90°	12 V 60°	12 V 90°
Engine capacity (cm^3)	2991.7	2992	2991
Bore x stroke (mm)	85.7 x 64.8	79.7 x 50.0	78.5 x 51.5
Peak power	382 kW 520 bhp at 10,500	375 kW 510 bhp at 11,600	387 kW 525 bhp at 12,300
Stroke/bore	0.75	0.63	0.66
Piston speed (m/sec)	22.6	19.3	21.1
Compression ratio	11.4:1	11.1:1	11:1
Fuel injection	Lucas	Lucas	Lucas
Engine weight (kg)	156	187	180
Power output per litre	137kW 173 bhp	125 kW 170 bhp	129 kW 175 bhp
Valve angle	32°	32°	26°
Raced as of	1967	1968/70, 1972/75, 1976, 1978/81, 1982	1979

The Turbo Marques: Teams and Specs

As at Monaco 1983

	BMW	RENAULT	FERRARI
Teams	Brabham, ATS	Renault, Lotus	Ferrari
Cylinders: number and configuration	4 in-line	6 V 90°	6 V 120°
Engine capacity	1499 cc	1498 cc	1496 cc
Bore x stroke	89.2 x 60 mm	86.0 x 43.0 mm	81.0 x 48.4 mm
Peak power at standard *race* (i.e. not qualifying) charge pressure	441 kW 600 bhp at 9,500 rpm	426 kW 580 bhp at 10,500 rpm	441 kW 600 bhp at 11,000 rpm
Stroke/bore	0.67	0.5	0.59
Piston speed (m/sec)	19.0	15.0	17.7
Compression ratio	6.7:1	7:1	6.5:1
Fuel injection	Kugelfischer	Kugelfischer	Lucas-Ferrari
Chargers	1 KKK	2 KKK	2 KKK
Charge pressure	ca. 1.9 bar	1.8 bar	1.7 bar
Engine weight	165 kg	180 kg	177 kg
Power output per litre	294 kW 400 bhp	284 kW 386 bhp	294 kW 400 bhp
Valve angle	40°	22°	38°
Raced as of	1982	1977	1981

* Estimated or extrapolated.

HART	ALFA ROMEO	TAG TURBO P01 (Porsche Development)	HONDA
Toleman	Alfa Romeo	McLaren	
4 in-line	8 V 90°	6 V 80°	6 V 80°
1494 cc	1497 cc	1498 cc	1498 cc
88.0 x 61.5 mm	74 x 43.5 mm	82 x 47.3	
580 bhp at 10,000 rpm	441 kW 600 bhp at 11,200 rpm	441 kW 600 bhp at 11,000 rpm*	441 kW 600 bhp at 11,000 rpm
0.7	0.59	0.576	
20.5	16.2	17.3	
7:1	7:1*	7:1*	7:1*
Lucas		Kugelfischer or Bosch Elektronik	Honda PGMF I
1 Garret	Alfa Avio	2 KKK	2 KKK
1.85 bar	1.8 bar*	1.9 bar*	1.9 bar*
135 kg	175 kg*	145 kg*	160 kg*
386 bhp	294 kW* 400 bhp*	294 kW* 400 bhp*	294 kW 400 bhp
40°	25°*	30°	
1981	1983	Mid-season 1983	Mid-season 1983

Structure and Safety

The Happy Medium Between Performance and Survival

Pictures such as these highlight the exaggerated upfront position of the driver in ground effect Formula I cars – dictated by the need to accommodate fuel tank, engine, oil tank and transmission behind the driver. As a result, the latter's legs were in a highly exposed and vulnerable position.

The real legacy of the ground effect era is the fact that driver safety is today greater than ever before. This was partly fortuitous – fuel tank placement in the ground effect generation had to be changed out of design necessity – and partly a result of deliberate corrective action taken by the FIA. Because of the close link between coachwork/superstructure design and driver safety, it seems appropriate to deal with them under a separate heading.

At least as far as the leading makes are concerned, the typical Formula I superstructure has evolved into a very strong, long, slender unit which starts ahead of the pedals and ends at the engine mountings behind the tank. Minimum width at the front is dictated exclusively by current requirements relating to cockpit width, namely that it shall be not less than 45 centimetres. This rule was a must to prevent designers from going to extremes and proposing even tighter cockpits with even less room for the drivers' legs. In fact, before the 45 cm rule came into force, the old McLaren cockpit was built so narrow that my legs used to rest against the spring/damper units. The monocoque widens to some 60 cm at shoulder level to accommodate the tank and at the rear – that is, where the engine begins – it is exactly wide enough to match the width of the engine (in the case of the Cosworth, 67 cm). Thus you have a harmonious transition from monocoque to engine: the engine is mounted directly behind the monocoque and, all other things being equal, can be bolted directly to it.

MONOCOQUE FABRIC AND DESIGN

The designer has a very big hand in determining the overall safety of a car when he decides on the material and the dimensions used for the monocoque. There are rules and regulations, of course, but there are never checks on compliance: there is no way there could be, because doing so would often involve using complicated and expensive testing apparatus. There is therefore nothing else for it but to appeal to the designer's conscience and trust him to design a safe car. It is often not until the first shunt occurs that it turns out that the appeal has been in vain.

Riccardo Paletti's horrifying shunt at the start of the Canadian Grand Prix in 1982 is a case in point: it is unforgivable that the tank surrounds should have collapsed and ruptured the fuel cell. Admittedly, this did not cause Paletti's death (he died instantly as a result of a ruptured aorta), but there is no excuse for a modern Formula I car catching fire – even after such a serious collision. The aluminium tore and ripped the fuel cell open, something that simply shouldn't happen any more.

The most modern, most rigid and also most expensive fabric used for monocoque construction these days is carbon fibre reinforced plastic. McLaren pioneered its use, and most other manufacturers have since followed suit.

In order to achieve good superstructure characteristics in a very narrow and, at cockpit level, open structure, it is imperative to make the whole monocoque as rigid as possible. The new-fangled plastics are in fact so rigid that under

The Lotus monocoque – still a ground effect car in this photograph – is an integrated carbon fibre design and incorporates the fuel tank, which extends from the seat back to the front of the engine.

(albeit enormous) stress they no longer distort – *i.e.*, exhibit high elasticity – but simply shatter.

My own feeling is that this is the best solution currently available to us, because the whole superstructure is tailored to the driver's body to such a degree that there is simply no room for distortion. In effect, distortion is synonymous with broken bones. At any rate, I have the certainty of being protected in the first instance by an extremely rigid structure: if it should come to a shunt, I can only cross my fingers and hope that the bits and pieces around it – radiators, bodywork, air vents, wheels, and so on) will absorb the impact to such a point that the safety harness and my body will cope with the residual strain. This would seem to be a fair assumption judging by the fact that, when he was driving for McLaren, de Cesaris was involved in no less than eighteen shunts without being seriously injured.

Unfortunately, the comparative 'safety' of the erstwhile ground effect cars is now somewhat dissipated, at least in terms of lateral protection. The wing cars were anything but safe as far as handling was concerned, but in terms of driver protection they were good, despite there being too little leg room. What I mean by this is that the wide air intakes and all the equipment housed in them, such as water and oil coolers, offered very good lateral protection. With the 1983 rule changes, some cars (notably Brabham) have dispensed with side pods since they are no longer needed to boost ground effect. Today's Brabham looks for all the world like a dragster, with its narrow bodywork and all the major components in the region of the rear wheels: this, of course, has been done in the interests of traction.

Personally speaking, I was delighted that McLaren retained side pods, complete with water and oil radiators, in the 1983 design.

Carbon fibre monocoques lend a futuristic look to a stripped-down Formula I car. The sinister reticulated black of the plastic contrasts strongly with the bright and generally glinting metal parts screwed or riveted to it. The individual parts of the monocoque superstructure – complete with all the requisite bolt holes, cut-outs, connector points and outlets – are readied in the McLaren works and shipped to the U.S. company Hercules which puts them through a special secondary bonding process. Back comes the finished monocoque ready for the final touches.

This new type of monocoque is far and away the most expensive, but it does offer the designer scope for optimum driver protection without weight penalties. Traditional monocoque construction techniques entail the use of aluminium components (panels, flanges and profiled sections) which are

Entente cordiale: the British Lotus with its French Renault Turbo engine. . .

riveted together as and where necessary. Parts can be replaced or added more readily than in the case of an integral carbon fibre monocoque, but reinforcement must be provided at specific stress points; the new trend is towards the use of honeycomb or sandwich panels plus carbon fibre to heighten rigidity. It is also possible to opt for a hybrid construction – half carbon fibre, half light-metal alloy.

It is a mistake to think of the driving seat as an upholstered or foam-rubber padded bucket seat. In actual fact, the driving seat is a singularly uncomfortable affair – at least in the McLaren – consisting of a thin carbon fibre shell moulded to the contours of the driver's body. Bits of foam rubber and strips of insulating tape afford improvised padding where it hurts most.

The new Formula I safety regulations can be divided into two categories: constructional safety features and safety equipment.

Constructional Safety Features

Impact Absorbing Zones: The crushable structures between the wheels are required to be 10 cm wide and 35 cm long. Formerly, they came about virtually of necessity as a result of the side pod profiles and the cooling units housed in them. In fact, the side pods offered more than the rules called for in terms of size and protection As of the 1983 season, we were back to the point in some marques where you have to get out your magnifying glass to identify the 'real' impact absorbing zones – what the FIA Handbook refers to as crushable structures – *i.e.*, those elements that really *are* capable of absorbing impact energy.

The rules prescribe 'box members' which extend from a fixed point behind the driver to at least 50 cm in front of the soles of his feet: in practice, these are so thin that they are virtually equivalent to the thickness of the monocoque. In other words, they are hardly adequate to absorb energy.

The impact absorbing zone in front of the driver's feet is particularly important. In the ground effect days, designers would have loved to push us so far forward that the 'zone' would have been the soles of our feet – the farther forward the driver was positioned, the easier it was to design an aerodynamic underbody. A 25 cm zone was prescribed – precious little. This was increased to 50 cm for the 1983 championship season; the designers are not as insistent as formerly on an extreme up-front position for the driver.

In this respect the new Brabham is a typical and, for the driver, pleasant example. Generally speaking, however, the designers are still very miserly when it comes to space, since every possible centimetre of length has to be used to accommodate the engine and the fuel and oil tanks.

The new 50 cm impact absorbing zone in front is normally made of aluminium and generally houses the brake cylinders. It can absorb an astonishing amount of impact energy. However effective it may be in the event of a small or even medium-size shunt, I am still acutely aware of how vulnerable my legs would be if something really serious happened: after all, the heavier components in a rear or transverse engine car – *i.e.*, the engine and the transmission – cannot be brought to a standstill immediately. In the event of a collision, they will 'follow through'.

Roll Hoops: Two main roll hoops are prescribed. The first of these has to be no more than 25 cm ahead of the steering wheel and must be at least as high as the upper rim of the steering wheel. Its function is to protect the driver's hands and legs in the event of the car somersaulting. Today's designers, almost without exception, exploit the front roll hoop to house the instruments – or what is left of them. The front roll hoop has to be more than a short piece of metal tubing bent across the front of the cockpit: it must be designed in such a way that stresses acting on it are completely aborbed down through the monocoque.

The rules relating to the size of material used in safety structures specify that they must be capable of withstanding certain minimum stresses, namely one and a half times car weight laterally, five and a half times car weight longitudinally, and seven and a half times car weight vertically.

The second roll hoop is more readily identified by the layman as the one which is mounted behind the driver's head. The rules say that it must be positioned no less than 50 cm behind the first and must be high enough that an imaginary line between the top of the first roll hoop and the top of the second passes above the driver's helmet when he is belted into his normal driving position.

Fuel Tank: The safe central position of the fuel tank between engine and driver has already been alluded to on several occasions. Fuel is not actually carried in the tank but in a rubber safety cell which is fitted inside it, the so-called 'fuel cell' which must be of recognised manufacture.

Even when the tank is full (maximum capacity 1983 = 250 litres), the use of a fuel cell permits the tank to distort without any spillage. All connections have to be metallic and permanently bonded – vulcanised – to the fuel cell. The main tank intake must be at least 25 cm behind the cockpit, and must not project beyond the contours of the bodywork. Fuel fillers are usually of the aircraft variety, to ensure a perfect seal for all eventualities. The regulation requiring tanks to be no more than five years old is somewhat superfluous, inasmuch as there can hardly ever have been a Formula I car that has seen five years' service.

Fire extinguishers: Two separate fire extinguishers are prescribed – a 5 kg cockpit unit and a 2.5 kg unit for the engine area. The larger bottle has to be installed in the cockpit and is usually mounted transversely under the driver's knees. The unit is triggered electrically via an independent circuit, which has to function irrespective of whether the main circuit has been cut, and the activating lever or switch must be easily reached by the driver from his belted-in driving position.

Life Support Breathing System: A further requirement is for a compressed

A carbon fibre reinforced plastic monocoque (Alfa Romeo).

The front impact absorbing zone in my McLaren. It is built of aluminium sheeting riveted directly to the carbon fibre monocoque. Brake and clutch fluid reservoirs are located here, together with a small transmitter unit for the lap timing system. When the car is driven over a contact loop set into the track at the start/finish line, its lap time is automatically recorded and printed out.

air cylinder connected via a heat-resistant cable to the driver's helmet. This unit is activated at the same time as the fire extinguishers. Despite what is often said and written, the cylinder contains *air*, not oxygen: if the car should catch fire, oxygen would only make matters worse. Although this life support system is prescribed, some drivers do not use it because they are not convinced as to its efficiency.

Safety Harness: Two shoulder, one abdominal and two leg straps are obligatory, all of them to be firmly anchored. The free ends come together in the safety harness release buckle. Strapping yourself in is such an awkward business in the tiny cockpit that you can't manage the operation alone – you have to have help from the pit crew. The release mechanism has, of course, to be very simple: the harness comes apart in your lap.

Starter Unit: Starter units have to be regarded as safety features, since a car stranded out on the circuit constitutes a hazard to other drivers. Although the rules call for onboard starters, it has to be admitted that there

Keeping tabs on the competition during qualifying. Times are displayed on a portable print-out.

are serious sins of omission in this respect. This is all the more worrying since a stalled engine can spell danger for innocent bystanders, particularly the race marshals called on to push the car off to the side of the track.

The rulebook provides that, for the duration of the race meeting, each car must be equipped with a starter unit which can be activated by the driver from his normal driving position and which is plugged into an independent power source capable of providing 'at least two starts'. At the beginning of the race and after a pit stop we are allowed to hook into a temporary 'external power source' – normally a huge compressed air cylinder. By contrast, the actual onboard starter has been scaled down mercilessly.

I feel it would be a good idea to institute some kind of functional check procedure, since the phrase 'at least two starts' is meaningless: you often have to try half a dozen times before a hot racing engine catches again.

The starter unit has been a major topic of discussion on account of the increasing number of planned pit stops during races. In Brazil this year, when his engine stalled as a result of the car catching fire during a pit stop, Keke Roesberg was simply 'push-started' by his pit crew. Because he was actually in the race proper, this is prohibited and he was, quite rightly, disqualified. Normally all drivers keep their engines running throughout these short pit stops, but most teams have an external air cylinder handy to be on the safe side.

on Systems

Priorities in the Ground Effect Car Era and After

In the classic days of Grand Prix racing, a car's success or failure used to hinge on its suspension. 'Kinematics' – *i.e.*, how tension and compression of a car's springs affect toe-in and camber – was a major determining factor in overall performance. Then along came ground effect and we had to revise our ideas as far as suspension systems were concerned. Adjusting the suspension by itself had suddenly become pointless, and trying out various types of springs and dampers was equally irrelevant (other than as a means of helping to gauge the car's overall aerodynamic performance). Since all manner of elements interacted and each influenced the other, it was exceedingly difficult to identify them individually: this meant that testing was more complex than ever before, and that results more often than not were inconclusive.

In fact, in the final analysis, the suspension of a ground effect car was only there to bring out the best in the car's aerodynamic design features and to accommodate the enormous downforce generated by them. Putting it another way, you might say that the best suspension was the one which made for least possible afflux and tailflow disruption, and which best ensured consistency in the size of the intake gaps which permitted airflow to reach the underbody.

The role of the suspension was so clearly delineated that designer response was immediate and apparent. You wouldn't find a ground effect car, for example, with its springs and dampers installed out in the open in the space between chassis and wheels where they would have contributed to drag. Instead, everything was moved as far inboard as possible.

Nor would you have found a car in those days with outboard anti-roll bars; they, too, would have increased drag, so they had to be revamped: they were scaled down drastically, mounted on the monocoque, and operated by complicated linkages.

The springs used on ground effect cars were so stiff that they disengaged from the upper and lower spring collars when the car was not under load. The rocker (2) transmits wheel deflections to the inboard coil spring/shock absorber unit. In the Renault, the very small compressed air cylinder for the starter unit (3) was located behind the cylinder head on the left and activated by a draw switch (4).

In essence, a suspension system comprises moving and non-moving parts, the latter being of virtually no consequence in a single-seater racing car since their role is effectively taken over by the monocoque itself as a result of the moving parts being bolted directly to it (as opposed to being mounted on rubber bushes in the standard passenger saloon).

Seen from the outside, the moving parts begin with the uprights, complete with the wheel bearings and stub axle. These uprights are normally aluminium or magnesium castings, and incorporate lugs to which the brake calipers are bolted. Most cars now have two calipers for each brake disc, the idea being to cut down caliper size without losing braking power, and thereby allowing the largest possible discs to be fitted inside the wheel rims. Twin calipers are also becoming increasingly common on rear brakes, the aerodynamics of current racing cars allowing a surprising amount of the total braking effort to be handled by the rear tyres.

Formula I dragster style: the springs and dampers of the 1983 Osella are sited ahead of the driver to obtain as slim a design as possible. The design features push-rod suspension fed diagonally through the wishbones.

The transfer of braking power to the front axle as a result of the displacement of the centre of gravity during braking is effectively cancelled out by the downforce acting on the car as a whole. In addition, because of their larger diameter, the rear wheel brakes acquire more leverage. This explains the present trend towards mounting discs and calipers of the same size at both front and rear.

Braking power is transmitted via two hydraulic cylinders, which respond to the brake pedal via a balance bar mechanism; one cylinder serves the front, the other the rear. The balance bar can be adjusted (from the cockpit if necessary) to adapt brake performance to specific track conditions. As a general rule, however, the brake circuitry is only adjusted in response to unusual circumstances such as vapour bubbles in the brake fluid or worn brake linings. Excessive rear braking is particularly unpleasant, by the way, because it unbalances the whole car.

The brake pipes which transmit fluid to the calipers are no longer allowed to flap around in the breeze. In the leading makes, at least, these cables are neatly tucked away into the wishbones or, at worst, aligned in their slipstream so as to cause minimum drag.

The wheel unit – upright, disc, caliper and wheel – is attached to the monocoque by means of wishbones. The layout of these linkages used to be very much a trade secret in the days before ground effect, because it determined the handling of the car and thus its circuit performance. Once ground effect cars came into their own, however, oversteer and understeer in the conventional sense of the terms had next to no relevance; the cars whipped through the corners as if they were on hidden rails. In the ground effect era, we only tinkered with the spring collars when we wanted to raise or lower the car for aerodynamic reasons. That apart, there was precious little experimentation with the car's suspension during qualifying or even in testing.

Most FI cars use air ducts to cool the brakes. The rear ducts are set high to exploit oncoming airflow. 'Captured' air is channelled to the middle of the brake disc, whence it flows through cooling slits into the wheel rim. The entire brake system is designed to operate at very high temperatures. In cold or wet weather the air ducts are progressively taped over to ensure that the brake pads reach their optimum working temperature.

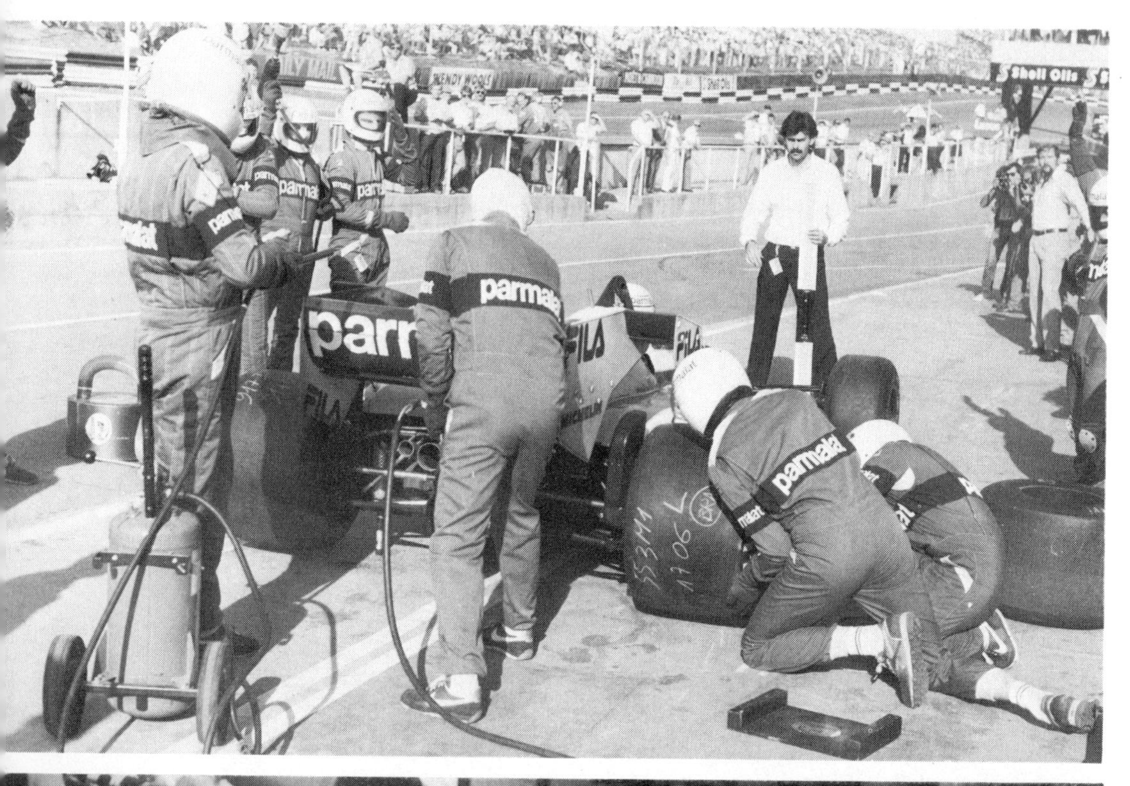
Shell Oils
parmalat
FILA

BMW MPower
parmalat
KONI

(Top left) The Brabham-BMW pit crew came out best in championship season 1983 when it came to refuelling. On-board pneumatic jacks are used to lift the car. The mechanic in the centre is connecting the compressed air cylinder to lift the car some 10 cm. (Bottom left) For transport and for accurate measurement the cars are mounted on narrow aluminium wheels.
(Top right) All the leading makes feature two brake calipers per disc – at least at the front. The disc is connected to the wheel hub via an aluminium cup.
(Centre right) Carbon fibre reinforced carbon brake disc on the McLaren.
(Below) Changing rear brake pads. The linings are being marked to facilitate the collation of data on wear, running performance and overall brake system temperature.

The wishbones themselves are normally oval tubes (round tubes flattened to reduce drag) secured at either end by universal joints. Progressively slimmer monocoque design has resulted in them becoming longer and longer to bridge the gap between the chassis and the wheels. Broad-based triangular front wishbones are now used by almost everyone, though one or two teams still have upper rocker arms. The wide spread inboard anchorage of the wishbones, particularly the bottom ones, is dictated by the need to take out wheel loads over as broad a base as possible.

Since the overall stresses that had to be accommodated were greatly increased in ground effect cars, and since it was vital to retain a constant skirt gap, very stiff springs were used during that era. These springs did not operate across a broad range of up-and-down movement: their tension and compression range was very limited indeed, and they readily disengaged from their upper and lower collars when not subjected to load.

To be honest, when you really thought about it, you began to wonder why there was any springing at all and why there wasn't more experimentation with rubber blocks of one sort or another. It is just possible that these would have proved a better solution than conventional springs – to the extent that they might even have stopped the cars porpoising.

Since the springs had been designed to accommodate high-speed driving, they were completely insensitive at low speeds. When the driver got into the car or when one of the mechanics stood on it to carry out an adjustment, the car didn't budge; it was virtually rock solid. Nor did fiddling with the dampers make any difference, since they too had been tailored to high-speed driving.

The practice of transmitting suspension loads inboard facilitated the installation of the anti-roll bars in the same area. Anti-roll bars themselves are now extremely compact, and are activated by lever arms which are designed to exert different amounts of resistance when subject to torsion. These "blades" can best be thought of in terms of leaf-springs, which provide high resistance in one plane and low resistance in the other; as a result, when the blade is horizontal to the anti-roll bar, relatively little load is communicated because the leaf itself bends. On the other hand, when the blade lies vertically (*i.e.*, upright and on edge) to the anti-roll bar, a lot of power can be transmitted because the arm will not flex in this direction. Since the driver can adjust the angle of the arm via a Bowden cable, he does have the advantage of being able to adjust the stiffness of the anti-roll bars while the car is in motion.

Monitoring brake disc temperatures: The outer edge of the disc is coated with a white paint which has special properties allowing it to change colour to reflect changes in temperature. The highest temperature registered can be 'read off' by reference to the colour shade. This approach to temperature measurement may not be completely accurate, but it has the advantage of being simple and does not require the installation of complex thermometric devices.

Continental
DUNLOP
GOOD YEAR
LONGINES
Agip
27
MAGNETI MARELLI
olivetti
GOOD YEAR

Above: The authorities found themselves forced to stipulate a minimum cockpit width of 45 centimetres to prevent the driver (in this instance P. Tambay in a Ferrari) being even more cramped.
Left: Tyre-change rehearsal in a typical race weekend. A complete change of tyres should not take more than ten seconds.

Time allotted to change engines in the McLaren was 100 minutes. With the introduction of the TAG turbo it has taken longer because there is much more to connect on a turbo engine.

If it is necessary to make adjustments, either to the anti-roll bars or to the brake balance, it is obviously best to do so on the smoothest and straightest part of the circuit. It is customary for anti-roll bars to be adjusted quite frequently during qualifying, to obtain optimum handling for individual corners, but adjustments in the course of a race only commend themselves where there is a major change in the car's handling characteristics, due to something like deteriorating tyres. Adjustment from the cockpit is normally carried out via control knobs or slides, which are notched to prevent inadvertent repositioning.

Before the ground effect era, a car's handling characteristics could be varied over a wide range of speeds by making appropriate adjustments to the anti-roll bars. In a ground effect car, however, adjustment of the anti-roll bar was effective at low speeds only – generally on corners taken in first or second gear. Once you got above a certain speed – and a relatively low one at that – the car's handling characteristics were totally controlled by aerodynamics.

One result of the ground effect era is that rear suspension systems have become increasingly similar to front end layouts. Triangular wishbones are also used for rear suspensions, whereby the upper wishbone – like the one in front – is very stiff to accommodate stresses transmitted inboard. Traditional radius rods have fallen by the wayside because they got in the way of the side-pods. Upper rear wishbones usually have a secondary bracket to keep stress ratios within reasonable limits. This bracket unit will be used to house the shocks and springs and the anti-roll bar, the last being practically identical to its front-wheel equivalent in terms of size and function.

It was extremely important that suspension components did not lie too close to the side pods and thus disrupt tailflow.

Today's Suspensions

In 1983 things are looking up again – we are back to cars in which everything else is not totally subservient to ground effect. As far as suspension systems are concerned, this has clearly resulted in considerable improvements for the drivers. Today's cars, with their completely new settings for springs and dampers, are much more pleasant to drive.

However, although I personally shed few tears at the banning of ground effect cars, I must concede that they taught us a few things about suspension systems. And we have taken over a lot that made sense. Today, for example, you won't find cars with anti-roll bars or dampers mounted in the airflow; and, but for ground effect, we might never have had pull-rod or push-rod suspension.

At the start of 1983 my McLaren was fitted with new front suspension. I'd like to go into this in more detail, since other teams have also made similar changes.

The underbody of a ground effect car had to be as smooth and uncluttered as possible if aerodynamics aids were to be exploited to the full. This is the key requirement in chassis design. In this shot we can see how effectively the skirts sealed the underbody zone.

My new suspension system owes its existence to simple acknowledgement of the fact that its predecessor was not 'pulling its weight': in 1982 the upper wishbone had the job of transferring wheel loadings inboard to the spring damper unit and, as such, had to be big enough and heavy enough to withstand flexing. Brabham tried for a long time to get around this difficulty by using what they called 'pull-rod' suspension. What this meant was that the spring-damper unit, mounted inboard, was activated not via the upper wishbone but instead via a diagonal strut and a lever arm. The whole system was distinctly lighter, but it had the disadvantage that it operated the heavier end of the shock absorber – the lighter end (rod and eye) was fixed to the upper part of the chassis, whereas the thicker, heavier end containing the oil had to be activated by the lever to compensate up-and-down movement. On the face of it, the answer seemed to be simply to turn the whole thing round, with the oil up top. When it was discovered that the system didn't work as well like that, they came up with a new solution – 'push-rod' suspension.

In effect, the diagonal strut leading inboard from the upright responds to 'push' rather than 'pull' and runs from low on the outside to high on the inside, exactly the reverse of the previous set-up. This means that the heavy end of the shock absorber can be fixed to the lower part of the chassis and the lighter end activated from above via the push-rod and lever unit.

By using different ratio levers, the new suspension system can be progressively adjusted to accommodate increasing load. The whole is simpler, lighter and more adaptable than its predecessor, so much so that Renault, for example, have already adopted it for their rear suspension.

Now that the cars no longer have sliding skirts, it has once again become practical for them to be 'sprung'. Spring rates are now back to between a sixth and a fifth of what they were in ground effect days, with the result that we again have a complex and fascinating interplay of springs, dampers, toe-in and camber, understeer and oversteer.

Tyres

Racing With Radials

Tyre manufacturers have been a mainstay of Grand Prix racing from its earliest beginnings. Michelin's involvement has latterly meant not only that a new firm has come on the scene but also a new product category – it was Michelin, of course, who first developed radial tyres for passenger cars and successfully marketed them worldwide. Today, virtually all high performance tyres are manufactured in accordance with radial design principles because they offer the best results in terms of roadholding, wear-and-tear and safety.

It is only a few years since Michelin entered the arena in a bid to prove that radials could successfully challenge the cross-ply tyres which traditionally dominated Formula I. (To recapitulate: the individual layers of the cross-ply carcass are arranged diagonally to the direction of travel whereas the steel or synthetic 'belts' which impart rigidity to the contact surface of the radial tyre are aligned in the direction of travel.) Last season (1982) Michelin supplied McLaren, Ligier, Renault and Alfa, while Goodyear supplied Lotus, Tyrrell, Ferrari, Brabham and Williams; the other teams used Pirelli and Avon. In 1983, following the withdrawal of Avon, Pirelli supplied Lotus, Toleman and March.

Personally speaking, I believe it is important to be able to work with a manufacturer who has as few teams as possible clamouring for his attention, so that you can develop close ties and a working relationship which ensures a quick response to individual requirements. I see a real future for radials in Formula I: what is still missing is experience – and that is where Goodyear have a tremendous edge.

I am often asked if a Formula I driver can really sense a difference between radials and cross-plies. The answer is a definite 'yes'. The steel belt structure of the radials contributes to a rigid, flat contact patch, which means that they can stand up to somewhat higher cornering speeds. It also means that they can cause problems when you are driving close to the limit. In fact, at or around the limit, the slightly curved contact patch of the Goodyears is more forgiving. The radials – the Michelins – are definitely a plus on slow circuits like Monte Carlo.

The first determinant factor as regards tyre quality is the tyre's physical make-up, or construction; the second is the rubber compound. There is not all that much to be said about tyre profiles, at least not as far as dry-weather tyres are concerned: the completely smooth 'slicks' are far and away the best because there is maximum contact between tyre surface and track and optimum heat dispersion from the wide surface.

As the 1982 Monaco Grand Prix proved, however, the situation is very different when the track is wet. When it starts raining, water simply cannot be dispersed from the broad, smooth contact patch between a slick tyre and the track; as a result, the tyres start to float. The average driver really has no conception of how helpless we are when a Formula I car starts to aquaplane – a situation aggravated by accumulated pick-up of rubber particles and oil slicks on the ideal line.

Race organisers adhere to a specific set of rules to deal with sudden changes in weather conditions during a race. A sudden downpour – as opposed to a steady drizzle – means that the race has to be stopped. If less than two laps have been completed, it's back to square one: a restart is scheduled for no more than thirty minutes later. If the race is halted after two laps have been completed but before three-quarters of the total race distance has been covered, the race is run in two parts and the result decided on aggregate. Finally, if the race is interrupted after three-quarters of the scheduled distance has been covered, the race is considered run and full championship points are allocated.

It is only when a re-start is impossible that either no points are awarded (less than two laps completed) or half points are allocated (less than three-quarters completed). It goes without saying that these rules apply not only in the event of stoppage due to rain but also to suspension of a race for any other reason of *force majeure*.

On the other hand, if it is raining when the race starts, and more than half of the cars appear on the grid fitted with rain tyres, the conditions are officially designated 'wet' and the race will not be stopped even in the event of a cloudburst.

It is worth recalling in this context that race organisers can stipulate the overall length of a Grand Prix as being anywhere between 250 and 320 kilometres. When a race is run in the wet, it is quite possible that correspondingly slower lap times will result in the requisite number of laps not being completed. When this happens, the lead driver is flagged down after the lap in which the two-hour limit is exceeded, this being the maximum race time permitted.

Rain tyres – wets – are readily distinguished by their pronounced tread. They do not always come 'ready-made' from the factory, however, and cutting the tread profiles by hand is a tedious, time-consuming business.

Rubber Compounds

The rule of thumb is as follows: the softer the compound, the faster the lap time – and the greater the wear on the tyre. Rain tyre compounds are manufactured even softer than normal and are water compatible. The extremely soft rain compounds only survive because rainwater acts as an excellent coolant.

Millions at stake: Goodyear supplies tyres to several Formula I teams, but the firm's previous monopoly is being challenged by Michelin and Pirelli.

Wet tyres deteriorate rapidly on a drying track, and soon start to get sticky. If a driver is in two minds about going in for a change to slicks, he will normally move off line and drive on the comparatively wet surface just outside the normal racing line. This way, you can hedge your bets for a couple of laps, bearing in mind that changing tyres is always a difficult decision – the track *may* be drying out but, then again, there *may* be a threat of more rain. It is not all that easy to assess weather conditions from the cockpit, not least because they vary at different points around the circuit. An added complication is that each driver is usually unaware of what the others are doing or have done.

Since most of today's circuits tend to be short, a tyre change can cost you the best part of half a lap, because you have to take into account not only the actual time spent at the pits but also the time lost in decelerating before the stop and accelerating away again afterwards.

Actual contact between tyre and track is a highly complex affair. It is customary to express the performance of any given tyre compound in terms of a friction coefficient (μ) which represents the tyre's capacity to transfer forces of acceleration; typical Formula I tyres have a friction coefficient of 1.6, *i.e.*, they are capable of transferring forces of acceleration amounting to 1.6 times g, the acceleration due to gravity.

In an everyday saloon car the friction coefficient of the tyres is around 1, which is to say that gravitational and accelerating forces are approximately equal. Clearly, the coefficient of a racing tyre is significantly higher: as a result, an interface effect must exist to the extent that tyre and track 'grip' or 'interlock'. This effect can only be achieved at quite specific temperatures; when a tyre is too cold it will not be soft enough to grip, and when it is too hot it will smear and become sticky.

The proper choice of compound is clearly vital. So too is tyre permutation. Since the individual tyres on a Formula I car are each subjected to very distinctive stresses, we not only vary the dimensions (small front, large rear) but also the compound used in each. Thus, for a circuit which mainly features righthanders, we would select a hard front left, a relatively soft front right and (probably) two medium hard rear tyres. It is far from uncommon to see a car racing with three quite distinct compounds.

The ideal situation is where all four tyres reach optimum running temperature at full speed. Although it is possible to reduce tyre temperatures by varying your driving technique, you have to bear in mind that this means slower lap times. On the other hand, easing off to let the tyres recuperate is clearly a better option than being forced into the pits to change tyres that are no longer serviceable. It is very rare that you see a driver pulling off a *coup* like Alain Prost did at Kyalami in 1982, namely stopping for a change of tyres and then going on to win the race.

Choosing the right tyres for the actual race is doubly difficult because conditions in practice are often quite different in terms of weather and so on. Also, you normally can't predict how the circuit will change in the course of the race as a result of sand, wind or rubber on the track. All in all, it is something of a gamble. This explains why some drivers who were nowhere in practice suddenly speed up on the day of the race, or why there are sudden dramatic changes in race positions for no apparent reason.

Pit stop and tyre change: about ten people are involved and, if all goes well, the whole operation will be over in about ten seconds.

It is possible to keep a running check on how your tyres are holding up even when they are turning at high speed: you can see the front two without any difficulty, and use your rear-view mirrors to keep an eye on the others. In addition, you can sense in the corners whether a tyre has reached its optimum grip or gone beyond it. If all else fails, of course, the lap times on your pit signals will put you in the picture.

If you keep pushing too hard, rubber will fly off the tyre and it will be completely ruined. There's nothing for it then but to go in for a tyre change – in which case, you might as well change all four, since an experienced pit crew can mount a complete set in little more time than it takes to change an individual tyre.

The ground effect era posed a new problem as regards tyres, to the extent that they had to absorb immense lateral acceleration loads. The rear tyres coped better than the front, thanks to their greater width and stability. However, when you cornered at very high speed in a ground effect car, it would sometimes jump or shudder sideways, a very nasty sensation because you had little or no warning: suddenly the car would skip two or three metres sideways towards the kerb before it righted itself. This happened because the tyre sidewalls were subjected to too much load and were incapable of absorbing it. Fortunately this phenomenon only occurred in qualifying, when the car was absolutely on the limit. To counteract it we increased rim diameters, to give the tyres more stability.

Qualifying

The fact that lap times are distinctly faster during qualifying than in the race proper can be attributed to some small extent to the minimum amount of fuel the cars carry during qualifying. The main reason, however, is that the cars are fitted with qualifying tyres, which only last for a few laps and only work well when the car is as light as possible.

The weight differences in a Formula I car with an empty, half-full or full fuel tank are considerable, and bear absolutely no comparison with conditions applicable to a standard passenger saloon. A Formula I car built to the prescribed weight limit of 540 kg weighs around 610 kg with the driver in the cockpit and a virtually empty tank. If the engine develops 600 bhp the car has a power to weight ratio of .98 bhp/kg in qualifying trim. Put in 200 litres of fuel and you have a starting weight of 760 kg and the power/weight

Aircraft-style refuelling connection on the F1 Renault. On the other side is a similar coupling to permit ventilation; this is connected to an overflow churn.

ratio drops to 0.78 bhp/kg – a fall-off of some 20 per cent, which is considerable by any standards.

Qualifying tyres will only stand up to a couple of warm-up laps and one or two laps flat-out – after which they start to break up or, at best, lose most of their grip. All of us know full well that we can pull out an extra couple of seconds when we are driving on qualifying tyres, assuming, of course, that we do all the right things and aren't held up in any way. To me, these qualifying laps are 'chaos laps', because driving them means you are at much greater risk than otherwise. If I drive one just right, then I know that there is no way I can go any faster; I don't even have to check the stopwatch, I simply pull off into the pit lane and call it a day.

The rules stipulate that each driver has a maximum of eight qualifying tyres at his disposal each day. The tyres are laid out in readiness in front of the pits and are painstakingly marked by race officials to prevent any hanky-panky. You only put them on when you know that the car has been thoroughly sorted out and is genuinely ready to attempt a fast time. As I have said, qualifying lap times are appreciably faster – one or two seconds is a lot on a short circuit – partly because of the softer compound but also because of a rubber agglutinant, a binding agent, which is sweated out of the tyre when it starts to get really hot for the first time, and which greatly enhances the tyre's adhesive properties. In other words, it is not only a question of hard or soft compound, it is also a question of 'chemistry'.

Gilles Villeneuve's death is a tragic reminder of the incredible danger implicit in the present qualifying procedure. It only takes a split second of inattention to provoke a serious accident. A change in format would be welcome, perhaps to the effect that only a handful of drivers are trying for qualifying times at any given moment. Not only would this make things less dangerous, it would also be more attractive from the spectator's point of view.

I have already mentioned the options open to the turbo marques during qualifying – boosting charge pressure to 2.5 and using additional cooling. As I said, my Porsche does not take kindly as yet to being boosted above standard race pressure This doesn't mean to say, of course, that I have anything against qualifying in the first or second row of the grid: on a tight circuit that kind of position is worth its weight in gold!

Material Developments

New Formula I Component Technology

Aluminium engines, magnesium blocks and uprights, specially-insulated electrical circuitry pioneered by the aircraft industry, titanium springs and teflon hoses – all of these are so commonplace in today's Formula I cars that there is no need to discuss them in any detail here.

What does invite comment, however, is the growing use of carbon fibre-reinforced plastic materials for monocoques and for finely detailed components such as the inlet manifold on the BMW Turbo.

We are even experimenting with brake discs made of carbon fibre-reinforced *carbon*, a material derived from carbon fibre reinforced plastic that has been put through a special heat process. This is yet another breakthrough that can be sourced to aviation technology: Concorde has been fitted with brakes like these for some time now.

Their distinctive features are their very low weight (remember that discs are unsprung) and their exceptionally high thermal resistance at temperatures in excess of 2000° Centigrade, which means that they do not even have to be internally cooled. Brake linings are now being manufactured in more or less the same material. The significant advantage over conventional materials is that far less braking pressure has to be applied. When they are first used, the brakes are a little slower to react than normal, but retardation becomes very impressive once the temperature has built up.

Initially these brakes were used only in test runs. A few problems had to be solved, the main one being how best to secure the disc to the aluminium hub. Once we had solved that one we felt confident enough to use the brakes in a Grand Prix. A second problem emerged, however, once disc and hub had been properly connected, namely the incredible heat – 2000° Centigrade and above in some instances – which was generated in the narrow wheel rim.

Today, McLaren always use these new brakes, as do some other teams.

They have been important in getting down to the new 540 kg limit. The brake discs are protected by two carbon fibre-reinforced shields which keep them warm and reduce heat loss to the immediate environment. Mind you, when we switched to the turbo engine, the brakes promptly gave out. They simply were not up to the distinctly improved engine performance and higher top speed. It took us longer than anticipated to get our hands on internally-cooled carbon fibre reinforced carbon brakes such as Renault has been using for ages, with the result that I had to call it a day in one of the early races because of brake failure.

The principal use for carbon fibre reinforced plastic in modern racing car construction is in the monocoque, the specific qualities of which were described at greater length in preceding chapters. Carbon fibre reinforced plastic has a lot going for it when it comes to building a racing chassis. First of all, it is unrivalled in terms of weight (1.45 kg/dm^3 as opposed to 2.7 for aluminium, 4.5 for titanium and 7.9 for steel); second – and even more crucial – the fibres can be woven and aligned so as to meet specific demands in terms of tensile elongation.

The material is essentially a reinforced plastic. What makes it so special (and so expensive) is the fact that extremely high tensile strength carbon fibre has been substituted for the more familiar fibreglass weave. The abbreviation CFRP (carbon fibre reinforced plastic) will soon be as familiar as FRP (fibreglass reinforced plastic) is today.

CFRP certainly opens up an exciting new range of possibilities when you consider that it has the stiffness and the tensile strength of steel at respectively one-half and a staggering one-tenth of the latter's weight. The material's properties can also be varied by judicious selection of fibre grades and weaves. Where the fibre itself has a high tensile strength coefficient, then the finished compound will also exhibit good stress behaviour and will be particularly appropriate to the manufacture of load-bearing components in the car. (Where the coefficient is low, on the other hand, the fibre will rip without prior deformation: this makes for high rigidity but, in stress situations – such as in a shunt – can result in the material shattering: you might even say that the material 'explodes' into fragments under stress.)

CFRP is also being used in the manufacture of sandwich panels, *i.e.*, where CFRP sheets are bonded to either side of a relatively thick lightweight core, often in extruded polyester resin. The resultant panel is very light and very rigid and, as such, is ideally suited for use in monocoque parts which are under stress.

Titanium Engine Components

Titanium is a shiny silvery metal that has made its presence felt in the aircraft industry: it is used, for example, in the manufacture of the thick bolts for the powerful swing wing joints of the Tornado.

Titanium is much more expensive than steel. It is also considerably lighter – by about fifty percent – and has a modulus of elasticity which is barely half that of steel. What this means is that, under stress, titanium will distort roughly twice as much. This property means that titanium is particularly useful in the manufacture of certain engine components such as connecting rods and bolts, and less useful in the case of parts such as crankshafts, where minimum elasticity is desirable.

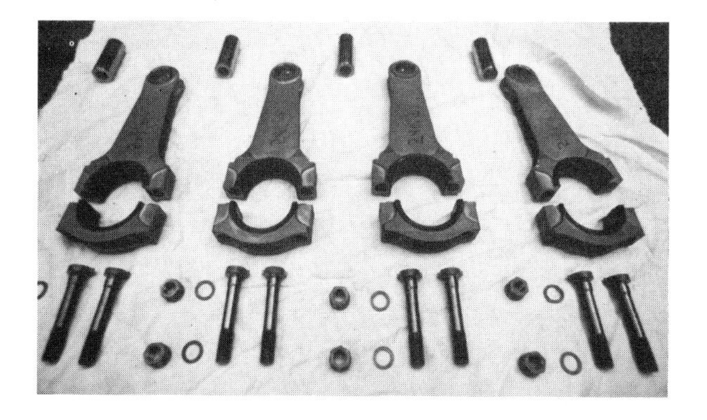

The four titanium connecting rods and bolts of a BMW Turbo – a cool £1,000 worth. The forged blanks are completely tooled on every face.

As a result, today's high-performance engines are quite liable to have titanium connecting rods, for example, but unlikely to use titanium crankshafts: in order to achieve the same rigidity as steel, a titanium crankshaft would have to be thicker, at which point the inherent advantage of lower specific weight is clearly lost.

The most impressive titanium components used in Formula I today are the connecting rods in the BMW Formula I Turbo. The titanium alloy is first forged to the approximate shape before being completely machined to the final form and weight required. Once the surface has been machined, the rod is shot peened to improve notch sensitivity. The connecting rod cross section (big end hole to small end hole) is in the form of an 'H' to provide maximum rigidity. The finished rod weighs just over 500 grams – very light indeed given its unusual length of 153.6 mm. Connecting rods like these don't come cheap : they cost the best part of £250* each.

When it comes to bearings, you only have to glance at the bearing bush to see that titanium isn't an ideal material. It has been found necessary to use roller bearings to take up not only direct stress but also to accommodate axial forces. This is not necessary in conjunction with steel connecting rods, which run directly up against the crank arm. Logically – to allow for expansion – the big end bolts are also made of titanium; only the nuts are made of steel.

* DM 1,000 / US$350.

Michele Alboreto

René Arnoux ▶

RENAULT
elf
ICHELIN

Elio de Angelis *Andrea de Cesaris* ▶

MARTINI

LANCIA
Marlboro
Marlboro
MARTINI
RACING

MARTI

Marlb

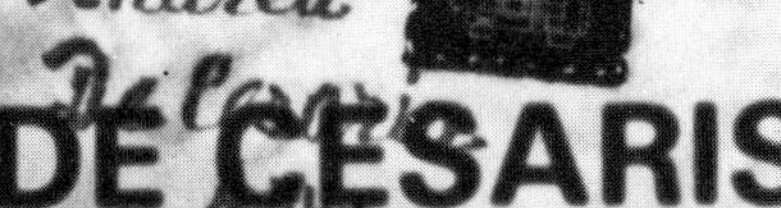
Andrea
Simpson
DE CESARIS

Eddie Cheever

Bruno Giacomelli ▶

agv
SaMar
formsport
Marlboro
WORLD CHAMPIONSHIP TEAM
MiSURA

◀ *Jacques Laffite*

Nigel Mansell

parmalat
Piquet
parmalat
GOODYEAR

◀ *Nelson Piquet*

Riccardo Patrese

elf
RENAULT elf
stand21
VETEMENTS LECONTE
MICHELIN
ellesse
Marlboro
Marlboro
WORLD CHAMPIONSHIP TEAM

Alain Prost

Keijo (Keke) Rosberg

Patrick Tambay

Marc Surer ▶

BIRELL
Quaker

Derek Warwick

Gilles Villeneuve (killed May 8, 1982 at Zolder) ▶

Labatt
CHRONOGRAPH
HEUER

John Watson

Manfred Winkelhock

The Race

There is so much to do and so little time to think on race days, that mental stress is not so great as it otherwise might be.

The first priority is to get down to the circuit ahead of the heavy race-day traffic and get yourself ready for the warm-up session. This only lasts 30 minutes, and for most of that time the track is dirty; in other words, the ideal line has not yet been swept clean by our tyres. Consequently, you must beware of any hasty conclusions as to how the car is handling. Usually, a few finishing touches have to be made to the car – a hectic business in so short a time. Final tyre selection must also be made during this brief period, now that ambient weather and air temperature conditions have been established.

My next step is to find out how fast I really am relative to my rivals. For this, the warm-up gives a much better indication than the pre-race qualifying

runs on the previous days. In the first place, practically all the cars have put on race tyres and are fuelled for the race itself; in the second, the turbos are using normal boost pressure as opposed to the increased amount used for qualifying. Thus, for the first time in the whole weekend, I have a chance to see how my car is going to perform. The warm-up either bolsters your confidence for the race or leaves you with a frustrated feeling that it isn't going to be your day.

We've now got three hours to race time. If necessary this is enough to instal a complete new engine – although that happens very rarely nowadays. I spend the time in the relative calm of the team motor home. Then, half an hour before the start, we drive the cars round to their grid positions. This is a relatively slow lap on cold tyres, during which you can do very little except check that everything is okay mechanically. When the cars are on the grid we get out again.

Five or six minutes before the off I make my final careful preparations. Trivial things, things that you might otherwise ignore, suddenly assume great importance: adjusting your fireproof balaclava to make sure that your hair is in the right place and won't tickle you to distraction later on, making sure that your ear plugs are comfortably in position, and so on. Only when I have done all this, and got my helmet on, do I get back into the car.

One minute before the green flag comes the command: start your engines. I leave this as long as possible, to avoid any possibility of my engine overheating. When I get the feeling from the noise around me that a good two-thirds of the engines have been started, I start my own.

The green flag releases us for a one further warm-up lap. I try to hold as clean a line as possible, to prevent the tyres picking up dirt. At the same time, however, you have to zig-zag to heat the tyres up. Coming up to a corner, you drop back a bit so as to be able to drive through it as fast as possible. This doesn't always come off, because you can't hold back the drivers behind you. I am usually irritated by the drivers on the front row slowing down too early, thereby forcing the others to become really bunched up.

We all trundle back to our starting positions in first gear, and everything gets unbearably hot. It would be much better if we all drove the warm-up lap as fast as possible, but it is always very difficult to avoid the concertina effect.

The Start

You find your way back to your starting position, not always as easily as you might think since your field of vision is limited by the driving position. Now comes the interminable wait for the red light. Your water temperature gauge climbs to 120° Centigrade. The engine revs have to be kept up (you'll stall below 4,000). The electrical fuel pump has been switched off and the gear lever is in neutral.

Red light. Everybody is now stationary. The race will start in anything from six to ten seconds.

Starting shunts (in the 1982 championship season particularly) prove how difficult it is to get a Formula I field away simultaneously. It is a fact that every driver still finds the start of a race incredibly hairy. Let me try to explain.

1982: A vintage year for shunts coming away from the grid. One of the less disastrous is this one involving the two Alfas of Bruno Giacomelli and Andrea de Cesaris at Oesterreich-Ring.

Starting shunt at Brands (1982): Patrese jumps out of first gear and Arnoux ploughs into his Brabham; nobody was hurt. Out front are Derek Daly (Williams) and Alain Prost (Renault).

One factor is a constant, namely the ideal rev speed for letting out the clutch. This is computed on the basis of first gear ratio and the fuel quantity injected, *i.e.*, weight; this can be worked out exactly, taken as an empirical value and checked out in practice by means of a single trial start at a quiet spot somewhere out on the circuit. One trial start is all you have, because the clutch will only handle two starts in all – one in practice and one in the race itself. Things get sticky where a race has to be restarted. Starting revs are 9,500 for a short first gear, as used on a slow circuit such as Monaco, and up to 11,000 for a long first gear, in other words, close to maximum revs.

As soon as the red light comes on you select first gear. To be more precise, you jam it in to the accompaniment of a terrible grinding, rasping and crashing in the gearbox. Why? Because the clutch is very tight and has very little travel in order to avoid slippage. When the car is hot – and, at the start, it is *really* hot – the clutch doesn't disengage one hundred percent, hence the violence needed to engage bottom gear.

A hot clutch is the cause of most false starts. If it does not engage completely, the car will start to creep forward. If you don't get it under control immediately, you'll jump the start and incur a time penalty. You can either ease back on the accelerator (and risk a stall) or brake with your toes and blip the accelerator with your heel. This heel-and-toe movement is standard procedure in rally and sports car driving, but it isn't easy in Formula I because the pedal space is very cramped.

Once you've engaged bottom gear – immediately after the red comes on –

My McLaren TAG Turbo was genuinely competitive for the first time at the end of championship season 1983.

it is important that the green light come on immediately, or at worst no more than ten seconds later; otherwise you are likely to end up with either a burnt-out clutch or a stalled engine.

To recapitulate: bottom gear, check forward roll, and come up to starting revs, let's say 10,000 rpm. There is no way you can listen for the revs, you've got to watch the rev counter – this is a delicate operation given the sensitivity of the engine. After about three seconds you should have steadied the revs and only be watching the rev counter out of the corner of your eye.

As soon as the green comes on, let the clutch out with a bang. Letting it slip at 10,000 rpm would burn it out immediately.

I know that 15 percent wheelspin makes for an ideal start. If I'm revving too high and spinning the wheels too much, I have to ease up on the accelerator, check the wheelspin and accelerate again. If I decelerate too much the wheels won't spin enough, and the engine won't have enough torque to permit a fast start. The shuddering sound you can hear when this happens has nothing to do with the clutch.

Only when you have these purely mechanical factors of the start under control can you begin to worry about the other drivers. In theory, the start to a Grand Prix should be a smooth and harmonious affair, since everybody has to do the same things and move off in the same pattern.

I keep looking forward, perhaps glancing slightly to either side, shift into second and wait for it. Do I have a drama on my hands? That smooth and harmonious start can be shattered if someone at the back makes a super start and bulldozes his way through half the pack, weaving in and out as Gilles Villeneuve used to. It's even more traumatic, of course, if someone ahead of me is stationary because of a stalled engine or a burnt-out clutch. My golden rule in such cases is: follow the pack. If it snakes out left, go with it. The last thing to do is try to be smart and come through on the right!

Whenever there is a foul-up at the start, your reactions must be instinctive. Even if you have already gone over in your mind's eye all the possible permutations, the only thing you can rely on now is intuition. You can check what's going on behind you in your rear mirror, but it's only a quick glance, you can't really take a good look. In front of you, behind you, next to you, there are others who are also reacting instinctively. From one second to the next completely new situations develop, and you have to feel your way through them like lightning and at greatly increased personal risk.

The safest place to be, of course, is up front on the first row of the grid.

Race Routine and Jockeying for Position

A rough-and-ready comparison of lap times ver the last few years suggests that there have been spectacular improvements, bearing in mind that a proper statistical analysis is precluded because additional chicanes have been built in to most circuits. In spite of these, however, today's lap times are generally faster than those of, say, five years ago.

When it comes to a one-on-one battle for the lead between two cars that are roughly equal, the old adage still applies: wait for the man in front to make a mistake. Jockeying for position can create anomalous situations, however, when the two cars involved exhibit different characteristics. Typically, this is where you have one car with a 'big' engine and a high top speed (usually a turbo) and the other with better cornering speed. I remember once settling my McLaren in behind Tambay's Ferrari. Tambay pulled away easily on the straights thanks to his turbo engine, but I closed right up on him in the corners. He made a couple of minor mistakes, but nothing serious. I had to wait thirty laps until he made a real mistake coming into a long straight: his top speed evaporated and I was through.

One of the most exciting races in 1982, in terms of battling for position, was the US Grand Prix in Detroit. The race had been restarted after a shunt and positions in the first 'heat' were due to be taken into account in determining finishing positions.

I was in sixth place, and doing everything I could to get past Bruno Giacomelli. As a result I kept locking my front wheels and throwing my brakes out of balance. This was unfortunate, but it didn't immediately affect the car's handling. I closed up on Pironi and Cheever, who were trailing Prost (who later retired) and Rosberg. I wondered how I was going to take Pironi and Cheever: both the Ferrari Turbo and the Twelve Cylinder Ligier were more powerful cars, and I never got close enough to outbrake them without taking unreasonable risks. In addition I must admit that my wild attack on Giacomelli had made me a little more cautious. So there I was, tucked in behind Cheever and Pironi, hoping for the best. Meanwhile, the signals kept coming: John Watson was creeping closer and closer – +20, +15, +10.

I wasn't all that worried about Watson, and when he came up behind me I was happy to let him through, more or less on the following basis: on you go, show me how to get past those two. I had a front row seat.

Nelson Piquet (Brabham-BMW), Kyalami 1982.

Above: René Arnoux (Renault) leading the field at Monaco between Ste. Dévote and the Casino.
Left: Winkelhock (ATS) heads Laffite (Talbot Ligier) through the Station Curve overlooking the harbour in Monte Carlo.

Above: There are very few places where you can safely overtake during the Monaco Grand Prix – and coming down to Mirabeau is certainly not one of them. Pironi (Tyrrell) tries to take me and puts us both out of the race. At that time I was driving a Brabham-Alfa.

Right: The famous Tarzan Corner at Zandvoort: Tambay (Ferrari) ahead of Lauda (McLaren).

You probably remember what happened. It took Watson less than half a lap to get past both of them. I was furious, I just couldn't believe it. Watson had pulled off a beautiful overtaking manoeuvre – twice. He took advantage of the relatively wide circuit not to outbrake them normally (that is, more or less parallel) but to brake inwards from right to left. Neither Cheever nor Pironi knew what was happening. They both braked in normal fashion and made to take the corner, but there was Watson, wheels locked, braking into the apex of the bend. His tactic worked twice in a row, albeit with a deal of luck, because the driver who is under attack can't see that someone is forcing himself diagonally through from behind.

At any rate, I was furious at the way Watson had simply left me standing. I steeled myself to do what he had done and I was lucky both times. With Cheever and Pironi behind me I really put my foot down, and was soon right up with Keke Rosberg – who by this time had also fallen prey to Watson. Now that Prost was out of the race, Watson was leading, Rosberg was second and I was lying third.

There was no way I was going to let Watson get away from me. I was so keyed up about this, so fixated, that I completely forgot about the first race, the restart and the fact that overall times were going to be aggregated. When the race was stopped I was twelve seconds up on Watson, so all I had to do was settle in comfortably behind him: if Rosberg didn't hold me up too long, the race was in the bag.

Instead of taking it easy and waiting for an opportune moment to pass Rosberg, I kept telling myself I mustn't let Watson get too far ahead. I had forgotten all about my twelve seconds in hand.

I tried to outbrake Rosberg at the end of the straight. I moved left out of his slipstream, beating him for speed. Then he started to pull left, left, left, and farther left at the braking point until I had nowhere else to go to *my* left except into the wall. Then his rear wheel caught my front and flipped me up into the air just like a Mystère 10 – nose up, twelve degrees. Suddenly, all I could see was blue sky. You wait for the crunch, you brace yourself, then – wham! – down you come. The car came down at a sharp angle, pitching forward on to the monocoque instead of bouncing back on its wheels. The front end was bent right out of shape.

Afterwards, Rosberg denied that he had closed the door intentionally, but what other reason could he have had for pulling left away from the ideal line? In spite of that, I didn't feel angry towards him – it was up to me to expect him to behave that way, just like he always does. There is no getting away from it, the fault was basically mine. I should have kept my cool and I could have won. That's the way it goes after a lay-off, I told myself. Two years in the air instead of on the track; things are different there . . .

Changing Conditions During The Race

Tactics in the older sense of the term are very much a thing of the past. Nowadays, everybody simply keeps on driving as fast as possible, except perhaps during the final ten or twenty laps if the outcome of the race has already been more or less decided. As a result, any change in driving technique during a race is basically conditional upon changes in the set-up of the car.

The turbo marques have a definite edge over the normally aspirated cars when it comes to adapting to race conditions as they develop. Hand adjustment of boost pressure from the cockpit means nothing more or less than the facility to increase or decrease power – to go faster or to save fuel. In this respect, the turbo driver has a much more impressive arsenal at his disposal than his rival in a normally aspirated car. It's a bit like riding a 2-stroke motorcycle where you can vary the mixture: you develop a feeling for these hand adjustments – just enough to get the most from the engine but not so much as to kill it off. Nelson Piquet has a particular talent for this, as one might expect from such a gifted driver.

Once we have smaller fuel tanks and have to cope with reduced consumption it will be very interesting indeed to watch how boost pressure tactics evolve.

The most important changes that set in during a race relate to the tyres. There are two quite distinct ways in which tyres can be ruined.

First, they overheat so much that they blister. Once that starts happening, it is only a matter of time before they are useless and you have to stop for a tyre change. The tiny bubbles are visible from the cockpit – quite distinctly in the case of the front tyres, less so in the rear.

The second way is when 'graining' occurs. It is difficult to describe this condition, other than by saying that it is reminiscent of the traces left by a rubber eraser on a table-top. Little shards or granules of rubber collect on the tyre surface, first on the inner edge then spreading across the tyre. The net effect is that the tyres lose their grip. You can counteract this by slowing down as soon as you spot a thin black strip on the inner edge of the tyre: you

First signs of 'graining': the signal to ease up.

find that it will then clean itself off automatically. If you keep forcing the pace, on the other hand, the tyre will gradually 'grain' to the point where it becomes unserviceable.

There is another problem that I notice in the case of Michelin radials. A black 'wreath' develops on the inner edge and spreads over the entire tyre width. This is not 'graining' but 'pick up' of dirt and debris from the track surface. When this happens, of course, the tyre gets greasier and the car is more difficult to handle – but this extra layer is not malignant and doesn't destroy the tyre. It's still a major headache for me trying to distinguish between graining and pick-up. The fact is, it takes a lot of experience of each particular make of tyre to be able to identify one condition as opposed to the other. The switch from Goodyear to Michelin was, in this sense, a traumatic experience for me.

Meanwhile, Back at the Pits

Once the race is under way, the pit crew's only major job is to get ready for a tyre change and keep the signals coming to let the driver know his race position. There is no longer any question of race tactics emanating from the pits – for that to happen, we would have to have radio contact as at Indianapolis. In any case, what could they possibly have to tell the driver out there on the track? A Grand Prix is far too short for that kind of refinement. If I do have to come in, I can exchange a few quick words with the team boss by means of a two-way inter-com plugged into my helmet. But that is really the limit to today's contact between pilot and ground control.

Above:
Ex-rally star Gérard Larrousse, flanked here by René Arnoux (left) and Alain Prost, is now Renault Sport's Competitions Director.

Right:
Gordon Murray, technical mastermind at Brabham.

Above: Mauro Forghiere – two decades of technical genius at Ferrari. Left: Frank Williams – now, after years in the wilderness, one of the top team bosses.

Above: My two technicians at McLaren in 1982, John Barnard (centre) and Tyler Alexander.

Right: BMW – duo: Designer Paul Rosche (left) and racing chief Dieter Stappert.

Top: Lotus boss Colin Chapman, a pioneer of two Formula I generations, who died in December 1982.
Bottom left: Ken Tyrrell.
Bottom right: Brabham No. 1 Bernie Ecclestone, spokesman for the Grand Prix circus.

Circuits

Leading Grand Prix Circuits and How To Drive Them

Brands Hatch

A magnificent circuit and a very demanding one. It has a special harmony that allows you to set the car up properly. You can make all kinds of minute adjustments in practice to bring out the absolute best in your car. The most striking feature at Brands is that most of the curves are banked.

Flat-out at start and finish, touch the brakes coming up to Paddock Bend, select fourth gear, steer into the bend and give it everything you've got – even though you know the car will bottom out in the dip. Up to Druids, through in second, shift up to third, fourth, the left hand curve behind the pits has a new surface, very slippery; then the old surface again; the car shudders and oversteers.

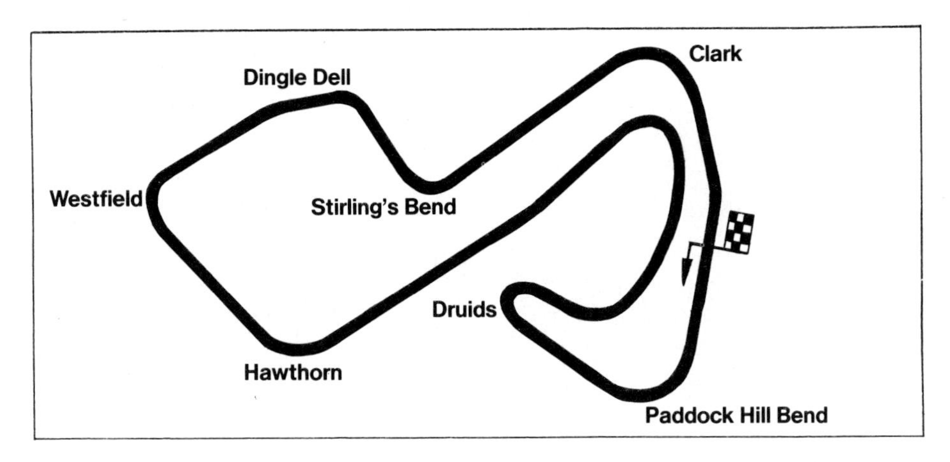

Brands Hatch (United Kingdom), 20 miles south east of London. Length 4.20 kilometres (2.61 miles). Minimum circuit width 9 metres. Current (1983) lap record: 1 min. 12.37 sec. (209.24 kmh/130.015 mph) by Didier Pironi 1980.

Then the most important bend on the circuit, the left-hander that opens into the long straight. Fifth at the end of the straight, then down into fourth and accelerate hard through the right-hander (Hawthorn Bend). Fantastic the punishment these cars can take. Two more right-handers, a tighter left and then the rush down to Clearways – from which it is vital to come out perfectly to reach maximum top speed on the start/finish straight.

Detroit

This one has all the drawbacks of a city circuit – and an American city into the bargain. This means that it can only change direction where one highway intersects with another, so the whole circuit is a boring succession of right-angle bends, roughly speaking, not one of them long enough to make any real demands on the driver. The only real threat to man and machine are the bumpy track where different road surfaces meet and the vapours gushing up through the manhole covers.

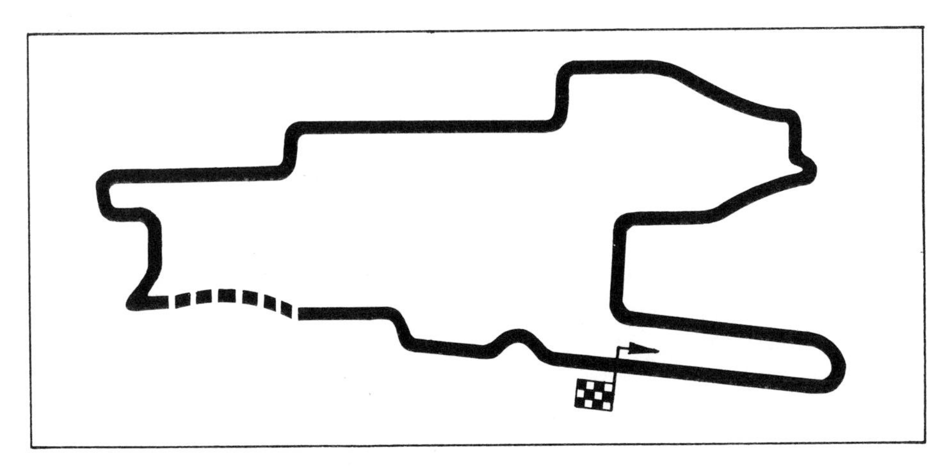

Detroit (USA). Length 4.17 kilometres (2.59 miles). Minimum circuit width 11 metres. Current (1983) lap record: 1 min. 47.66 sec. (134.49 kmh/ 83.568 mph) by Watson 1983.

Dijon

Not the shortest circuit perhaps (Long Beach and Monaco are even shorter) but certainly the one with the shortest lap times. Dijon is very demanding because the surface has become uneven over the years. The toughest sections from the driver's point of view are the two final right-handers before the long straight. The first of these is banked, and it takes a lot of nerve to hold it in fourth. Then comes a big bump and you are out into the last right-hander, which is taken flat-out at around 160 mph plus. No doubt about it, this was one of the hardest *g*-force corners of all in the ground effect car era.

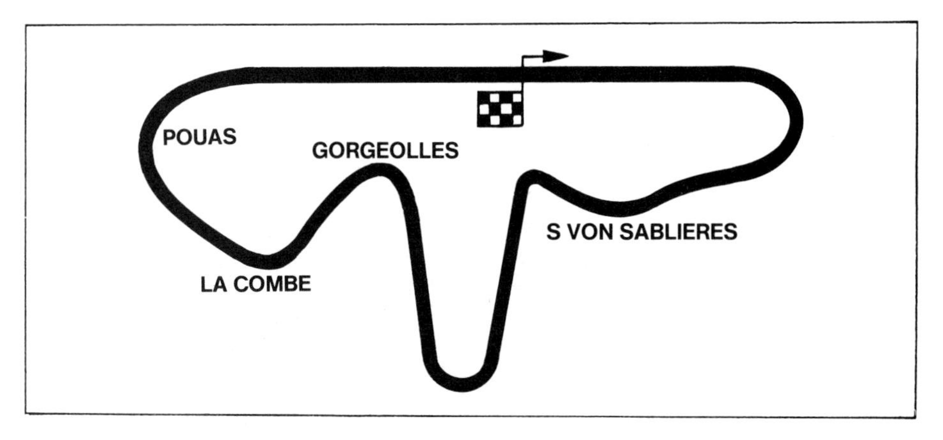

Dijon (France), 200 miles south-east of Paris. Length 3.80 kilometres (2.36 miles). Minimum circuit width 10 metres. Current (1983) lap record: 1 min. 07.48 sec. (202.74 kmh/125.98 mph) by Alain Prost 1982.

Hockenheim

There are now three chicanes at Hockenheim, one of them a fast one – between the *Ostkurve* and the *Motodrom* – and the other two slow – one on the opening straight and the other built into the *Ostkurve*. The first chicane has now been made much, much narrower: it hooks sharp right and you may even be forced to take it in bottom gear. After that, it's full speed ahead towards the *Ostkurve* and chicane number two (the newest one), back into second, through again into the *Ostkurve*. Then comes the long straight with the fast chicane. This was a tricky one in a ground effect car because the rapid zig-zag taken in third gear could damage the skirts and ruin the aerodynamics.

Then the stadium: you roar up to it in fifth, brake, slip down into fourth, line the car up into the bend, put your foot down hard, and go through it as if you were on rails. Then it is second gear for the *Sachs-Kurve*, foot down again up to the tight right-hander, brake lightly and sweep into the finishing straight in third. In a normally aspirated car, Hockenheim is a boring circuit: when the turbos scream past you on the long straights you feel as if you're going to get a parking ticket. The most dramatic manoeuvre on the whole circuit is the brutal braking just before the two slow chicanes.

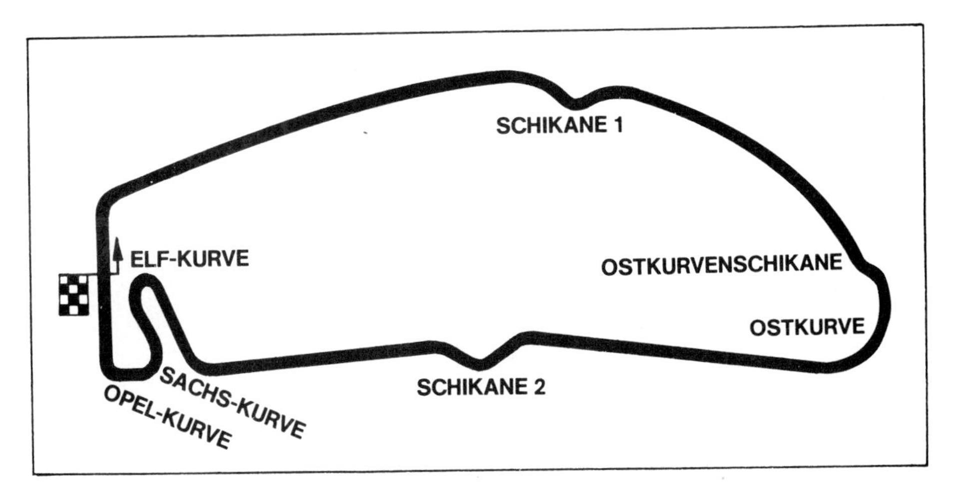

Hockenheim (West Germany), 53 miles south of Frankfurt. Length 6.69 kilometres (4.22 miles). Minimum circuit width 8.5 metres. Current (1983) lap record: 1 min. 53.938 sec. (214.758 kmh/133.444 mph) by Arnoux 1983.

Imola

A terribly bumpy circuit that leaves you bruised and battered. Flat-out through the long fast left-hander after the pits, second for Tosa, double back up the hill to a fast left almost flat-out in fourth, down the hill and brake into the 'S', which you take in second. ('Take' is a bit of an exaggeration – you simply bounce from one side of the track to the other.) Then flat-out again uphill into two right-handers, through the small chicane, and down towards the two left-handers, which are so bumpy that you can scarcely see where you are going. Then comes a fast 'S', a chicane and we're back at the pits.

There are no corners at Imola that I would single out for special mention. They are all important because they all open out into sections of the circuit where you have to accelerate, often uphill. It goes without saying that you have to come out of them all at full tilt.

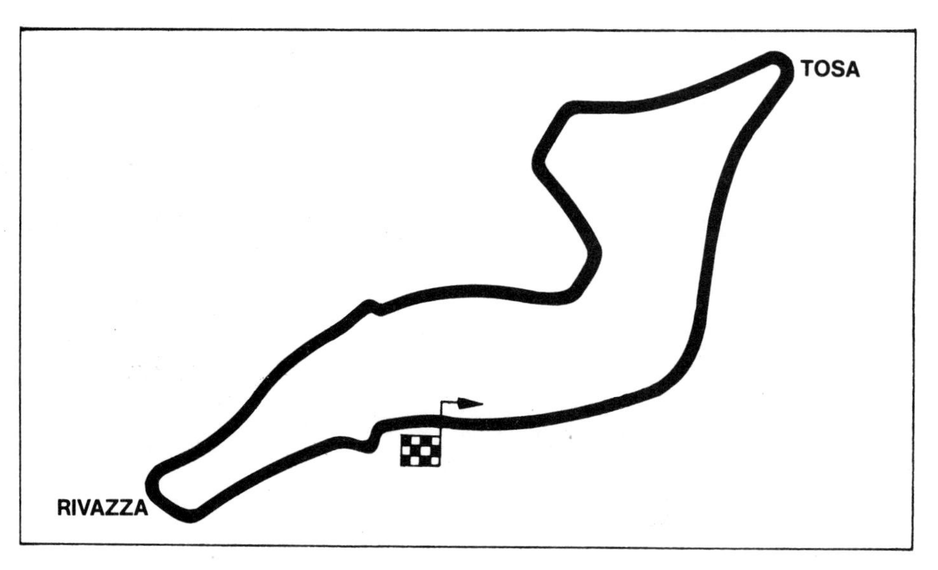

Imola (Italy), 19 miles east of Bologna. Length 5.04 kilometres (3.13 miles). Minimum circuit width 9 metres. Current (1983) lap record: 1 min. 34.43 sec. (192.12 kmh/119.377 mph) by Patrese 1983.

Wish you were here: the picture postcard Grand Prix with the Casino on the left and the Hôtel de Paris on the right. Derek Daly is in the foreground, with Niki Lauda tucked in behind.

Right: Oesterreich-Ring is currently the fastest Formula I circuit – and is picturesque into the bargain. The spectators have a magnificent view of the track.
Insert: The run-off areas might seem to be over-generous but Riccardo Patrese is grateful for every last inch. . .

HYPO BANK
Steiermark

Castrol

Brands Hatch: A magnificent natural setting and a classic cornucopia of corners. . .
Left: The 1.8 kilometre (1.12 mile) straight at Paul Ricard, the longest straight in Grand Prix racing today. The fastest cars reach 340 kmh/210 mph.

Left: Police and race marshals in the perennial battle to maintain law and order at Imola.

Insert: The turbos fight it out among themselves: Prost and Arnoux are leading.

Kyalami

I find Kyalami the easiest of all Grand Prix circuits. There is a ridiculously long straight where you can take a breather – all you have to do is keep your foot hard down and hold the steering wheel steady. You reach a top speed of about 195 mph – depending on the car you are driving – but there is no real problem. The right-hander at the end of the long straight is relatively slow – third gear – then you open up again down through the 'S' bends. After the second 'S' there is a fourth-gear right-hander; if you don't enter the bend ideally, you are in deep trouble. After that, there is a sharp left-hander, another S-bend and the hairpin which leads back onto the long straight. Not very exciting.

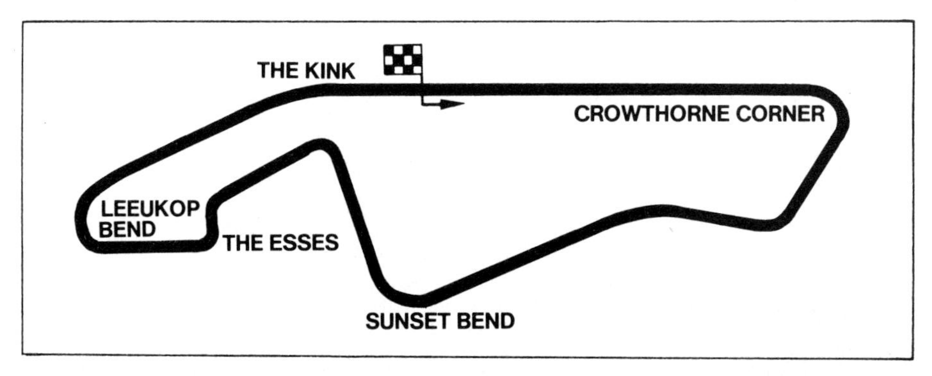

Kyalami (South Africa), 15 miles north of Johannesburg. Length 4.10 kilometres (2.55 miles). Minimum circuit width 11 metres. Current (1983) lap record: 1 min. 08.28 sec. (216.38 kmh/134.45 mph) by Alain Prost 1982.

Long Beach

Most of what has to be said about Long Beach is valid for any race that is run on a street circuit, including Monaco. In the case of a race on a 'real' – *i.e.*, permanent – circuit, you can test in the preceding weeks and come to the race itself pretty much ready, with only the usual fine tuning to worry about. On a street circuit, however, you simply don't know what to expect: all you can do is try one set of tyres after another and set up the car on the basis of past experience. You just have to keep your fingers crossed that the car doesn't understeer or oversteer too much. All you can do is jump in and drive by the seat of your pants. If our designer asks me how the car is handling, what it's doing at this point and at that, there's no answer I can give him; the car simply has to be driven forcefully through the corners, otherwise you will be nowhere on the grid. As far as 'fine tuning' is concerned, forget it. There isn't enough time and there is too much traffic.

On circuits like this the qualifying laps really take it out of you. Slicing past those slabs of concrete, often just centimetres away, and at the same time contending with a bumpy circuit – there you have one of the most exhilarating and frightening jobs a racing driver is expected to do. The streets are so narrow by comparison with a normal circuit that you almost get claustrophobic. Even if you can keep that sort of feeling under control, you still have to cope with the enormous pressures of concentration. There is precious little room on a normal circuit for any kind of error: what little there is is even more curtailed on a circuit like Long Beach.

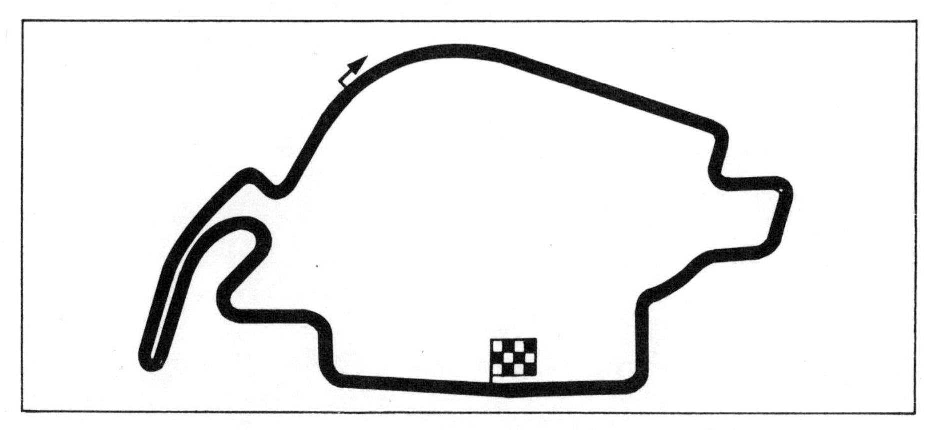

Long Beach (USA), 20 miles north of Los Angeles. Length 3.43 kilometres (2.13 miles). Minimum circuit width 9.1 metres. Current (1983) lap record: 1 min. 28.33 sec. (133.46 kmh/82.928 mph) by Niki Lauda 1983.

Monaco

The Monaco circuit is still the most attractive in the world from the spectator point of view, and the Grand Prix there is clearly the highlight of the championship season. That being the case, I would like to go into Monaco in more detail, and attempt to describe what it looks like from behind the wheel.

When you take up your starting position you try as far as possible to get your wheels on a zebra crossing where the road surface is smoother. One way or another, the chances are that only seconds after the start you'll find yourself in the middle of absolute bedlam as the field tries to squeeze through Sainte Dévote – where anything can happen. But if the guy in pole position can lay down two beautiful black tyre marks, tapering off to a lighter and lighter grey in the first ten metres, then all he needs is to be half a car's length up and in the right-hand lane to come out of Sainte Dévote clearly in the lead and roar up the hill. It looks like a simple uphill straight, but nothing is straight at 170 mph – there are dips and bumps and waves and manhole covers and ugly craters that thump the car down against the road. You've really got your hands full trying to stay on top of it.

Just before the entrance to Casino Square there is a bump. You can't brake before it – that would be too early – and you can't brake when you reach it because that would dig the nose of the car into the track. What you're left with is a tenth of a second to touch the brake if you are to have any hope of taking the left-hander. The right-hand curve which follows is slippery and gets narrower, but you have to keep your foot down. Half way through it there is a huge bump which makes your stomach leap and throws you towards the guard rails, which seem to attract you like a magnet. The closer you are to them when you whistle past, the faster and more rhythmically you make it through the whole Casino section.

Straight down the hill now, slam on the brakes for the upper Mirabeau, accelerate sharply and then brake almost to a standstill for the Station Hairpin (the station has long since disappeared, to be replaced by Loew's Hotel). All of us take the corner slowly in bottom gear, good little boys, all in a row. At the beginning of the race, when the pack is closed up, the ones at the back have to get into single file: if you're lying worse than sixth you almost have to 'park' and wait your turn.

A quick surge of acceleration now, down to the lower Mirabeau, gently through the Portier and then flat-out into the tunnel – third gear, fourth, fifth. The lighting in the tunnel has been gradually improved over the years but it is still not bright enough. You can see where you are going, but there isn't enough light to see if there is any oil on the road. Can you imagine what it would be like if somebody were to skid at 160 mph with several other cars right behind him? Furthermore, the right-hand kink in the tunnel is very tricky: you can take it almost flat out and feel your stomach lurch.

The small undulation after the tunnel acts like a ramp. You take off and land, hitting the brake immediately and staying well out to the right to line yourself up for the chicane. Braking hard on the cratered surface pulls you even farther to the right, however, and you streak through perilously close to the guard rail. You take the chicane in fourth gear – very fast – and the rapid left-right zig-zag makes the car aerodynamically unstable. Together with the sheer driving ability required to get into position, this narrow section is the most critical one on the circuit. You have to drive with absolute precision: if you touch the kerb, you can normally kiss the race goodbye.

As you come out of the chicane you instinctively pull your head in, because everything is so tight and narrow. Then you're bumping through the wide but uneven Tabac bend, still in third. Two sharp esses round the swimming pool, accelerate briefly, brake hard for the Rascasse bend, stay in second for the old Gasworks Corner and then give it everything you've got back into the finishing straight.

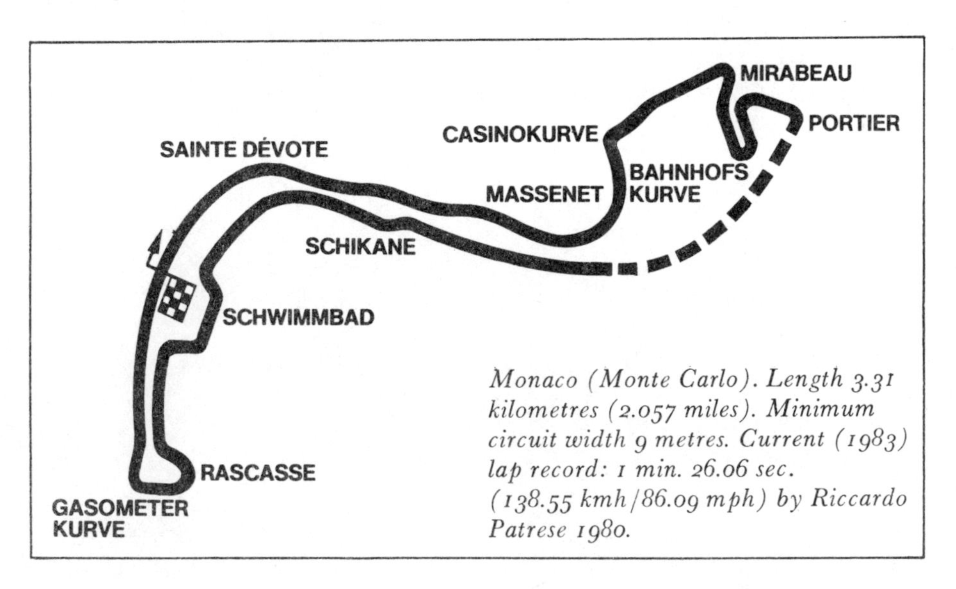

Monaco (Monte Carlo). Length 3.31 kilometres (2.057 miles). Minimum circuit width 9 metres. Current (1983) lap record: 1 min. 26.06 sec. (138.55 kmh/86.09 mph) by Riccardo Patrese 1980.

Montreal

A tedious circuit apart from the natural beauty of the St Lawrence and the impressive skyscrapers. There isn't one single corner that has to be 'driven' in the real racing sense of the term. The whole race is a staccato succession of braking and accelerating, braking and accelerating, interspersed with a completely uninteresting sequence of chicane-like curves. The surface is rather uneven and the car getes shaken about a bit.

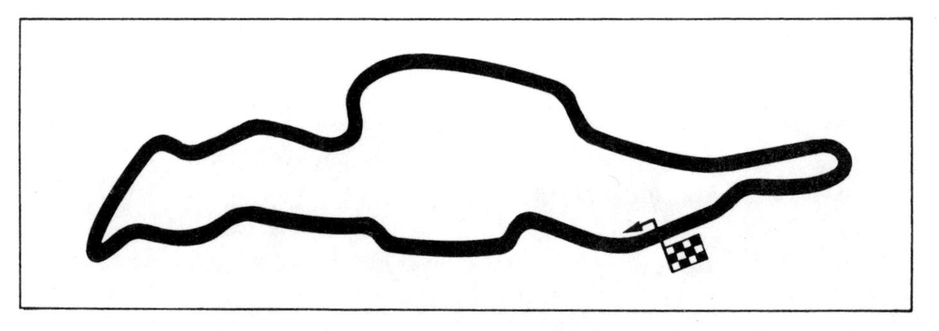

Montreal (Canada). Length 4.41 kilometres (2.74 miles). Minimum circuit width 10 metres. Current (1983) lap record: 1 min. 28.32 sec. (179.75 kmh/ 111.69 mph) by Didier Pironi 1982.

Monza

The classic spaghetti circuit: absolute bedlam, seething crowds and near-hysteria and all that goes with it, including collapsing stands and fisticuffs with the forces of law and order. For the driver, however, Monza is a demanding and interesting circuit. The high speeds on the start/finish straight and the approach to the Curva Grande have been cut back appreciably by the addition of a second-gear chicane There is another second-gear chicane ahead of the two Lesmo corners, and then we come to the most difficult section – Lesmo itself. You could put a 1982 McLaren through the first Lesmo in fourth, a bit uncomfortably because it is so very narrow, the run-off areas are tight, and you are really shifting. The second bend could comfortably be taken flat-out, but it really took guts to drive the first one that way. Coming out of Lesmo there is a straight, a third-gear chicane, another straight and then you brake hard for the Parabolica. Steer into it in third, step on the gas, accelerate out in fourth and shift up to fifth. As you can see, the Curva Grande and the Parabolica no longer quite live up to their earlier notoriety, whereas Lesmo has become much more exciting.

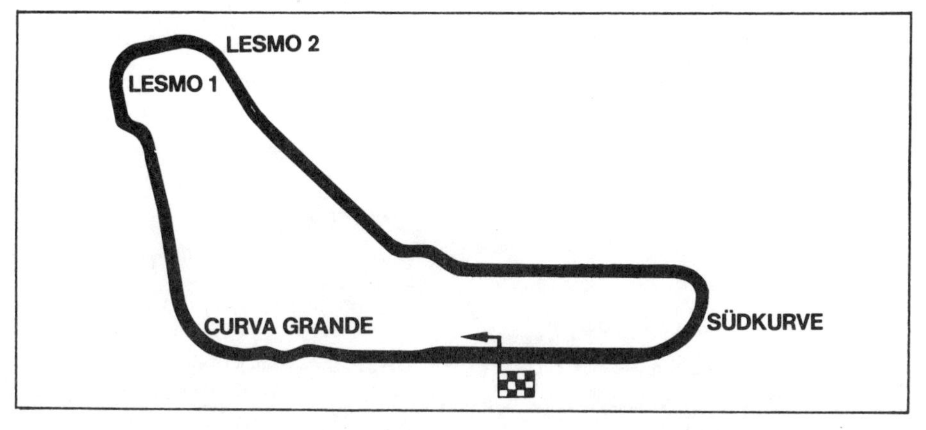

Monza (Italy), 10 miles north of Milan. Length 5.80 kilometres (3.60 miles). Minimum circuit width 9 metres. Current (1983) lap record: 1 min. 33.619 sec. (223.031 kmh/138.585 mph) by René Arnoux 1982.

Öesterreichring

At the time of writing, this is the fastest Grand Prix circuit in the world, with *average* lap speeds in excess of 150 mph. Apart from the very high speeds, the circuit is a relatively easy one, with decent run-out areas and a pretty good surface (although the first signs of wear are noticeable). The chicane immediately after the start/finish line has to be taken in second gear. Move up to third as you come out of it, head for the *Glatz-Kurve* in fifth and, if you are using a Cosworth engine, take a crack at it in fourth: line it up, clench your teeth, and go. Back up into fifth immediately after Glatz. You'll be travelling at 180 to 190 mph before you brake down for the *Bosch Kurve.* In a ground effect car it was a lot less traumatic than it used to be – providing you got the line right, you could hurtle through flat-out in fourth. The chicanes that come up next call for fourth and third, and the *Bosch Kurve*. The chicanes that come up next call for fourth and third, and the *Rindt Kurve* can be taken in fourth. It's easy to see why Öesterreichring is so fast: there isn't a single slow corner on the whole circuit.

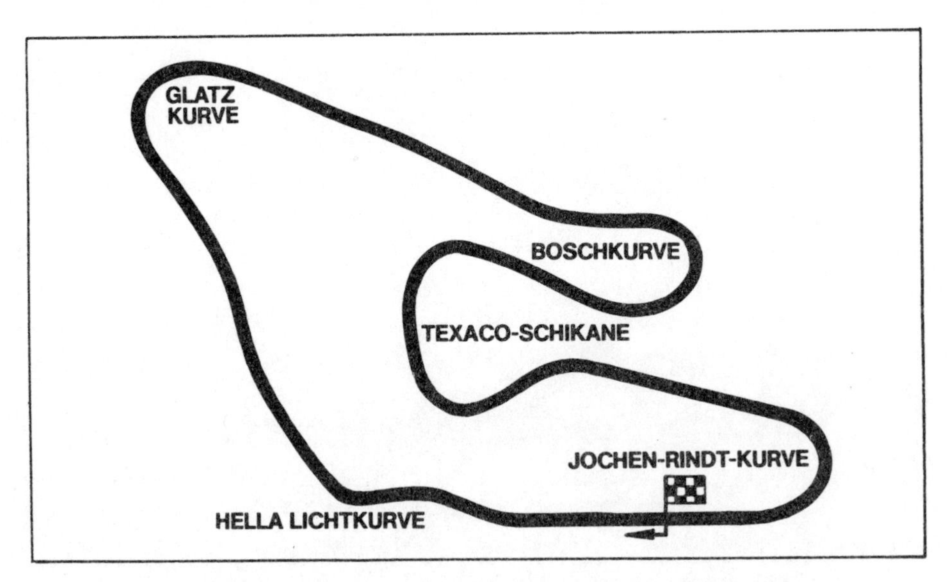

Öesterreich-Ring (Austria), 125 miles south west of Vienna. Length 5.94 kilometres (3.69 miles). Minimum circuit width 10 metres. Current (1983) lap record: 1 min. 32.53 sec. (231.20 kmh/143.66 mph) by René Arnoux 1980.

Paul Ricard (Le Castellet)

The Paul Ricard circuit is famous above all for having the longest straight in Grand Prix racing, the 1.8 kilometre Mistral. (This is, of course, short by comparison with sports car standards: Les Hunaudières at Le Mans is all of four kilometres.) The Mistral isn't much fun in a normally aspirated car since the turbos have an almost 20 mph edge. But, whether you're travelling at 190 or 210 mph, every engine has to cope with the same problem – running at top revs for the best part of 40 seconds, a stretch unheard of on any other Grand Prix circuit.

In a ground effect car, the really exciting part about the Mistral was the end of it. The right-hander could be taken flat-out in fifth, allowing for a little bump going in, which meant just over 180 mph and, at the same time, a three-ton load on the car. Even after the first ten laps you felt the strain building up on your neck muscles and had great difficulty turning your head. Just after this right-hander comes another bend tailor-made for ground effect cars. Although the radius of this bend closes up – *i.e.*, it gets tighter as you drive through it – it could be taken flat-out in third in a ground effect car: the tighter the radius, the greater the ground effect. I leave you to imagine the g-force acting on the driver's head.

There is another interesting stretch after the start/finishing straight, which is effectively a very fast chicane. If you're driving a Cosworth you can take this in fifth, although the turbo drivers change down a gear. Then the car is braked from about 190 mph to 50 mph to take the two right-handers which lead into the Mistral.

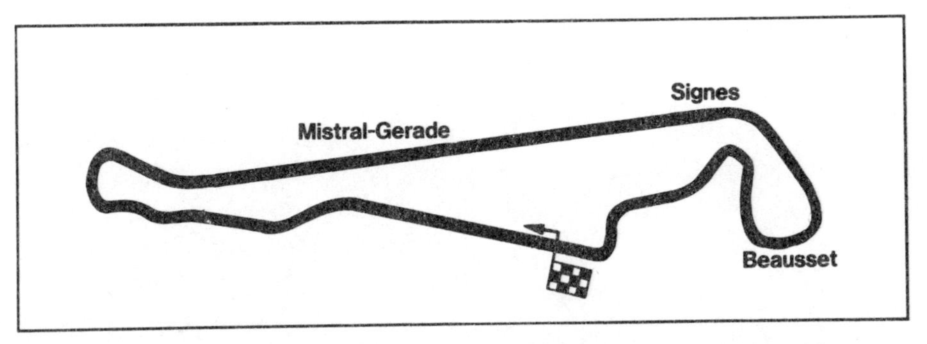

Paul Ricard/Le Castellet (France), 21 miles east of Marseilles. Length 5.81 Kilometres (3.61 miles). Minimum circuit width 12 metres. Current (1983) lap record: 1 min. 40.07 sec. (209.00 kmh/129.86 mph) by Riccardo Patrese 1982.

Rio

The best example of barely tolerable centrifugal force acting on a ground effect car was Rio, mentioned earlier in the chapter on aerodynamics. There are several bends that have a very long radius and are also slightly banked. One of the niceties of the track is the way the straight tapers out into a high speed curve. Rio is the toughest circuit I know in terms of the physical demands made on the driver. Your hands, your feet and your head are buffeted by g-force and your head is jerked out of position. To cap it all, the race is run at the height of the Brazilian summer, so you have to contend with incredible heat and humidity. But centrifugal force is infinitely worse for the driver than heat alone. The long fast bends are taken in third gear at about 125 mph.

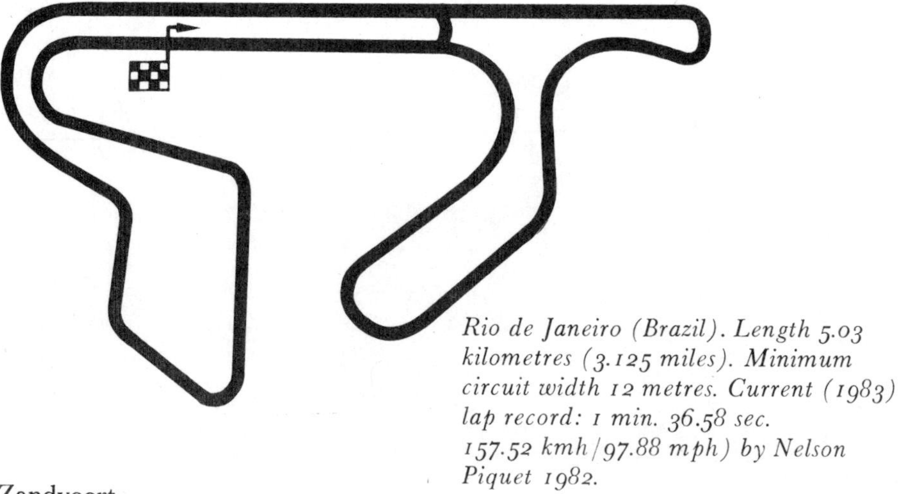

Rio de Janeiro (Brazil). Length 5.03 kilometres (3.125 miles). Minimum circuit width 12 metres. Current (1983) lap record: 1 min. 36.58 sec. 157.52 kmh/97.88 mph) by Nelson Piquet 1982.

Zandvoort

Zandvoort's trademark – apart from the rolling sand dunes all around it – is the Tarzan corner, where the ground effect cars braked from 190 mph to 70 mph in less than 100 metres. The fact that the wheels didn't lock was an indication of the downforce being developed. Furthermore, this is the only safe place on the circuit for passing, so this is where most of the outbraking manoeuvres occur.

In spite of all this, the Tarzan bend is not as exciting as Scheivlak: you come over the hill in fifth, brake imperceptibly, slip down into fourth and go through the corner flat-out There is tremendous loading on both car and driver as you hop round the corner at 155 to 160 mph, and when you come out of it, there is an unusually high kerb: touch that and you are out of the running.

SCHEIVLAK

HUGENHOLTZ

TARZANKURVE

Zandvoort (Holland), 15 miles west of Amsterdam. Length 4.25 kilometres (2.64 miles). Minimum circuit width 9 metres. Current (1983) lap record: 1 min. 19.35 sec. (192.91 kmh/ 119.87 mph) by René Arnoux 1980.

Zolder

A dangerous circuit, because the run-off areas are inadequate for today's speeds and the guard rails are too close to the track all the way round. There are also different grades of asphalt, which force you to choose a particular line at braking points. The most important part of the circuit is the right-hander before the long straight. You can take this almost flat-out in fourth: line it up, bang your foot down and keep your fingers crossed.

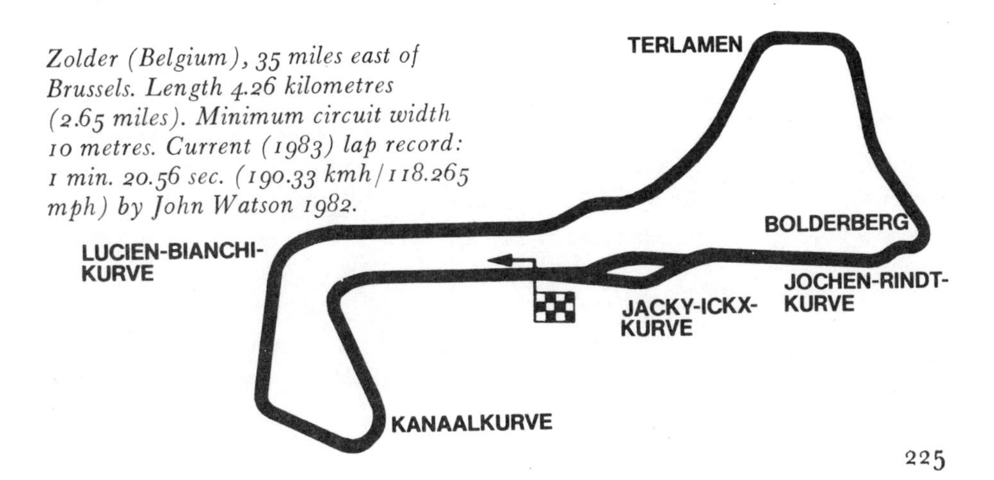

Zolder (Belgium), 35 miles east of Brussels. Length 4.26 kilometres (2.65 miles). Minimum circuit width 10 metres. Current (1983) lap record: 1 min. 20.56 sec. (190.33 kmh/118.265 mph) by John Watson 1982.

Physical Fitness

The Grand Prix Driver and His Body

By Willy Dungl

Willy Dungl is a 45-year-old masseur and physical fitness specialist who lives in Vienna. He first hit the headlines as a result of his contribution to the Olympic Gold Medal triumphs of the Austrian national ski-ing team. After my serious accident at Nürburgring in 1976, Dungl took charge of me virtually from the time I left the intensive care unit and worked out my physical fitness training programme. By then, Dungl was far more than a common-or-garden masseur: he was responsible for overall physical condition and performance, not to mention psychic motivation. After my two-year lay-off it was again Dungl who honed me back to fitness. His knowledge, his techniques and his successes within the realm of sport and outside it are nothing short of sensational. – NL

It was not until 1976 that telemetric measurement techniques (using two-way radio transmission equipment) were exploited to monitor the physical condition and well-being of Grand Prix drivers. It was established that, on the day of a race, the driver's pulse rate is a constant 140 to 160 for periods of five, six or even seven hours at a stretch; moreover, the pulse rate can peak as high as 200. This is one symptom of physical stress that has scarcely been acknowledged. Telemetric measurement at Nürburgring also established that drivers who are not fit or who have not gone through fitness training programmes are prone to 'mini-blackouts' at the end of a long practice session: they lose consciousness for fractions of a second at a time. It was then that everyone concerned acknowledged that no driver can be successful without proper physical training. Since then, the drivers have become much fitter and much more resilient all round. You only have to compare a 1976 Laffite

Circulatory stress is only one of three essential factors which affect a Grand Prix driver's physical well-being. The second is static stress, centred on the arms and shoulders, which take a lot of punishment, and on the efforts of centrifugal force. Without special treatment, Lauda would not have been able to race on a couple of occasions – Jarama and Le Castellet most readily come to mind – because he had displaced a vertebra during training as a result of the g-forces. The dislocated vertebra was pushing down on a nerve and was agonisingly painful. It was only once we had gone through an intensive programme to re-educate the muscles of his spine that this problem resolved itself: he built up enough muscle to withstand the forces acting on him during a race.

The third factor is metabolic stress. The Grand Prix driver has to school his body to husband vast reserves of energy. This means that his diet must be calibrated over the longer term and monitored particularly closely just before a race.

Let's take a closer look at these three stress categories – circulation, muscles and metabolism.

Circulation

Build-up begins with a series of short runs at a moderate pace. The idea is to run twenty minutes – about three miles – without racing your pulse.

Then you move up to longer distances by means of interval training, *i.e.*, we run two minutes, walk two minutes, run three, walk two, run four, walk two, and so on until we are running ten-minute bursts; then we work back down. The net effect is to run about twelve miles. Clearly you can vary the distances and intervals to correspond to individual requirements.

There are standard tests – such as the Cooper Test and the Harvard Test – for purposes of monitoring circulatory stress. Good test values indicate that the body is using up less oxygen under stress than would be the case for someone who is not in training or who is less fit. The relevance of this in the case of a Grand Prix driver is obvious: the less oxygen his body uses, the more he has for his brain, thereby maintaining mental alertness and lightning reaction times.

Musculature

We begin by building up the hands, wrists and lower arms. I have designed a special piece of equipment for this: what it involves is a length of tubing from which I have suspended a seven kilogram weight. All you have to do is wind up the weight by turning the tubing. This is an exercise to start strengthening the lower arm muscles in particular. When Niki begins training he can barely manage the exercise three times, but once he is race-fit he can do it ten times without difficulty.

Circuit training to build up muscle tone takes in a whole range of shoulder, neck and pectoral expansion exercises. As I said earlier, back muscle exercises are especially important. I get Niki to lie face down over a table with only his legs and pelvis supported and the upper part of his body jack-knifed downwards, hands clasped behind the neck: he now has to pull himself up thirty times. This exercise is repeated three times in each session, the body movements being varied from left to right to work on different groups of muscles. In between, there are other routines to strengthen the stomach muscles, and loosening-up exercises involving stretching and bending to avoid undue stress on the spinal column.

Rio is the toughest track of all as far as back stress is concerned, and we have to work up to it weeks in advance. I also put together a special horseshoe-shaped foam-rubber cushion that helps to stop Niki's helmet being jerked to one side by the centrifugal force.

When I work on a Grand Prix driver's musculature, I take care not to turn him into a body builder. I have to give him the muscles he needs for racing, no more, no less – anything beyond that is pure ballast. This is because every muscle and every fibre in the body needs blood and oxygen; and, when a muscle gets hot, it has to be cooled down. If you're built like Mr Universe, you need that much more energy to keep your muscles nourished. As a result, the body's overall energy needs are greater and you are under stress. It doesn't make sense, therefore, to turn a Grand Prix driver into a superb athlete.

Metabolism and Diet

A Grand Prix driver is under stress by nine o'clock at the latest on the morning of a race. He just can't bring himself to eat sensibly to take on energy for the race. On top of this, he needs extra reserves, say, for a race in the heat of the summer: cooling down the human 'engine' also burns up energy. Without the right training, the body is only able to store a limited amount of body sugar, then it has to be replenished. The racing driver, however, has to go for a long period without eating, so he has to educate his body to store a larger reserve.

Digestion is also hard work. When we complain of sluggishness, what we mean is that blood is being used for digestive purposes and the supply of blood is being channelled to the stomach rather than the brain. Digestive energy requirements vary with the kind of food we eat. If I take in 100 calories of protein, my body has to expend 30 calories to convert the 100 into energy. What is more, it will be a few hours before I can derive energy from the protein intake. What happens, in fact, is that converting 100 calories of protein into energy entails using up in the first instance 30 calories from the body's immediate energy reserves. The worst thing you can do to a driver just before the race, obviously, is serve him up, say, a plate of ham and eggs: this will more than likely induce sluggishness, and it will be some time before his metabolic balance can be restored.

Details like these are fairly obvious. What is more important, and more difficult to achieve, is a longer-term nutritional programme to enable the driver to condition his body metabolism. We have run comparative tests under qualified medical supervision to monitor the metabolism and blood sugar levels of several drivers eating different types of meal:

* A 'wholemeal breakfast' (consisting of wholemeal bread, 100-percent wheat *muesli*, about 100 grams of carbohydrate and about 500 calories): Niki ran 4.5 kilometres about an hour afterwards, then we took a sugar count immediately and once again an hour later. The count was 90 before running, between 75 and 80 when he finished, and back to normal an hour later;

* A 'normal' breakfast (consisting of white bread or rolls, sugar, honey, *i.e.*, rapidly-absorbed carbohydrates): Niki had a sugar count between 140 and 150 one hour after eating, tired during the 4.5 kilometre run, and was in difficulties towards the end. It was not until three hours later that the count was normal. Explanation: when sugar is absorbed quickly, the stomach glands release a significant amount of insulin; the sugar quickly disappears, the insulin remains. An excess of sugar is followed by a deficiency, hence the ensuing sluggishness;

* 'Ham and eggs' breakfast: Niki started running an hour later, just as the digestive process was getting under way. Accordingly, as explained above, he had to syphon off 30 percent of his available energy (oxygen) to convert the protein. This is obviously counter-productive: it would be much wiser simply to run on an empty stomach.

On race day – or even on qualifying days – the racing driver has to keep his diet rich in carbohydrates and low on proteins. In between times, on the other hand, when there are regular breaks and he has a chance to 'top up', he will need a higher intake of vital protein.

Finally, after training sessions, it is important to scrub down properly to get rid of residual matter. There's an old Russian recipe that calls for seven minutes under a hot shower followed by a cold rinse. An alternative is a thirty-second dip in a cold stream during a cross-country run. This helps you to go long distances without your body going stale with excretions of meat, sugar and lactic acid. Once cleansed, it has to be reconditioned – perhaps by means of raw vegetable intake – ready for the next work-out.

Grand Prix Winners Since 1950

1950. Britain: Farina (*Alfa Romeo*). Monaco: Fangio (*Alfa Romeo*). Switzerland: Farina (*Alfa Romeo*). Belgium: Fangio (*Alfa Romeo*). France: Fangio (*Alfa Romeo*). Italy: Farina (*Alfa Romeo*).

1951. Switzerland: Fangio (*Alfa Romeo*). Belgium: Farina (*Alfa Romeo*). France: Fagioli/Fangio (*Alfa Romeo*). Britain: Gonzalez (*Ferrari*). Germany: Ascari (*Ferrari*). Italy: Ascari (*Ferrari*). Spain: Fangio (*Alfa Romeo*).

1952. Switzerland: Taruffi (*Ferrari*). Belgium: Ascari (*Ferrari*). France: Ascari (*Ferrari*). Britain: Ascari (*Ferrari*). Germany: Ascari (*Ferrari*). Holland: Ascari (*Ferrari*). Italy: Ascari (*Ferrari*).

1953. Argentina: Ascari (*Ferrari*). Holland: Ascari (*Ferrari*). Belgium: Ascari (*Ferrari*). France: Hawthorn (*Ferrari*). Britain: Ascari (*Ferrari*). Germany: Farina (*Ferrari*). Switzerland: Ascari (*Ferrari*). Italy: Fangio (*Maserati*).

1954. Argentina: Fangio (*Maserati*). Belgium: Fangio (*Maserati*). France: Fangio (*Mercedes*). Britain: Gonzalez (*Ferrari*). Germany: Fangio (*Mercedes*). Switzerland: Fangio (*Mercedes*). Italy: Fangio (*Mercedes*). Spain: Hawthorn (*Ferrari*).

1955. Argentina: Fangio (*Mercedes*). Monaco: Trintignant (*Ferrari*). Belgium: Fangio (*Mercedes*). Holland: Fangio (*Mercedes*). Britain: Moss (*Mercedes*). Italy: Fangio (*Mercedes*).

1956. Argentina: Fangio/Musso (*Ferrari*). Monaco: Moss (*Maserati*). Belgium: Collins (*Ferrari*). France: Collins (*Ferrari*). Britain: Fangio (*Ferrari*). Germany: Fangio (*Ferrari*). Italy: Moss (*Maserati*).

1957. Argentina: Fangio (*Maserati*). Monaco: Fangio (*Maserati*). France: Fangio (*Maserati*). Britain: Brooks/Moss (*Vanwall*). Germany: Fangio (*Maserati*). Pescara: Fangio (*Maserati*). Italy: Moss (*Vanwall*).

1958. Argentina: Moss (*Cooper*). Monaco: Trintignant (*Cooper*). Holland: Moss (*Vanwall*). Belgium: Brooks (*Vanwall*). France: Hawthorn (*Ferrari*). Britain: Collins (*Ferrari*). Germany: Brooks (*Vanwall*). Portugal: Moss (*Vanwall*). Italy: Brooks (*Vanwall*). Morocco: Moss (*Vanwall*).

1959. Monaco: Brabham (*Cooper*). Holland: Bonnier (*BRM*). France: Brooks (*Ferrari*). Britain: Brabham (*Cooper*). Germany: Brooks (*Ferrari*). Portugal: Moss (*Cooper*). Italy: Moss (*Cooper*). USA: McLaren (*Cooper*).

1960. Argentina: McLaren (*Cooper*). Monaco: Moss (*Lotus*). Holland: Brabham (*Cooper*). Belgium: Brabham (*Cooper*). France: Brabham (*Cooper*). Britain: Brabham (*Cooper*). Portugal: Brabham (*Cooper*). Italy: P. Hill (*Ferrari*). USA: Moss (*Lotus*).

1961. Monaco: Moss (*Lotus*). Holland: von Trips (*Ferrari*). Belgium: P. Hill (*Ferrari*). France: Baghetti (*Ferrari*). Britain: von Trips (*Ferrari*). Germany: Moss (*Lotus*). Italy: P. Hill (*Ferrari*). USA: Ireland (*Lotus*).

1962. Holland: G. Hill (*BRM*). Monaco: McLaren (*Cooper*). Belgium: Clark (*Lotus*). France: Gurney (*Porsche*). Britain: Clark (*Lotus*). Germany: G. Hill (*BRM*). Italy: G. Hill (*BRM*). USA: Clark (*Lotus*). South Africa: G. Hill (*BRM*).

1963. Monaco: G. Hill (*BRM*). Holland: Clark (*Lotus*). Belgium: Clark (*Lotus*). France: Clark (*Lotus*). Britain: Clark (*Lotus*). Germany: Surtees (*Ferrari*). Italy: Clark (*Lotus*). USA: G. Hill (*BRM*). Mexico: Clark (*Lotus*). South Africa: Clark (*Lotus*).

1964. Monaco: G. Hill (*BRM*). Holland: Clark (*Lotus*). Belgium: Clark (*Lotus*). France: Gurney (*Brabham*). Britain: Clark (*Lotus*). Germany: Surtees (*Ferrari*). Austria: Bandini (*Ferrari*). Italy: Surtees (*Ferrari*). USA: G. Hill (*BRM*). Mexico: Gurney (*Brabham*).

1965. South Africa: Clark (*Lotus*). Monaco: G. Hill (*BRM*). Belgium: Clark (*Lotus*). France: Clark (*Lotus*). Britain: Clark (*Lotus*). Germany: Clark (*Lotus*). Italy: Stewart (*BRM*). USA: G. Hill (*BRM*). Mexico: Ginther (*Honda*).

1966. Monaco: Stewart (*BRM*). Belgium: Surtees (*Ferrari*). France: Brabham (*Brabham*). Britain: Brabham (*Brabham*). Holland: Brabham (*Brabham*). Germany: Brabham (*Brabham*). Italy: Scarfiotti (*Ferrari*). USA: Clark (*Lotus*). Mexico: Surtees (*Cooper*).

RENAULT elf
16
elf

Page 233: Réné Arnoux in the Rascasse Corner at Monaco.
Left: Lauda (McLaren) in Detroit.
Above: Pironi (Ferrari).
Watson (McLaren).

EBEL
SWISS
WATCHES
Marlboro
McLAREN INTERNATIONAL
EBEL
Marlboro
McLAREN INTERNATIONAL

1967. South Africa: Rodriguez (*Cooper*). Monaco: Hulme (*Brabham*). Holland: Clark (*Lotus*). Belgium: Gurney (*Eagle*). France: Brabham (*Brabham*). Britain: Clark (*Lotus*). Germany: Hulme (*Brabham*). Canada: Brabham (*Brabham*). Italy: Surtees (*Honda*). USA: Clark (*Lotus*). Mexico: Clark (*Lotus*).

1968. South Africa: Clark (*Lotus*). Spain: G. Hill (*Lotus*). Monaco: G. Hill (*Lotus*). Belgium: McLaren (*McLaren*). Holland: Stewart (*Matra*). France: Ickx (*Ferrari*). Britain: Siffert (*Lotus*). Germany: Stewart (*Matra*). Italy: Hulme (*McLaren*). Canada: Hulme (*McLaren*). USA: Stewart (*Matra*). Mexico: G. Hill (*Lotus*).

1969. South Africa: Stewart (*Matra*). Spain: Stewart (*Matra*). Monaco: G. Hill (*Lotus*). Holland: Stewart (*Matra*). France: Stewart (*Matra*). Britain: Stewart (*Matra*). Germany: Ickx (*Ferrari*). Italy: Stewart (*Matra*). Canada: Ickx (*Brabham*). USA: Rindt (*Lotus*). Mexico: Hulme (*McLaren*).

1970. South Africa: Brabham (*Brabham*). Spain: Stewart (*March*). Monaco: Rindt (*Lotus*). Belgium: Rodriguez (*BRM*). Holland: Rindt (*Lotus*). France: Rindt (*Lotus*). Britain: Rindt (*Lotus*). Germany: Rindt (*Lotus*). Austria: Ickx (*Ferrari*). Italy: Regazzoni (*Ferrari*). Canada: Ickx (*Ferrari*). USA: Fittipaldi (*Lotus*). Mexico: Ickx (*Ferrari*).

1971. South Africa: Andretti (*Ferrari*). Spain: Stewart (*Tyrrell*) Monaco: Stewart (*Tyrrell*). Holland: Ickx (*Ferrari*). France: Stewart (*Tyrrell*). Britain: Stewart (*Tyrrell*). Germany: Stewart (*Tyrrell*). Austria: Siffert (*BRM*). Italy: Gethin (*BRM*). Canada: Stewart (*Tyrrell*). USA: Cevert (*Tyrrell*).

1972. Argentina: Stewart (*Tyrrell*). South Africa: Hulme (*McLaren*). Spain: Fittipaldi (*Lotus*). Monaco: Beltoise (*BRM*). Belgium: Fittipaldi (*Lotus*). France: Stewart (*Tyrrell*). Britain: Fittipaldi (*Lotus*). Germany: Ickx (*Ferrari*). Austria: Fittipaldi (*Lotus*). Italy: Fittipaldi (*Lotus*). Canada: Stewart (*Tyrrell*). USA: Stewart (*Tyrrell*).

1973. Argentina: Fittipaldi (*Lotus*). Brazil: Fittipaldi (*Lotus*). South Africa: Stewart (*Tyrrell*). Spain: Stewart (*Tyrrell*). Belgium: Fittipaldi (*Lotus*). Monaco:. Stewart (*Tyrrell*). Sweden: Hulme (*McLaren*). France: Peterson (*Lotus*). Britain: Revson (*McLaren*). Holland: Stewart (*Tyrrell*). Germany: Stewart (*Tyrrell*). Austria: Peterson (*Lotus*). Italy: Peterson (*Lotus*). Canada: Revson (*McLaren*). USA: Peterson (*Lotus*).

1974. Argentina: Hulme (*McLaren*). Brazil: Fittipaldi (*McLaren*). South Africa: Reutemann (*Brabham*). Spain: Lauda (*Ferrari*). Belgium: Fittipaldi (*McLaren*). Monaco: Peterson (*Lotus*). Sweden: Scheckter (*Tyrrell*). Holland: Lauda (*Ferrari*). France: Peterson (*Lotus*). Britain: Scheckter (*Tyrrell*). Germany: Regazzoni (*Ferrari*). Austria: Reutemann (*Brabham*). Italy: Peterson (*Lotus*). Canada: Fittipaldi (*McLaren*). USA: Reutemann (*Brabham*).

1975. Argentina: Fittipaldi (*McLaren*). Brazil: Pace (*Brabham*). South Africa: Scheckter (*Tyrrell*). Spain: Mass (*McLaren*). Monaco: Lauda (*Ferrari*). Belgium: Lauda (*Ferrari*). Sweden: Lauda (*Ferrari*). Holland: Hunt (*Hesketh*). France: Lauda (*Ferrari*). Britain: Fittipaldi (*McLaren*). Germany: Reutemann (*Brabham*). Austria: Brambilla (*March*). Italy: Regazzoni (*Ferrari*). USA: Lauda (*Ferrari*).

1976. Brazil: Lauda (*Ferrari*). South Africa: Lauda (*Ferrari*). USA West: Regazzoni (*Ferrari*). Spain: Hunt (*McLaren*). Belgium: Lauda (*Ferrari*). Monaco: Lauda (*Ferrari*). Sweden: Scheckter (*Tyrrell*). France: Hunt (*McLaren*). Britain: Lauda (*Ferrari*). Germany: Hunt (*McLaren*). Austria: Watson (*Penske*). Holland: Hunt (*McLaren*). Italy: Peterson (*March*). Canada: Hunt (*McLaren*). USA: Hunt (*McLaren*). Japan: Andretti (*Lotus*).

1977. Argentina: Scheckter (*Wolf*). Brazil: Reutemann (*Ferrari*). South Africa: Lauda (*Ferrari*). USA West: Andretti (*Lotus*). Spain: Andretti (*Lotus*). Monaco: Scheckter (*Wolf*). Belgium: Nilsson (*Lotus*). Sweden: Laffite (*Ligier*). France: Andretti (*Lotus*). Britain: Hunt (*McLaren*).

Germany: Lauda (*Ferrari*). Austria: Jones (*Shadow*). Holland: Lauda (*Ferrari*). Italy: Andretti (*Lotus*). USA: Hunt (*McLaren*). Canada: Scheckter (*Wolf*). Japan: Hunt (*McLaren*).

1978. Argentina: Andretti (*Lotus*). Brazil: Reutemann (*Ferrari*). South Africa: Peterson (*Lotus*). USA West: Reutemann (*Ferrari*). Monaco: Depailler (*Tyrrell*). Belgium: Andretti (*Lotus*). Spain: Andretti (*Lotus*). Britain: Reutemann (*Ferrari*). Germany: Andretti (*Lotus*). Austria: Peterson (*Lotus*). Holland: Andretti (*Lotus*). Italy: Lauda (*Brabham*). USA: Reutemann (*Ferrari*). Canada: Villeneuve (*Ferrari*).

1979. Argentina: Laffite (*Ligier*). Brazil: Laffite (*Ligier*). South Africa: Villeneuve (*Ferrari*). USA West: Villeneuve (*Ferrari*). Spain: Depailler (*Ligier*). Belgium: Scheckter (*Ferrari*). Monaco: Scheckter (*Ferrari*). France: Jabouille (*Renault*). Britain: Regazzoni (*Williams*). Germany: Jones (*Williams*). Austria: Jones (*Williams*). Holland: Jones (*Williams*). Italy: Scheckter (*Ferrari*). Canada: Jones (*Williams*). USA: Villeneuve (*Ferrari*).

1980. Argentina: Jones (*Williams*). Brazil: Arnoux (*Renault*). South Africa: Arnoux (*Renault*). USA West: Piquet (*Brabham*). Belgium: Pironi (*Ligier*). Monaco: Reutemann (*Williams*). France: Jones (*Williams*). Germany: Laffite (*Ligier*). Austria: Jabouille (*Renault*). Holland: Piquet (*Brabham*). Italy: Piquet (*Brabham*). Canada: Jones (*Williams*). USA: Jones (*Williams*).

1981. USA West: Jones (*Williams*). Brazil: Reutemann (*Williams*). Argentina: Piquet (*Brabham*). Belgium: Reutemann (*Williams*). Monaco: Villeneuve (*Ferrari*). Spain: Villeneuve (*Ferrari*). France: Prost (*Renault*). Britain: Watson (*McLaren*). Germany: Piquet (*Brabham*). Austria: Laffite (*Talbot*). Holland: Prost (*Renault*). Canada: Laffite (*Talbot*). USA: Jones (*Williams*).

1982. South Africa: Prost (*Renault*). Brazil: Piquet (*Brabham*). USA West: Lauda (*McLaren*). San Marino: Pironi (*Ferrari*). Belgium: Watson (*McLaren*). Monaco: Patrese (*Brabham*). USA East: Watson (*McLaren*). Canada: Piquet (*Brabham*). Holland: Pironi (*Ferrari*). Britain: Lauda (*McLaren*). France: Arnoux (*Renault*). Germany: Tambay (*Ferrari*). Austria: de Angelis (*Lotus*). Switzerland: Rosberg (*Williams*).

1983. Brazil: Piquet (*Brabham*). USA-West/Long Beach: Watson (*McLaren*). France: Prost (*Renault*). San Marino: Tambay (*Ferrari*). Monaco: Rosberg (*Williams*). Belgium: Prost (*Renault*). USA-East/Detroit: Alboreto (*Tyrrell*). Canada: Arnoux (*Ferrari*). Britain: Prost (*Renault*). Germany: Arnoux (*Ferrari*). Austria: Prost (*Renault*). Holland: Arnoux (*Ferrari*). Italy: Piquet (*Brabham*). Europe: Piquet (*Brabham*). South Africa: Patrese (*Brabham*).

International Formula I Constructors' Cup

Up to and including 1958, the trophy was always awarded to the make of car driven by the winner of the drivers' championship. Since 1958, however, the Constructors' Cup has been awarded on the basis of a points system identical to that for the individual driver's championship.

1950: Alfa Romeo
1951: Alfa Romeo
1952: Ferrari
1953: Ferrari
1954: Maserati and Mercedes-Benz
1955: Mercedes-Benz
1956: Ferrari
1957: Maserati
1958: Ferrari
1959: Cooper
1960: Cooper
1961: Ferrari
1962: BRM
1963: Lotus
1964: Ferrari
1965: Lotus
1966: Brabham
1967: Brabham
1968: Lotus
1969: Matra
1970: Lotus
1971: Tyrrell
1972: JPS-Lotus
1973: Lotus
1974: McLaren
1975: Ferrari
1976: Ferrari
1977: Ferrari
1978: Lotus
1979: Ferrari
1980: Williams
1981: Williams
1982: Ferrari
1983: Ferrari

Formula I Champions Since 1950

1950: Giuseppe Farina
1951: Juan Manuel Fangio
1952: Alberto Ascari
1953: Alberto Ascari
1954: Juan Manuel Fangio
1955: Juan Manuel Fangio
1956: Juan Manuel Fangio
1957: Juan Manuel Fangio
1958: Mike Hawthorn
1959: Jack Brabham
1960: Jack Brabham
1961: Phil Hill
1962: Graham Hill
1963: Jim Clark
1964: John Surtees
1965: Jim Clark
1966: Jack Brabham
1967: Denis Hulme
1968: Graham Hill
1969: Jackie Stewart
1970: Jochen Rindt
1971: Jackie Stewart
1972: Emerson Fittipaldi
1973: Jackie Stewart
1974: Emerson Fittipaldi
1975: Niki Lauda
1976: James Hunt
1977: Niki Lauda
1978: Mario Andretti
1979: Jody Scheckter
1980: Alan Jones
1981: Nelson Piquet
1982: Keke Rosberg
1983: Nelson Piquet

For The Record:
265 Starts in 16 Years

Abbreviations

A	Austria	H	Hungary
Arg	Argentina	I	Italy
Aus	Australia	Irl	Ireland
B	Belgium	NL	Netherlands
Can	Canada	NZ	New Zealand
CH	Switzerland	S	Sweden
CS	Czechoslovakia	SA	South Africa
D	Germany	SF	Finland
E	Spain	USA	United States of America
F	France	Yu	Yugoslavia
GB	United Kingdom	*	Class

1968

Bad Mühllacken (A) 15.4.
Cooper 1300, Placed 2*
Hill climb
Herbert Grünsteidl (A), Cooper*
Richard Gerin (A), Porsche 906

Dobratsch (A) 28.4.
Cooper 1300, Placed 1*
Hill climb
Lauda (A), Cooper*
Rudi Lins (A), Porsche 906

Alpl (A) 5.5.
Cooper 1300, Placed 1*
Hill climb
Lauda (A), Cooper*
Richard Gerin (A), Porsche 906

Engelhartszell (A) 26.5.
Cooper 1300, Placed 1*
Hill climb
Lauda (A), Cooper*
Gerhard Krammer (A), Brabham-Alfa

Kasten-Viechtenstein (A) 9.6.
Porsche 911, Retired (crashed)
Hill climb
Dieter Schmied (D), Lotus 23

Koralpe (A) 23.6.
Porsche 911, Placed 1*
Hill climb
Lauda (A), Porsche 911*
Richard Gerin (A), Porsche 906

Tulln-Langenlebarn (A) 14.7.
Porsche 911, Retired (engine failure)
Aerodrome
Klaus Reisch (A), Alfa Romeo GTA

Tauplitzalm 4.8.
Porsche 911, Placed 1*
Hill climb
Lauda (A). Porsche 911*
Giulio de Guidi (CH), Cooper-ATS

Stainz (A) 11.8.
Porsche 911, Placed 1*
Hill climb
Lauda (A), Porsche 911*
Jochen Rindt (A), Brabham F-2

Walding (A) 15.8.
Porsche 911, Placed 1*
Hill climb
Lauda (A), Porsche 911*
Peter Peter (A), Porsche 906

Zeltweg (A) 25.8.
Porsche 911, Placed 1
Aerodrome
Lauda (A), Porsche 911

Aspern (A) 6.10.
Porsche 911, Placed 3
Aerodrome
Ernst Furtmayer (D), BMW 2002

Aspern (A) 6.10.
Kaimann, Placed 8
Formula V
Ernst Breinberg (A), Kaimann

Innsbruck (A) 13.10.
Porsche 911, Retired
Aerodrome
P. Kaiser (D), Porsche 911

Dopplerhütte (A) 27.10.
Porsche 911, Placed 1*
Kaimann, Placed 2
Hill climb
Lauda (A), Porsche 911*;
Kaimann: Rudi Lins (A), Porsche 910

1969

Hockenheim (D) 12.4.
Kaimann, Placed 4
Formula V
Gerold Pankl (A), Austro-V

Aspern (A) 13.4.
Kaimann, Retired
Aerodrome, Formula V
Peter Peter (A), Austro-V

Belgrade (YU) 20.4.
Kaimann, Placed 2
Formula V
Gerold Pankl (A), Austro-V

Budapest (H) 11.5.
Kaimann, Placed 4
Formula V
Alfred Vogelberger (D) Olympic

Rossfeld (D) 8.6.
Kaimann, Placed 5
Hill climb
Alfred Vogelberger (D), Olympic

Hockenheim (D) 15.6.
Kaimann, Placed 2
Formula V
Erich Breinsberg (A), Kaimann

Nürburgring (D) 29.6.
Kaimann, Placed 2
Formula V Hansa-Pokal
Erich Breinsberg (A), Kaimann

Sopron (H) 6.6.
Kaimann, Placed 1
Formula V
Lauda (A), Kaimann-V

Tulln-Langenlebarn (A) 13.7.
Opel 1900, Retired (engine failure)
Peter Huber (A), Ford Escort TC
Formula V
Kaimann, Placed 3
Peter Peter (A), Austro-V

Oesterreich-Ring (A) 27.7.
Kaimann, Placed 8
Formula V
Helmut Marko (A), McNamara

Nürburgring (D) 3.8.
Kaimann, Placed 2
Formula V
Helmut Marko (A), McNamara

Oesterreich-Ring 10.8.
Lauda/Stuppacher (A), Porsche 910,
Placed 21
Siffert/Ahrens (CH/D), Porsche 917

Mantorp Park (S) 31.8.
Kaimann, Retired (fuel pump)
Formula V
Bertil Roos (S), RPB

Salzburgring (A) 21.9.
Kaimann, Placed 3
Formula V
Dieter Quester (A), Kaimann

Innsbruck (A), 5.10.
Kaimann, Placed 2
Aerodrome, Formula V
Erich Breinsberg (A), Kaimann

Nürburgring (D) 12.10.
Kaimann, Placed 20
Eifel Cup, Formula V
Peter Peter (A), Austro-V

Munich-Neubiberg (D) 26.10.
Opel 1900, Placed 5
Kaimann, Placed 1
Aerodrome
Dieter Basche (D), BMW 2002 ti
Lauda (A), Kaimann

1970

Nogaro (F) 29.3.
McNamara, Retired (crashed)
Formula 3
J.-P. Jaussaud (F), Tecno

Nürburgring (D) 19.4.
McNamara, Placed 16
300 kms, Formula 3
Freddy Kottulinsky (S), Lotus

Magny Cours (F) 3.5.
McNamara, Placed 5
Formula 3
J.-P. Jaussaud (F), Tecno

Hockenheim (D), 10.5.
McNamara, Retired (crash)
Formula 3
Hermann Unold (D), Tecno

Oesterreich-Ring (A) 17.5.
McNamara, Placed 6
Formula 3
Freddy Kottulinsky (S), Lotus

Brno (CS) 24.5.
McNamara, Placed 2
Formula 3
Jürg Dubler (CH), Chevron

Silverstone (GB) 7.6.
McNamara, Did not start
Formula 3
Mike Beuttler (GB), March

Norisring (D) 28.6.
Porsche 908, Placed 8
Jürgen Neuhaus (D), Porsche 917

Hockenheim (D) 5.7.
Porsche 908, Placed 12
Vic-Elford, McLaren-Chevy
McNamara, Placed 5
Formula 3
Gianni Salvati (I), Tecno

Nürburgring (D) 12.7.
Lauda/Herzog (A/CH), BMW 1600
Retired
6-Hours
de Adamich/Picchi (I), Alfa Romeo

Brands Hatch (GB) 17.7.
McNamara, Retired (crash)
Formula 3
Mike Beuttler (GB), Brabham

Diepholz (D) 19.7.
Porsche 908, Placed 1
Aerodrome
Lauda (A), Porsche 908

Karlskoga (S) 9.8.
McNamara, Placed 5
Formula 3
Peter Hanson (GB), Chevron
Porsche 908, Retired (gearbox)
Chris Craft (GB), McLaren-Cosworth

Knutstorp (S) 16.8.
McNamara, Retired (crash)
Formula 3
Ulf Svensson (S), Brabham

Keimola (SF) 23.8.
Porsche 908, Retired (bearings)
Gijs van Lennep (NL), Porsche 917

Zandvoort (NL) 30.8.
McNamara, Placed 4
Formula 3
Jürg Dubler (CH), Chevron

Brands Hatch (GB) 31.8.
McNamara, Retired
Formula 3
Gerry Birrell (GB), Brabham

Zolder (B) 6.9.
McNamara, Retired (crash)
Formula 3
James Hunt (GB), Lotus

Imola (I) 13.9.
Lauda/Kottulinsky (A/S), Porsche 908
Placed 5
Bell/Redman (GB), Porsche 917

Thruxton (GB) 20.9.
Porsche 908, Placed 5
Jürgen Neuhaus (D) Porsche 917

Oesterreich-Ring (A) 11.10.
Lauda/Peter (A) Porsche 908, Placed 6
1000 kms, World Endurance Championship
Siffert/Redman (CH/GB), Porsche 917

Nürburgring (D) 18.10.
Porsche 908, Placed 3
Helmut Kelleners (D), March-Chevy
Oesterreich-Ring (A) 25.10.
Porsche 908, Placed 1
Martha Grand National
Lauda (A), Porsche 908

1971

Mallory Park (GB), 14.3.
March/Ford, Retired (fuel pump)
Formula 2
Henri Pescarolo (F), March-Ford

Hockenheim (D) 4.4.
March/Ford, Retired (clutch)
Formula 2 European Championship (EC)
François Cevert (F), Tecno-Ford

Thruxton (GB) 12.4.
March/Ford, Placed 10
EC Formula 2
Graham Hill (GB), Brabham-Ford

Nürburgring (D) 2.5.
March/Ford, Placed 6
EC Formula 2
François Cevert (F), Tecno-Ford

Jarama (E), 16.5.
March/Ford, Placed 7
EC Formula 2
Emerson Fittipaldi (Brazil), Lotus-Ford

Salzburgring (A) 23.5.
Chevron-Ford, Placed 1
2-litre EC Sports
Lauda (A), Chevron-Ford

Crystal Palace (GB), 31.5.
March/Ford, Did not qualify
EC Formula 2
Emerson Fittipaldi (Brazil), Lotus-Ford

Monza (I) 20.6.
March/Ford, Retired (gearbox)
Formula 2
Dieter Quester (A), March-BMW

Rouen (F), 27.6.
March/Ford, Placed 4
EC Formula 2
Ronnie Peterson (S), March-Ford

Nürburgring (D) 11.7.
Lauda/Huber (A), BMW Alpina Coupé
EC Saloon
Marko/Glemser (A/D), Ford Capri RS

Spa-Francorchamps (B) 24/25.7.
Lauda/Larrousse (A/F), BMW Alpina Coupé
Retired
EC Saloon

Glemser/Soler-Roig (D/E), Ford Capri RS
Mantorp Park (S) 8.8.
March/Ford, Placed 13
EC Formula 2
Ronnie Peterson (S), March-Ford

Oesterreich-Ring (A), 15.8.
March F-1, Retired (engine)
Austrian Grand Prix, Formula 1
Jo Siffert (CH), BRM

Kinnekulle (S), 22.8.
March/Ford, Placed 6
Formula 2
Ronnie Peterson (S), March-Ford

Brands Hatch (GB) 30.8.
March/Ford, Placed 7
Formula 2
Ronnie Peterson (S), March-Ford

Tulln-Langenlebarn (A) 1.9.
March/Ford, Retired
EC Formula 2
Ronnie Peterson (S), March-Ford

Albi (F) 26.9.
March/Ford, Retired
EC Formula 2
Emerson Fittipaldi (Brazil), Lotus-Ford

Vallelunga (I) 10.10.
March/Ford, Placed 7
EC Formula 2
Ronnie Peterson (S), March-Ford

1972

Buenos Aires, 23.1.
March F-1, Placed 11
Formula 1, Argentinian GP
Jackie Stewart (GB), Tyrrell-Ford

Kyalami (SA) 4.3.
March F-1, Placed 7
Formula 1, South African GP
Denny Hulme (NZ), McLaren-Ford

Mallory Park (GB) 12.3.
March/Ford, Placed 2
EC Formula 2
Dave Morgan (GB), Brabham-Ford

Oulton Park (GB) 31.3.
March/Ford, Placed 1
Formula 2
Lauda (A), March-Ford

Thruxton (GB) 3.4.
March/Ford, Placed 3
EC Formula 2
Ronnie Peterson (S), March-Ford

Hockenheim (D) 16.4.
March/Ford, Retired (engine failure)
EC Formula 2
J.-P. Jaussaud (F), Brabham-Ford

Jarama (S), 1.5.
March F-1, Retired (jammed throttle)
Formula 1, Spanish GP
Emerson Fittipaldi (Brazil), Lotus-Ford

Pau (F) 7.5.
March/Ford, Retired (rear axle shaft)
EC Formula 2
Peter Gethin (GB), Chevron-Ford

Monte Carlo, 14.5.
March F-1, Placed 16
Formula 1 Monaco GP
Jean-Pierre Beltoise (F), BRM

Brno (CS), 21.5.
Alpina-BMW, Retired (engine failure)
EC Saloon
Dieter Glemser (D), Ford Capri

Crystal Palace (GB), 28.5.
March/Ford, Retired (crankshaft)
EC Formula 2
Jody Scheckter (SA), McLaren-Ford

Nivelles (B) 4.6.
March F-1, Placed 12
Formula 1 Belgian GP
Emerson Fittipaldi (Brazil), Lotus Ford

Hockenheim (D) 11.6.
March/Ford, Retired (engine failure)
EC Formula 2
Emerson Fittipaldi (Brazil), Lotus Ford

Vallelunga (I) 18.6.
March F-1, Did not start (crashed during training)
Rome Trophy
Emerson Fittipaldi (Brazil), Lotus Ford

Rouen (F) 25.6.
March/Ford, Retired (engine failure)
EC Formula 2
Emerson Fittipaldi (Brazil), Lotus Ford

Clermont-Ferrand (F) 2.7.
March F-1, Retired (rear suspension)
Formula 1 French Grand Prix
Jackie Stewart (GB), Tyrrell-Ford

Oesterreich-Ring (A) 9.7.
March/Ford, Retired (engine failure)
EC Formula 2
Emerson Fittipaldi (Brazil), Lotus-Ford

Brands Hatch (GB) 15.7.
March F-1, Placed 9
Formula 1 British Grand Prix
Emerson Fittipaldi (Brazil), Lotus-Ford

Imola (I), 23.7.
March/Ford, Placed 3
EC Formula 2
John Surtees (GB), Surtees-Ford

Nürburgring (D) 30.7.
March F-1, Retired (oil tank leak)
Formula 1 German Grand Prix
Jackie Ickx (B), Ferrari

Mantorp Park (S) 6.8.
March/Ford, Did not qualify
EC Formula 2
Mike Hailwood (GB), Surtees-Ford

Oesterreich-Ring (A) 13.8.
March F-1, Placed 10
Formula 1 Austrian Grand Prix
Emerson Fittipaldi (Brazil), Lotus-Ford

Zandvoort (NL) 20.8.
Lauda/Hezemans (A/INL) BMW Alpina Coupé, Placed 3
EC Touring
Mass/Soler-Roig (D/E), Ford Capri RS

Salzburgring (A) 3.9.
March/Ford, Placed 6
EC Formula 2
Mike Hailwood (GB), Surtees-Ford

Monza (I), 10.9.
March F-1, Placed 13
Formula 1 Italian Grand Prix
Emerson Fittipaldi (Brazil), Lotus-Ford

Oulton Park (GB) 16.9.
March/Ford, Placed 2
Formula 2
Ronnie Peterson (S), March-Ford

Mosport (Can) 24.9.
March F-1, Disqualified
Formula 1 Canadian GP
Jackie Stewart (GB), Tyrrell-Ford

Hockenheim (D) 1.10.
March/Ford, Placed 9
EC Formula 2
Tim Schenken (Aus), Brabham-Ford

Watkins Glen (USA) 8.10.
March F-1, Placed 17
Formula 1 United States Grand Prix
Jackie Stewart (GB), Tyrrell-Ford

Kyalami (SA) 4.11.
Lauda/Scheckter (A/SA), March-BMW Placed 4
9 hours endurance
Regazzoni/Merzario (CH/I), Ferrari

1973

Buenos Aires (Arg) 28.1.
BRM F-1, Retired (engine failure)
Formula 1 Argentinian Grand Prix
Emerson Fittipaldi (Brazil), Lotus-Ford

Interlagos (Brazil) 11.2.
BRM F-1, Placed 8
Formula 1 Brazilian Grand Prix
Emerson Fittipaldi (Brazil), Lotus-Ford

Kyalami (SA) 3.3.
BRM F-1, Retired (engine/pistons)
Formula 1 South African Grand Prix
Jackie Stewart (GB), Tyrrell-Ford

Brands Hatch (GB) 18.3.
BRM F-1, Retired (battery/tyres)
Race of Champions
Peter Gethin (GB), Chevron F 5000

Monza (I) 25.3.
Alpina BMW Coupé, Placed 1
EC Touring (4 hours)
Lauda/Muir, Alpina BMW Coupé

Aspern (A) 1.4.
BMW 2002 Gr. 1, Retired (tyres)
Aerodrome
Dieter Quester (A), BMW 2002/Gr. 1

Silverstone (GB) 8.4.
BRM F-1, Placed 5
Daily Express Trophy
Jackie Stewart (GB), Tyrrell-Ford

Barcelona (E) 29.4.
BRM F-1, Retired (tyres)
Formula 1 Spanish Grand Prix
Emerson Fittipaldi (Brazil), Lotus-Ford

Spa (B) 5.5.
Alpina-BMW Coupé, Placed 1
Coupe de Spa (Spa Trophy)
Lauda (A), Alpina-BMW-Coupé

Spa (B) 6.5.
Lauda/Stuck (A/D), Alpina-BMW-Coupé
Placed 7
1000 kms, Championship of Makes
Bell/Hailwood (GB), Gulf-Mirage-Ford

Zolder (B) 20.5.
BRM F-1, Placed 5
Formula 1 Belgian Grand Prix
Jackie Stewart (GB), Tyrrell-Ford

Nürburgring (D) 27.5.
Lauda/Muir (A/Aus) Alpina-BMW-Coupé
Did not start (Muir crashed in qualifying)
1000 kms
Ickx/Redman (B/GB), Ferrari

Monte Carlo, 3.6.
BRM F-1, Retired (gearbox/clutch)
Formula 1 Monaco Grand Prix
Jackie Stewart (GB), Tyrrell-Ford

Anderstorp (S) 17.6.
BRM F-1, Placed 13
Formula 1 Swedish Grand Prix
Denny Hulme (NZ), McLaren-Ford

Nürburgring (D) 23/24.6.
Alpina-BMW-Coupé, Placed 1
24-hours endurance
Lauda/Joisten (A/D), Alpina-BMW-Coupé

Le Castellet (F) 1.7.
BRM F-1, Placed 9
Formula 1 French Grand Prix
Ronnie Peterson (S), Lotus-Ford

Nürburgring (D) 8.7.
Lauda/Joisten (A/D), Alpina-BMW-Coupé
Placed 3
EC Saloon, 6 hours endurance
Stuck/Amon (D/NZ), BMW CSL

Silverstone (GB) 14.7.
BRM F-1, Placed 12
Formula 1 British Grand Prix
Peter Revson (USA), McLaren-Ford

Diepholz (D) 15.7.
Alpina-BMW-Coupé, Retired (engine failure)
Aerodrome
Rolf Stommelen (D), Ford Capri RS

Zandvoort (NL) 29.7.
BRM F-1, Retired (tyres, fuel pressure)
Formula 1 Dutch Grand Prix
Jackie Stewart (GB), Tyrrell-Ford

Nürburgring (D), 5.8.
BRM F-1, Retired (crash)
Formula 1 German Grand Prix
Jackie Stewart (GB), Tyrrell-Ford

Oesterreich-Ring (A) 19.8.
BRM F-1, Did not start (hand injury at Nürburgring)
Formula 1 Austrian Grand Prix
Ronnie Peterson (S), Lotus-Ford

Monza (I) 9.9.
BRM F-1, Retired (crash)
Formula 1 Italian Grand Prix
Ronnie Peterson (S), Lotus-Ford

Mosport, 23.9.
BRM F-1, Retired (differential)
Formula 1 Canadian Grand Prix
Peter Revson (USA), McLaren-Ford

Innsbruck (A), 30.9.
BMW 2002 Gr. 1, Placed 1*
Aerodrome
Lauda (A), BMW 2002*

Watkins Glen (USA) 7.10.
BRM F-1, Placed 18
Formula 1 United States Grand Prix
Ronnie Peterson (S), Lotus-Ford

Oesterreich-Ring (A) 14.10.
Ford Capri RS, Placed 1*
End-of-season trophy
Lauda (A), Ford Capri RS*

1974

Buenos Aires, 13.1.
Ferrari F-1, Placed 2
Formula 1 Argentinian Grand Prix
Denny Hulme (NZ), McLaren-Ford

Interlagos (Brazil) 27.1.
Ferrari F-1, Retired (engine failure)
Formula 1 Brazilian Grand Prix
Emerson Fittipaldi (Brazil), McLaren-Ford

Brands Hatch (GB), 17.3.
Ferrari F-1, Placed 2
Race of Champions
Jackie Ickx (B), Lotus-Ford

Kyalami (SA) 30.3.
Ferrari F-1, Retired (ignition)
Formula 1 South African Grand Prix
Carlos Reutemann (Arg), Brabham-Ford

Salzburgring (A) 14.4.
Lauda/Mass (A/D), Ford Capri RS
Retired (engine failure)
EC Saloon
Stuck/Ickx (D/B), BMW 3.0 CSL

Jarama (E) 28.4.
Ferrari F-1, Placed 1
Formula 1 Spanish Grand Prix
Lauda (A), Ferrari

Nivelles (B) 12.5.
Ferrari F-1, Placed 2
Formula 1 Belgian Grand Prix
Emerson Fittipaldi (Brazil), McLaren-Ford

Nürburgring (D) 19.5.
Lauda/Mass (A/D), Ford Capri RS, Retired
1000 kms, Championship of Makes
Beltoise/Jarier (F), Matra

Monte Carlo, 26.5.
Ferrari F-1, Retired (ignition)
Formula 1 Monaco Grand Prix
Ronnie Peterson (S), Lotus-Ford

Anderstorp (S) 9.6.
Ferrari F-1, Retired (rear suspension)
Formula 1 Swedish Grand Prix
Jody Scheckter (SA), Tyrrell-Ford

Zandvoort (NL) 23.6.
Ferrari F-1, Placed 1
Formula 1 Dutch Grand Prix
Lauda (A), Ferrari

Dijon (F) 7.7.
Ferrari F-1, Placed 2
Formula 1 French Grand Prix
Ronnie Peterson (S), Lotus-Ford

Nürburgring (D) 14.7.
Lauda/Glemser/Hezemans (A/D/NL),
Ford Capri RS, Placed 2
EC Saloon, 6 hours endurance
Heyer/Ludwig (D), Zakspeed-Escort

Brands Hatch (GB) 20.7.
Ferrari F-1, Placed 5
Formula 1 British Grand Prix
Jody Scheckter (SA), Tyrrell-Ford

Nürburgring (D) 4.8.
Ferrari F-1, Retired (crash)
Formula 1 German Grand Prix
Clay Regazzoni (CH), Ferrari

Oesterreich-Ring (A) 18.8.
Ferrari F-1, Retired (damaged valves)
Formula 1 Austrian Grand Prix
Carlos Reutemann (Arg), Brabham-Ford

Monza (I) 8.9.
Ferrari F-1, Retired (engine failure)
Formula 1 Italian Grand Prix
Ronnie Peterson (S), Lotus-Ford

Norisring (D) 15.9.
Ford Capri RS, Retired (gear change problems)
Hans-Joachim Stuck (D), BMW 3.0 CSL

Mosport (Can) 22.9.
Ferrari F-1, Retired (crash)
Formula 1 Canadian Grand Prix
Emerson Fittipaldi (Brazil), McLaren-Ford

Watkins Glen (USA) 6.10.
Ferrari F-1, Retired (shock absorbers)
Formula 1 United States Grand Prix
Carlos Reutemann (Arg), Brabham-Ford

1975

Buenos Aires (Arg) 12.1.
Ferrari F-1, Placed 6
Formula 1 Argentinian Grand Prix
Emerson Fittipaldi (Brazil), McLaren-Ford

Interlagos (Brazil) 26.1.
Ferrari F-1. Placed 5
Formula 1 Brazilian Grand Prix
Carlos Pace (Brazil), Brabham-Ford

Kyalami (SA) 1.3.
Ferrari F-1, Placed 5
Formula 1 South African Grand Prix
Jody Scheckter (SA), Tyrrell-Ford

Silverstone (GB) 12.4.
Ferrari F-1, Placed 1
International Trophy
Lauda (A), Ferrari

Barcelona (E) 27.4.
Ferrari F-1, Retired (crash)
Formula 1 Spanish Grand Prix
Jochen Mass (D), McLaren-Ford

Monte Carlo 11.5.
Ferrari F-1, Placed 1
Formula 1 Monaco Grand Prix
Lauda (A), Ferrari

Zolder (B) 25.5.
Ferrari F-1, Placed 1
Formula 1 Belgian Grand Prix
Lauda (A), Ferrari

Anderstorp (S) 8.6.
Ferrari F-1, Placed 1
Formula 1 Swedish Grand Prix
Lauda (A), Ferrari

Zandvoort (NL) 22.6.
Ferrari F-1, Placed 2
Formula 1 Dutch Grand Prix
James Hunt (GB), Hesketh-Ford

Le Castellet (F) 7.7.
Ferrari F-1, Placed 1
Formula 1 French Grand Prix
Lauda (A), Ferrari

Silverstone (GB) 19.7.
Ferrari F-1, Placed 8
Formula 1 British Grand Prix
Emerson Fittipaldi (Brazil), McLaren-Ford

Nürburgring (D) 3.8.
Ferrari F-1, Placed 3
Formula 1 German Grand Prix
Carlos Reutemann (Arg), Brabham-Ford

Oesterreich-Ring (A) 17.8.
Ferrari F-1, Placed 6
Formula 1 Austrian Grand Prix
Vittorio Brambilla (I), March-Ford

Monza (I) 7.9.
Ferrari F-1, Placed 3
Formula 1 Italian Grand Prix
Clay Regazzoni (CH), Ferrari

Watkins Glen (USA) 5.10.
Ferrari F-1, Placed 1
Formula 1 United States Grand Prix
Lauda (A), Ferrari

1976

Interlagos (Brazil) 25.1.
Ferrari F-1, Placed 1
Formula 1 Brazilian Grand Prix
Lauda (A), Ferrari

Kyalami (SA) 6.3.
Ferrari F-1, Placed 1
Formula 1 South African Grand Prix
Lauda (A), Ferrari

Brands Hatch (GB) 14.3.
Ferrari F-1, Retired (brakes)
Race of Champions
James Hunt (GB), McLaren

Long Beach (USA) 28.3.
Ferrari F-1, Placed 2
Formula 1 USA Grand Prix (West)
Clay Regazzoni (CH), Ferrari

Jarama (E) 2.5.
Ferrari F-1, Placed 2
Formula 1 Spanish Grand Prix
James Hunt (GB) McLaren-Ford

Zolder (B) 15.5.
Ferrari F-1, Placed 1
Formula 1 Belgian Grand Prix
Lauda (A), Ferrari

Monte Carlo 30.5.
Ferrari F-1, Placed 1
Formula 1 Monaco Grand Prix
Lauda (A), Ferrari

Anderstorp (S) 13.6.
Ferrari F-1, Placed 3
Formula 1 Swedish Grand Prix
Jody Scheckter (SA), Tyrrell-Ford

Le Castellet (F), 4.6.
Ferrari F-1, Retired (engine failure)
Formula 1 French Grand Prix
James Hunt (GB), McLaren-Ford

Brands Hatch (GB) 18.7.
Ferrari F-1, Placed 2
Formula 1 British Grand Prix
James Hunt (GB), McLaren-Ford

Nürburgring (D) 1.8.
Ferrari F-1, Retired (crash)
Formula 1 German Grand Prix
James Hunt (GB), McLaren-Ford

Oesterreich-Ring (A) 15.8.
Did not start
Formula 1 Austrian Grand Prix
John Watson (Irl), Penske-Ford

Zandvoort (NL) 29.8.
Did not start
Formula 1 Dutch Grand Prix
James Hunt (GB), McLaren-Ford

Monza (I) 12.9.
Ferrari F-1, Placed 4
Formula 1 Italian Grand Prix
Ronnie Peterson (S), March-Ford

Mosport (Can) 3.10.
Formula 1 Canadian Grand Prix
James Hunt (GB), McLaren-Ford
Ferrari F-1, Placed 8

Watkins Glen (USA) 10.10.
Ferrari F-1, Placed 3
Formula 1 USA Grand Prix (East)
James Hunt (GB), McLaren-Ford

Fuji (Japan) 24.10.
Pulled out of race voluntarily
Formula 1 Japanese Grand Prix
Mario Andretti (USA), Lotus-Ford

1977

Buenos Aires (Arg) 9.1.
Ferrari F-1, Retired (fuel injection)
Formula 1 Argentinian Grand Prix
Jody Scheckter (SA), Wolf-Ford

Interlagos (Brazil) 23.1.
Ferrari F-1, Placed 3
Formula 1 Brazilian Grand Prix
Carlos Reutemann (Arg), Ferrari

Kyalami (SA) 5.3.
Ferrari F-1, Placed 1
Formula 1 South African Grand Prix
Lauda (A), Ferrari

Long Beach (USA) 3.4.
Ferrari F-1, Placed 2
Formula 1 USA Grand Prix (West)
Mario Andretti (USA), Lotus-Ford

Jarama (E) 8.5.
Did not start (ribcage injury)
Formula 1 Spanish Grand Prix
Mario Andretti (USA), Lotus-Ford

Monte Carlo 22.5.
Ferrari F-1, Placed 2
Formula 1 Monaco Grand Prix
Jody Scheckter (SA), Wolf-Ford

Zolder (B) 5.6.
Ferrari F-1, Placed 2
Formula 1 Belgian Grand Prix
Gunnar Nilsson (S), Lotus-Ford

Anderstorp (S) 19.6.
Ferrari F-1, Pulled out voluntarily
Formula 1 Swedish Grand Prix
Jacques Laffite (F), Ligier-Matra

Dijon (F) 3.7.
Ferrari F-1, Placed 5
Formula 1 French Grand Prix
Mario Andretti (USA, Lotus-Ford

Silverstone (GB 16.7.
Ferrari F-1, Placed 2
Formula 1 British Grand Prix
James Hunt (GB, McLaren-Ford

Hockenheimring (D) 31.7.
Ferrari F-1, Placed 1
Formula 1 German Grand Prix
Lauda (A), Ferrari

Oesterreich-Ring (A) 14.8.
Ferrari F-1, Placed 2
Formula 1 Austrian Grand Prix
Alan Jones (Aus), Shadow-Ford

Zandvoort (NL) 28.8.
Ferrari F-1, Placed 1
Formula 1 Dutch Grand Prix
Lauda (A), Ferrari

Monza (I) 11.9.
Ferrari F-1, Placed 2
Formula 1 Italian Grand Prix
Mario Andretti (USA), Lotus-Ford

Watkins Glen (USA), 2.10.
Ferrari F-1, Placed 4
Formula 1 USA Grand Prix (East)
James Hunt (GB), McLaren-Ford

Mosport (Can) 9.10.
Did not start
Formula 1 Canadian Grand Prix
Jody Scheckter (SA), Wolf-Ford

Fuji (Japan) 23.10.
Did not start
Formula 1 Japanese Grand Prix
James Hunt (GB), McLaren-Ford

1978

Buenos Aires (Arg) 15.1.
Brabham-Alfa F-1, Placed 2
Formula 1 Argentinian Grand Prix
Mario Andretti (USA), Lotus-Ford

Rio de Janeiro (Brazil) 29.1.
Brabham-Alfa F-1, Placed 3
Formula 1 Brazilian Grand Prix
Carlos Reutemann (Arg), Ferrari

Kyalami (SA) 4.3.
Brabham-Alfa F-1, Retired (engine failure)
Formula 1 South African Grand Prix
Ronnie Peterson (S), Lotus-Ford

Long Beach (USA) 2.4.
Brabham-Alfa F-1, Retired (ignition)
Formula 1 USA Grand Prix (West)
Carlos Reutemann (Arg), Ferrari

Monte Carlo, 7.5.
Brabham-Alfa F-1, Placed 2
Formula 1 Monaco Grand Prix
Patrick Depailler (F), Tyrrell-Ford

Zolder (B) 21.5.
Brabham-Alfa F-1, Retired (crashed)
Formula 1 Belgian Grand Prix
Mario Andretti (USA), Lotus-Ford

Jarama (E) 4.6.
Brabham-Alfa F-1, Retired (engine)
Formula 1 Spanish Grand Prix
Mario Andretti (USA), Lotus-Ford

Anderstorp (S) 17.6.
Brabham-Alfa F-1, Placed 1
Formula 1 Swedish Grand Prix
Lauda (A), Brabham Alfa

Paul Ricard (F) 2.7.
Brabham-Alfa F-1, Retired (engine)
Formula 1 French Grand Prix
Mario Andretti (USA), Lotus-Ford

Brands Hatch (GB) 16.7.
Brabham-Alfa F-1, Placed 2
Formula 1 British Grand Prix
Carlos Reutemann (Arg), Ferrari

Hockenheim (D) 30.7.
Brabham-Alfa F-1, Retired (engine)
Formula 1 German Grand Prix
Mario Andretti (USA), Lotus-Ford

Oesterreich-Ring (A) 13.8.
Brabham-Alfa F-1, Retired (crash)
Formula 1 Austrian Grand Prix
Ronnie Peterson (S), Lotus-Ford

Zandvoort (NL) 27.8.
Brabham-Alfa F-1, Placed 3
Formula 1 Dutch Grand Prix
Mario Andretti (USA), Lotus-Ford

Monza (I) 10.9.
Brabham-Alfa F-1, Placed 1
Formula 1 Italian Grand Prix
Lauda (A), Brabham-Alfa

Watkins Glen (USA) 1.10.
Brabham-Alfa F-1, Retired (engine)
Formula 1 USA Grand Prix (East)
Carlos Reutemann (Arg), Ferrari

Montreal (Can) 8.10.
Brabham-Alfa F-1
Formula 1 Canadian Grand Prix
Gilles Villeneuve (Can), Ferrari

1979

Buenos Aires (Arg) 21.1.
Brabham-Alfa F-1, Retired (Fuel pressure)
Formula 1 Argentinian Grand Prix
Jacques Laffite (F), Ligier-Ford

Interlagos (Brazil) 4.2.
Brabham-Alfa F-1, Retired (gear lever)
Formula 1 Brazilian Grand Prix
Jacques Laffite (F), Ligier-Ford

Kyalami (SA) 3.3.
Brabham-Alfa F-1, Placed 6
Formula 1 South African Grand Prix
Gilles Villeneuve (Can), Ferrari

Long Beach (USA) 8.4.
Brabham-Alfa F-1, Retired (crash)
Formula 1 USA Grand Prix (West)
Gilles Villeneuve (Can), Ferrari

Brands Hatch (GB) 15.4.
Brabham-Alfa F-1, Placed 5
Race of Champions
Gilles Villeneuve (Can), Ferrari

Jarama (E) 29.4.
Brabham-Alfa F-1, Retired (water cooler)
Formula 1 Spanish Grand Prix
Patrick Depailler (F), Ligier-Ford

Zolder (B) 12.5.
BMW M1, Retired (damaged shocks)
Procar (Production Car) Grand Prix
Elio de Angelis (I), BMW M1

Zolder (B) 13.5.
Brabham-Alfa F-1, Retired (engine)
Formula 1 Belgian Grand Prix
Jody Scheckter (SA), Ferrari

Monte Carlo, 26.5.
BMW M1, Placed 1
Procar Grand Prix
Lauda (A), BMW M1

Monte Carlo, 27.5.
Brabham-Alfa F-1, Retired (crash)
Formula 1 Monaco Grand Prix
Jody Scheckter (SA), Ferrari

Dijon (F) 30.6.
BMW M1, Placed 8
Procar Grand Prix
Nelson Piquet (Brazil), BMW M1

Dijon (F) 1.7.
Brabham-Alfa F-1, Retired (crash)
Formula 1 French Grand Prix
Jean-Pierre Jabouille (F), Renault Turbo

Silverstone (GB) 13.7.
BMW M1, Placed 1
Procar Grand Prix
Lauda (A), BMW M1

Silverstone (GB) 14.7.
Brabham-Alfa F-1, retired (brakes)
Formula 1 British Grand Prix
Clay Regazzoni (CH), Williams-Ford

Hockenheim (D) 28.7.
BMW M1, Placed 1
Procar Grand Prix
Lauda (A), BMW M1

Hockenheim (D) 29.7.
Brabham-Alfa F-1, Retired (engine)
Formula 1 German Grand Prix
Alan Jones (Aus), Williams-Ford

Oesterreichring (A) 11.8.
BMW M1, Retired (clutch)
Procar Grand Prix
Jacques Laffite (F), BMW M1

Oesterreichring (A) 12.8.
Brabham-Alfa F-1, Retired (oil pressure)
Formula 1 Austrian Grand Prix
Alan Jones (Aus), Williams-Ford

Zandvoort (NL) 25.8.
BMW M1, Retired (electrics)
Procar Grand Prix
Hans-Joachim Stuck (D), BMW M1

Zandvoort (NL) 26.8.
Brabham-Alfa F-1, Retired (injured hand)
Formula 1 Dutch Grand Prix
Alan Jones (Aus), Williams-Ford

Monza (I) 8.9.
BMW M1, Placed 2
Procar Grand Prix
Hans-Joachim Stuck (D), BMW M1

Monza (I) 9.9.
Brabham-Alfa F-1, Placed 4
Formula 1 Italian Grand Prix
Jody Scheckter (SA), Ferrari

Imola (I) 16.9.
Brabham-Alfa F-1, Placed 1
Formula 1
Lauda (A), Brabham-Alfa

1982

Kyalami (SA) 23.1.
McLaren-Ford F-1, Placed 4
Formula 1 South African Grand Prix
Alain Prost (F), Renault Turbo

Rio de Janeiro (Brazil) 21.3.
McLaren-Ford F-1, Retired (collision)
Formula 1 Brazilian Grand Prix
Alain Prost (F), Renault Turbo

Long Beach (USA) 4.4.
McLaren-Ford F-1, Placed 1
Formula 1 USA Grand Prix (West)
Lauda (A), McLaren-Ford

Zolder (B) 9.5.
McLaren-Ford F-1, Disqualified
Formula 1 Belgian Grand Prix
John Watson (Irl), McLaren-Ford

Monte Carlo, 23.5.
McLaren-Ford F-1, Retired (engine)
Formula 1 Monaco Grand Prix
Riccardo Patrese (I), Brabham-Ford

Detroit (USA) 6.6.
McLaren-Ford F-1, Retired (collision)
Formula 1 USA Grand Prix (East)
John Watson (Irl), McLaren Ford

Montreal (Can) 13.6.
McLaren-Ford F-1, Retired (clutch)
Formula 1 Canadian Grand Prix
Nelson Piquet (Brazil),
Brabham-BMW Turbo

Zandvoort (NL) 3.7.
McLaren-Ford F-1, Placed 4
Formula 1 Dutch Grand Prix
Didier Pironi (F), Ferrari Turbo

Brands Hatch (GB) 18.7.
McLaren-Ford F-1, Placed 1
Formula 1 British Grand Prix
Lauda (A), McLaren-Ford

Le Castellet (F) 25.7.
McLaren-Ford F-1, Placed 8
Formula 1 French Grand Prix
René Arnoux (F), Renault Turbo

Hockenheim (D) 8.8.
McLaren-Ford F-1, Did not start (accident during qualifying)
Formula 1 German Grand Prix
Patrick Tambay (F), Ferrari Turbo

Oesterreich-Ring (A) 15.8.
McLaren-Ford F-1, Placed 5
Formula 1 Austrian Grand Prix
Elio de Angelis (I), Lotus-Ford
Dijon (F) 29.8.
McLaren-Ford F-1, Placed 3
Formula 1 Swiss Grand Prix
Keke Rosberg (SF), Williams-Ford

Monza (I) 12.9.
McLaren-Ford F-1, Retired (chassis)
Formula 1 Italian Grand Prix
René Arnoux (F), Renault

Las Vegas (USA) 25.9.
McLaren-Ford F-1, Retired (oil pressure)
Formula 1 USA Grand Prix (West)
Michele Alboreto (I), Tyrrell-Ford

1983

Rio de Janeiro (Brazil) 13.3.
McLaren-Ford F-1, Placed 2
Brazilian Grand Prix
Nelson Piquet (Brasil), Brabham-BMW Turbo

Long Beach (USA) 27.3.
McLaren-Ford F-1, Placed 2
Formula 1 USA Grand Prix (West)
John Watson (Irl), McLaren-Ford

Le Castellet (F) 17.4.
McLaren-Ford F-1, Retired (half wave)
Formula 1 French Grand Prix
Alain Prost (F), Renault

Imola (I) 1.5.
McLaren-Ford F-1, Retired (crash)
Formula 1 San Marino Grand Prix
Patrick Tambay (F), Ferrari

Monte Carlo (Monaco) 15.5.
McLaren-Ford F-1, Did not qualify
Formula 1 Monaco Grand Prix
Keke Rosberg (SF), Williams-Ford

Spa (B) 22.5.
McLaren-Ford F-1, Retired (engine)
Formula 1 Belgian Grand Prix
Alain Prost (F), Renault

Detroit (USA) 5.6.
McLaren-Ford F-1, Retired (shocks)
Formula 1 USA Grand Prix (East)
Michele Alboreto (I), Tyrell-Ford

Montreal (Can) 12.6.
McLaren-Ford F-1, Retired (spin)
Formula I Canadian Grand Prix
René Arnoux (F), Ferrari

Silverstone (GB) 16.7.
McLaren-Ford F-1, Placed 6
Formula 1 British Grand Prix
Alain Prost (F), Renault

Hockenheim (D) 7.8.
McLaren-Ford F-1, Disqualified for reversing in pit lane
Formula 1 German Grand Prix
René Arnoux (F), Ferrari

Oesterreichring (A) 14.3.
McLaren-Ford F-1, Placed 6
Formula 1 Austrian Grand Prix
Alain Prost (F), Renault

Zandvoort (NL) 28.8.
McLaren-TAG Turbo, Retired (brakes)
Formula 1 Dutch Grand Prix
René Arnoux (F), Ferrari

Monza (I) 11.9.
McLaren-TAG Turbo, Retired (engine)
Formula 1 Italian Grand Prix
Nelson Piquet (Brazil), Brabham-BMW Turbo

Brands Hatch (GB) 25.9.
McLaren-TAG Turbo, Retired (engine)
Formula 1 European Grand Prix
Nelson Piquet (Brazil), Brabham-BMW Turbo

Kyalami (SA) 15.10.
McLaren-TAG Turbo, Retired (electrics)
Formula 1 South African Grand Prix
Riccardo Patrese (I), Brabham-BMW Turbo

04574
61497

AMANDA MOYES
HILLFIELDS
GLOSSOP RD
CHISWORTH
GLOSSOP